Praise for Programming Kubernetes

Programming Kubernetes fills a gap in the Kubernetes ecosystem. There's a plethora of books and documentation on how to run Kubernetes clusters, but we're still working to fill in the space around writing software with Kubernetes. This book is a much-needed and well-written guide to "building with and on Kubernetes."

—Bryan Liles, Senior Staff Engineer, VMware

This is a book I wish had existed when I started writing Kubernetes controllers. It serves the reader as a comprehensive deep dive into the Kubernetes programming interface and system behavior, and how to write robust software.

—Michael Gasch, Application Platform Architect
in the Office of the CTO at VMware

A must-read if you want to extend Kubernetes.

—Dimitris-Ilias Gkanatsios, Technical Evangelist,
Microsoft Greece

Extending Kubernetes is the only way to deploy and manage the lifecycle of complex applications. This book shows how to create your own Kubernetes resources and how to extend the Kubernetes API.

—Ahmed Belgana, Cloud Build Engineer, SAP

Programming Kubernetes
Developing Cloud-Native Applications

Michael Hausenblas and Stefan Schimanski

Beijing · Boston · Farnham · Sebastopol · Tokyo

Programming Kubernetes

by Michael Hausenblas and Stefan Schimanski

Published by O'Reilly Media, Inc., 1005 Gravenstein Highway North, Sebastopol, CA 95472.

O'Reilly books may be purchased for educational, business, or sales promotional use. Online editions are also available for most titles (*http://oreilly.com*). For more information, contact our corporate/institutional sales department: 800-998-9938 or *corporate@oreilly.com*.

Development Editor: Virginia Wilson	**Indexer:** Judith McConville
Acquisitions Editor: John Devins	**Interior Designer:** David Futato
Production Editor: Katherine Tozer	**Cover Designer:** Karen Montgomery
Copyeditor: Rachel Monaghan	**Illustrator:** Rebecca Demarest
Proofreader: Arthur Johnson	

July 2019:   First Edition

Revision History for the First Edition
2019-07-18:   First Release

See *http://oreilly.com/catalog/errata.csp?isbn=9781492047100* for release details.

978-1-492-04710-0

[LSI]

Table of Contents

Preface

Welcome to *Programming Kubernetes*, and thanks for choosing to spend some time with us. Before we jump into the deep end, let's quickly get a few administrative and organizational things out of the way. We'll also share our motivation for writing this book.

Who Should Read This Book

You're a developer going cloud-native, or an AppOps or namespace admin wanting to get the maximum out of Kubernetes. Vanilla settings don't do it for you anymore, and you may have learned about extension points (*http://bit.ly/2XmoeKF*). Good. You're in the right place.

Why We Wrote This Book

Both of us have been contributing to, writing about, teaching, and using Kubernetes since early 2015. We have developed tooling and apps for Kubernetes and given workshops about developing on and with Kubernetes a couple of times. At some point we said, "Why don't we write a book?" This would allow even more people, asynchronously and at their own pace, to learn how to program Kubernetes. And here we are. We hope you have as much fun reading the book as we did writing it.

Ecosystem

In the grand scheme of things, it's still early days for the Kubernetes ecosystem. While Kubernetes has, as of early 2018, established itself as the industry standard for managing containers (and their lifecycles), there is still a need for good practices on how to write native applications. The basic building blocks, such as client-go (*http://bit.ly/2L5cUMu*), custom resources, and cloud-native programming languages, are in place. However, much of the knowledge is tribal, spread across people's minds and scattered over thousands of Slack channels and StackOverflow answers.

At the time of this writing, Kubernetes 1.15 was the latest stable version. The compiled examples should work with older versions (down to 1.12), but we are basing the code on newer versions of the libraries, corresponding to 1.14. Some of the more advanced CRD features require 1.13 or 1.14 clusters to run, CRD conversion in chapter 9 even 1.15. If you don't have access to a recent enough cluster, using Minikube (*http://bit.ly/2WT3k1l*) or kind (*https://kind.sigs.k8s.io*) on the local workstation is highly recommended.

Technology You Need to Understand

This intermediate-level book requires a minimal understanding of a few development and system administration concepts. Before diving in, you might want to review the following:

Package management

The tools in this book often have multiple dependencies that you'll need to meet by installing some packages. Knowledge of the package management system on your machine is therefore required. It could be *apt* on Ubuntu/Debian systems, *yum* on CentOS/RHEL systems, or *port* or *brew* on macOS. Whatever it is, make sure that you know how to install, upgrade, and remove packages.

Git

Git has established itself as the standard for distributed version control. If you are already familiar with CVS and SVN but have not yet used Git, you should. *Version Control with Git* by Jon Loeliger and Matthew McCullough (O'Reilly) is a good place to start. Together with Git, the GitHub website (*http://github.com*) is a great resource for getting started with a hosted repository of your own. To learn about GitHub, check out their training offerings (*https://services.github.com*) and the associated interactive tutorial (*http://try.github.io*).

Go

Kubernetes is written in Go (*http://golang.org*). Over the last couple of years, Go has emerged as the new programming language of choice in many startups and for many systems-related open source projects. This book is not about teaching you Go, but it shows you how to program Kubernetes using Go. You can learn Go through a variety of different resources, from online documentation on the Go website (*https://golang.org/doc*) to blog posts, talks, and a number of books.

Conventions Used in This Book

The following typographical conventions are used in this book:

Italic
> Indicates new terms, URLs, email addresses, filenames, and file extensions.

`Constant width`
> Used for program listings, as well as within paragraphs to refer to program elements such as variable or function names, databases, data types, environment variables, statements, and keywords. Also used for commands and command-line output.

`Constant width bold`
> Shows commands or other text that should be typed literally by the user.

`Constant width italic`
> Shows text that should be replaced with user-supplied values or by values determined by context.

 This element signifies a tip or suggestion.

 This element signifies a general note.

 This element indicates a warning or caution.

Using Code Examples

This book is here to help you get your job done. You can find the code samples used throughout the book in the GitHub organization for this book (*https://github.com/programming-kubernetes*).

In general, if example code is offered with this book, you may use it in your programs and documentation. You do not need to contact us for permission unless you're reproducing a significant portion of the code. For example, writing a program that uses several chunks of code from this book does not require permission. Selling or distributing a CD-ROM of examples from O'Reilly books does require permission. Answering a question by citing this book and quoting example code does not require permission. Incorporating a significant amount of example code from this book into your product's documentation does require permission.

We appreciate, but do not require, attribution. An attribution usually includes the title, author, publisher, and ISBN. For example: "*Programming Kubernetes* by Michael Hausenblas and Stefan Schimanski (O'Reilly). Copyright 2019 Michael Hausenblas and Stefan Schimanski."

If you feel your use of code examples falls outside fair use or the permission given above, feel free to contact us at *permissions@oreilly.com*.

Kubernetes manifests, code examples, and other scripts used in this book are available via GitHub (*https://github.com/programming-kubernetes*). You can clone those repositories, go to the relevant chapter and recipe, and use the code as is.

O'Reilly Online Learning

 For almost 40 years, *O'Reilly Media* has provided technology and business training, knowledge, and insight to help companies succeed.

Our unique network of experts and innovators share their knowledge and expertise through books, articles, conferences, and our online learning platform. O'Reilly's online learning platform gives you on-demand access to live training courses, in-depth learning paths, interactive coding environments, and a vast collection of text and video from O'Reilly and 200+ other publishers. For more information, please visit *http://oreilly.com*.

How to Contact Us

Please address comments and questions concerning this book to the publisher:

O'Reilly Media, Inc.
1005 Gravenstein Highway North
Sebastopol, CA 95472
800-998-9938 (in the United States or Canada)
707-829-0515 (international or local)
707-829-0104 (fax)

We have a web page for this book where we list errata, examples, and any additional information. You can access this page at *https://oreil.ly/pr-kubernetes*.

Email *bookquestions@oreilly.com* to comment or ask technical questions about this book.

For more information about our books, courses, conferences, and news, see our website at *http://www.oreilly.com*.

Find us on Facebook: *http://facebook.com/oreilly*

Follow us on Twitter: *http://twitter.com/oreillymedia*

Watch us on YouTube: *http://www.youtube.com/oreillymedia*

Acknowledgments

A big "thank you!" goes out to the Kubernetes community for developing such amazing software and for being a great bunch of people—open, kind, and always ready to help. Further, we're very grateful to our technical reviewers: Ahmed Belgana, Michael Gasch, Dimitris Gkanatsios, Mingding Han, Jess Males, Max Neunhöffer, Ewout Prangsma, and Adrien Trouillaud. You all provided super valuable and actionable feedback and made the book more readable and useful to the reader. Thank you for your time and effort!

Michael would like to express his deepest gratitude to his awesome and supportive family: my wicked smart and fun wife, Anneliese; our kids Saphira, Ranya, and Iannis; and our almost-still-puppy Snoopy.

Stefan would like to thank his wife, Clelia, for being super supportive and encouraging whenever he was again "working on the book." Without her this book wouldn't be here. If you find typos in the book, chances are high that they were proudly contributed by the two cats, Nino and Kira.

Last but certainly not least, both authors thank the O'Reilly team, especially Virginia Wilson, for shepherding us through the process of writing this book, making sure we'd deliver on time and with the quality expected.

## CHAPTER 1

Introduction

Programming Kubernetes can mean different things to different people. In this chapter, we'll first establish the scope and focus of this book. Also, we will share the set of assumptions about the environment we're operating in and what you'll need to bring to the table, ideally, to benefit most from this book. We will define what exactly we mean by programming Kubernetes, what Kubernetes-native apps are, and, by having a look at a concrete example, what their characteristics are. We will discuss the basics of controllers and operators, and how the event-driven Kubernetes control plane functions in principle. Ready? Let's get to it.

What Does Programming Kubernetes Mean?

We assume you have access to a running Kubernetes cluster such as Amazon EKS, Microsoft AKS, Google GKE, or one of the OpenShift offerings.

 You will spend a fair amount of time developing *locally* on your laptop or desktop environment; that is, the Kubernetes cluster against which you're developing is local, rather than in the cloud or in your datacenter. When developing locally, you have a number of options available. Depending on your operating system and other preferences you might choose one (or maybe even more) of the following solutions for running Kubernetes locally: kind (*https://kind.sigs.k8s.io*), k3d (*http://bit.ly/2Ja1LaH*), or Docker Desktop (*https://dockr.ly/2PTJVLL*).[1]

---

1 For more on this topic, see Megan O'Keefe's "A Kubernetes Developer Workflow for MacOS" (*http://bit.ly/2WXfzu1*), *Medium*, January 24, 2019; and Alex Ellis's blog post, "Be KinD to yourself" (*http://bit.ly/2XkK9C1*), December 14, 2018.

We also assume that you are a Go programmer—that is, you have experience or at least basic familiarity with the Go programming language. Now is a good time, if any of those assumptions do not apply to you, to train up: for Go, we recommend *The Go Programming Language* (*https://www.gopl.io*) by Alan A. A. Donovan and Brian W. Kernighan (Addison-Wesley) and *Concurrency in Go* (*http://bit.ly/2tdCt5j*) by Katherine Cox-Buday (O'Reilly). For Kubernetes, check out one or more of the following books:

- *Kubernetes in Action* by Marko Lukša (Manning)
- *Kubernetes: Up and Running*, 2nd Edition (*https://oreil.ly/2SaANU4*) by Kelsey Hightower et al. (O'Reilly)
- *Cloud Native DevOps with Kubernetes* (*https://oreil.ly/2BaE1iq*) by John Arundel and Justin Domingus (O'Reilly)
- *Managing Kubernetes* (*https://oreil.ly/2wtHcAm*) by Brendan Burns and Craig Tracey (O'Reilly)
- *Kubernetes Cookbook* (*http://bit.ly/2FTgJzk*) by Sébastien Goasguen and Michael Hausenblas (O'Reilly)

Why do we focus on programming Kubernetes in Go? Well, an analogy might be useful here: Unix was written in the C programming language, and if you wanted to write applications or tooling for Unix you would default to C. Also, in order to extend and customize Unix—even if you were to use a language other than C—you would need to at least be able to read C.

Now, Kubernetes and many related cloud-native technologies, from container runtimes to monitoring such as Prometheus, are written in Go. We believe that the majority of native applications will be Go-based and hence we focus on it in this book. Should you prefer other languages, keep an eye on the kubernetes-client (*http://bit.ly/2xfSrfT*) GitHub organization. It may, going forward, contain a client in your favorite programming language.

By "programming Kubernetes" in the context of this book, we mean the following: you are about to develop a Kubernetes-native application that directly interacts with the API server, querying the state of resources and/or updating their state. We do not mean running off-the-shelf apps, such as WordPress or Rocket Chat or your favorite enterprise CRM system, oftentimes called *commercially available off-the-shelf* (COTS) apps. Besides, in Chapter 7, we do not really focus too much on operational issues, but mainly look at the development and testing phase. So, in a nutshell, this book is about developing genuinely cloud-native applications. Figure 1-1 might help you soak that in better.

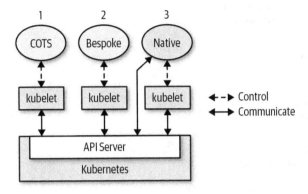

Figure 1-1. Different types of apps running on Kubernetes

As you can see, there are different styles at your disposal:

1. Take a COTS such as Rocket Chat and run it on Kubernetes. The app itself is not aware it runs on Kubernetes and usually doesn't have to be. Kubernetes controls the app's lifecycle—find node to run, pull image, launch container(s), carry out health checks, mount volumes, and so on—and that is that.

2. Take a bespoke app, something you wrote from scratch, with or without having had Kubernetes as the runtime environment in mind, and run it on Kubernetes. The same modus operandi as in the case of a COTS applies.

3. The case we focus on in this book is a cloud-native or Kubernetes-native application that is fully aware it is running on Kubernetes and leverages Kubernetes APIs and resources to some extent.

The price you pay developing against the Kubernetes API pays off: on the one hand you gain portability, as your app will now run in any environment (from an on-premises deployment to any public cloud provider), and on the other hand you benefit from the clean, declarative mechanism Kubernetes provides.

Let's move on to a concrete example now.

A Motivational Example

To demonstrate the power of a Kubernetes-native app, let's assume you want to implement at—that is, schedule the execution of a command (*http://bit.ly/2L4VqzU*) at a given time.

We call this cnat (*http://bit.ly/2RpHhON*) or cloud-native at, and it works as follows. Let's say you want to execute the command echo "Kubernetes native rocks!" at 2 a.m. on July 3, 2019. Here's what you would do with cnat:

```
$ cat cnat-rocks-example.yaml
apiVersion: cnat.programming-kubernetes.info/v1alpha1
kind: At
metadata:
  name: cnrex
spec:
  schedule: "2019-07-03T02:00:00Z"
  containers:
  - name: shell
    image: centos:7
    command:
    - "bin/bash"
    - "-c"
    - echo "Kubernetes native rocks!"

$ kubectl apply -f cnat-rocks-example.yaml
cnat.programming-kubernetes.info/cnrex created
```

Behind the scenes, the following components are involved:

- A custom resource called `cnat.programming-kubernetes.info/cnrex`, representing the schedule.

- A controller to execute the scheduled command at the correct time.

In addition, a `kubectl` plug-in for the CLI UX would be useful, allowing simple handling via commands like `kubectl at "02:00 Jul 3" echo "Kubernetes native rocks!"` We won't write this in this book, but you can refer to the Kubernetes documentation for instructions (*http://bit.ly/2J1dPuN*).

Throughout the book, we will use this example to discuss aspects of Kubernetes, its inner workings, and how to extend it.

For the more advanced examples in Chapters 8 and 9, we will simulate a pizza restaurant with pizza and topping objects in the cluster. See "Example: A Pizza Restaurant" on page 149 for details.

Extension Patterns

Kubernetes is a powerful and inherently extensible system. In general, there are multiple ways to customize and/or extend Kubernetes: using configuration files and flags (*http://bit.ly/2KteqbA*) for control plane components like the `kubelet` or the Kubernetes API server, and through a number of defined extension points:

- So-called cloud providers (*http://bit.ly/2FpHInw*), which were traditionally in-tree as part of the controller manager. As of 1.11, Kubernetes makes out-of-tree development possible by providing a custom `cloud-controller-manager` process to integrate with a cloud (*http://bit.ly/2WWlcxk*). Cloud providers allow the use of cloud provider–specific tools like load balancers or Virtual Machines (VMs).

- Binary kubelet plug-ins for network (*http://bit.ly/2L1tPzm*), devices (*http://bit.ly/2XthLgM*) (such as GPUs), storage (*http://bit.ly/2x7Unaa*), and container runtimes (*http://bit.ly/2Zzh1Eq*).
- Binary kubectl plug-ins (*http://bit.ly/2FmH7mu*).
- Access extensions in the API server, such as the dynamic admission control with webhooks (*http://bit.ly/2DwR2Y3*) (see Chapter 9).
- Custom resources (see Chapter 4) and custom controllers; see the following section.
- Custom API servers (see Chapter 8).
- Scheduler extensions, such as using a webhook (*http://bit.ly/2xcg4FL*) to implement your own scheduling decisions.
- Authentication (*http://bit.ly/2Oh6DPS*) with webhooks.

In the context of this book we focus on custom resources, controllers, webhooks, and custom API servers, along with the Kubernetes extension patterns (*http://bit.ly/2L2SJ1C*). If you're interested in other extension points, such as storage or network plug-ins, check out the official documentation (*http://bit.ly/2Y0L1J9*).

Now that you have a basic understanding of the Kubernetes extension patterns and the scope of this book, let's move on to the heart of the Kubernetes control plane and see how we can extend it.

Controllers and Operators

In this section you'll learn about controllers and operators in Kubernetes and how they work.

Per the Kubernetes glossary (*http://bit.ly/2IWGlxz*), a *controller* implements a control loop, watching the shared state of the cluster through the API server and making changes in an attempt to move the current state toward the desired state.

Before we dive into the controller's inner workings, let's define our terminology:

- Controllers can act on core resources such as deployments or services, which are typically part of the Kubernetes controller manager (*http://bit.ly/2WUAEVy*) in the control plane, or can watch and manipulate user-defined custom resources.
- Operators are controllers that encode some operational knowledge, such as application lifecycle management, along with the custom resources defined in Chapter 4.

Naturally, given that the latter concept is based on the former, we'll look at controllers first and then discuss the more specialized case of an operator.

The Control Loop

In general, the control loop looks as follows:

1. Read the state of resources, preferably event-driven (using watches, as discussed in Chapter 3). See "Events" on page 7 and "Edge- Versus Level-Driven Triggers" on page 9 for details.

2. Change the state of objects in the cluster or the cluster-external world. For example, launch a pod, create a network endpoint, or query a cloud API. See "Changing Cluster Objects or the External World" on page 11 for details.

3. Update status of the resource in step 1 via the API server in etcd. See "Optimistic Concurrency" on page 14 for details.

4. Repeat cycle; return to step 1.

No matter how complex or simple your controller is, these three steps—read resource state > change the world > update resource status—remain the same. Let's dig a bit deeper into how these steps are actually implemented in a Kubernetes controller. The control loop is depicted in Figure 1-2, which shows the typical moving parts, with the main loop of the controller in the middle. This main loop is continuously running inside of the controller process. This process is usually running inside a pod in the cluster.

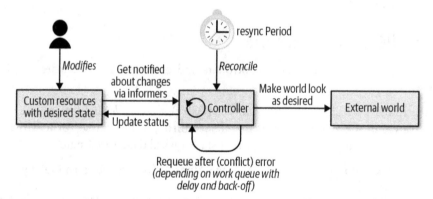

Figure 1-2. Kubernetes control loop

From an architectural point of view, a controller typically uses the following data structures (as discussed in detail in Chapter 3):

Informers

Informers watch the desired state of resources in a scalable and sustainable fashion. They also implement a resync mechanism (see "Informers and Caching" on page 56 for details) that enforces periodic reconciliation, and is often used to make sure that the cluster state and the assumed state cached in memory do not drift (e.g., due bugs or network issues).

Work queues

Essentially, a work queue is a component that can be used by the event handler to handle queuing of state changes and help to implement retries. In client-go this functionality is available via the *workqueue* package (*http://bit.ly/2x7zyeK*) (see "Work Queue" on page 61). Resources can be requeued in case of errors when updating the world or writing the status (steps 2 and 3 in the loop), or just because we have to reconsider the resource after some time for other reasons.

For a more formal discussion of Kubernetes as a declarative engine and state transitions, read "The Mechanics of Kubernetes" (*http://bit.ly/2IV2lcb*) by Andrew Chen and Dominik Tornow.

Let's now take a closer look at the control loop, starting with Kubernetes event-driven architecture.

Events

The Kubernetes control plane heavily employs events and the principle of loosely coupled components. Other distributed systems use remote procedure calls (RPCs) to trigger behavior. Kubernetes does not. Kubernetes controllers watch changes to Kubernetes objects in the API server: adds, updates, and removes. When such an event happens, the controller executes its business logic.

For example, in order to launch a pod via a deployment, a number of controllers and other control plane components work together:

1. The deployment controller (inside of kube-controller-manager) notices (through a deployment informer) that the user creates a deployment. It creates a replica set in its business logic.

2. The replica set controller (again inside of kube-controller-manager) notices (through a replica set informer) the new replica set and subsequently runs its business logic, which creates a pod object.

3. The scheduler (inside the kube-scheduler binary)—which is also a controller—notices the pod (through a pod informer) with an empty spec.nodeName field. Its business logic puts the pod in its scheduling queue.

4. Meanwhile the kubelet—another controller—notices the new pod (through its pod informer). But the new pod's spec.nodeName field is empty and therefore does not match the kubelet's node name. It ignores the pod and goes back to sleep (until the next event).

5. The scheduler takes the pod out of the work queue and schedules it to a node that has enough free resources by updating the `spec.nodeName` field in the pod and writing it to the API server.

6. The `kubelet` wakes up again due to the pod update event. It again compares the `spec.nodeName` with its own node name. The names match, and so the `kubelet` starts the containers of the pod and reports back that the containers have been started by writing this information into the pod status, back to the API server.

7. The replica set controller notices the changed pod but has nothing to do.

8. Eventually the pod terminates. The `kubelet` will notice this, get the pod object from the API server and set the "terminated" condition in the pod's status, and write it back to the API server.

9. The replica set controller notices the terminated pod and decides that this pod must be replaced. It deletes the terminated pod on the API server and creates a new one.

10. And so on.

As you can see, a number of independent control loops communicate purely through object changes on the API server and events these changes trigger through informers.

These events are sent from the API server to the informers inside the controllers via watches (see "Watches" on page 54)—that is, streaming connections of watch events. All of this is mostly invisible to the user. Not even the API server audit mechanism makes these events visible; only the object updates are visible. Controllers often use log output, though, when they react on events.

Watch Events Versus the Event Object

Watch events and the top-level `Event` object in Kubernetes are two different things:

- Watch events are sent through streaming HTTP connections between the API server and controllers to drive informers.

- The top-level `Event` object is a resource like pods, deployments, or services, with the special property that it has a time-to-live of an hour and then is purged automatically from `etcd`.

Event objects are merely a user-visible logging mechanism. A number of controllers create these events in order to communicate aspects of their business logic to the user. For example, the `kubelet` reports the lifecycle events for pods (i.e., when a container was started, restarted, and terminated).

You can list the second class of events happening in the cluster yourself using `kubectl`. By issuing the following command, you see what is going on in the `kube-system` namespace:

```
$ kubectl -n kube-system get events
LAST SEEN   FIRST SEEN   COUNT   NAME                                                KIND
3m          3m           1       kube-controller-manager-master.15932b6faba8e5ad     Pod
3m          3m           1       kube-apiserver-master.15932b6fa3f3fbbc              Pod
3m          3m           1       etcd-master.15932b6fa8a9a776                        Pod
...
2m          3m           2       weave-net-7nvnf.15932b73e61f5bc6                    Pod
2m          3m           2       weave-net-7nvnf.15932b73efeec0b3                    Pod
2m          3m           2       weave-net-7nvnf.15932b73e8f7d318                    Pod
```

If you want to learn more about events, read Michael Gasch's blog post "Events, the DNA of Kubernetes" (*http://bit.ly/2MZwbl6*), where he provides more background and examples.

Edge- Versus Level-Driven Triggers

Let's step back a bit and look more abstractly at how we can structure business logic implemented in controllers, and why Kubernetes has chosen to use events (i.e., state changes) to drive its logic.

There are two principled options to detect state change (the event itself):

Edge-driven triggers
> At the point in time the state change occurs, a handler is triggered—for example, from no pod to pod running.

Level-driven triggers
> The state is checked at regular intervals and if certain conditions are met (for example, pod running), then a handler is triggered.

The latter is a form of polling. It does not scale well with the number of objects, and the latency of controllers noticing changes depends on the interval of polling and how fast the API server can answer. With many asynchronous controllers involved, as described in "Events" on page 7, the result is a system that takes a long time to implement the users' desire.

The former option is much more efficient with many objects. The latency mostly depends on the number of worker threads in the controller's processing events. Hence, Kubernetes is based on events (i.e., edge-driven triggers).

In the Kubernetes control plane, a number of components change objects on the API server, with each change leading to an event (i.e., an edge). We call these components *event sources* or *event producers*. On the other hand, in the context of controllers, we're interested in consuming events—that is, when and how to react to an event (via an informer).

In a distributed system there are many actors running in parallel, and events come in asynchronously in any order. When we have a buggy controller logic, some slightly wrong state machine, or an external service failure, it is easy to lose events in the sense that we don't process them completely. Hence, we have to take a deeper look at how to cope with errors.

In Figure 1-3 you can see different strategies at work:

1. An example of an edge-driven-only logic, where potentially the second state change is missed.

2. An example of an edge-triggered logic, which always gets the latest state (i.e., level) when processing an event. In other words, the logic is edge-triggered but level-driven.

3. An example of an edge-triggered, level-driven logic with additional resync.

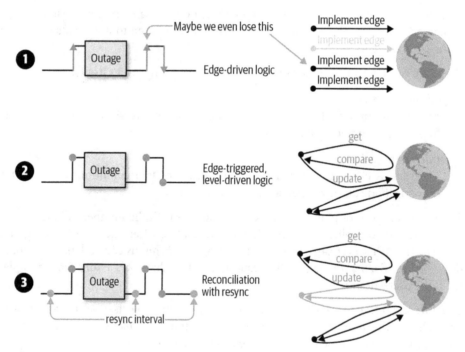

Figure 1-3. Trigger options (edge-driven versus level-driven)

Strategy 1 does not cope well with missed events, whether because broken networking makes it lose events, or because the controller itself has bugs or some external cloud API was down. Imagine that the replica set controller would replace pods only when they terminate. Missing events would mean that the replica set would always run with fewer pods because it never reconciles the whole state.

Strategy 2 recovers from those issues when another event is received because it implements its logic based on the latest state in the cluster. In the case of the replica set controller, it will always compare the specified replica count with the running pods in the cluster. When it loses events, it will replace all missing pods the next time a pod update is received.

Strategy 3 adds continuous resync (e.g., every five minutes). If no pod events come in, it will at least reconcile every five minutes, even if the application runs very stably and does not lead to many pod events.

Given the challenges of pure edge-driven triggers, the Kubernetes controllers typically implement the third strategy.

If you want to learn more about the origins of the triggers and the motivations for level triggering with reconciliation in Kubernetes, read James Bowes's article, "Level Triggering and Reconciliation in Kubernetes" (*http://bit.ly/2FmLLAW*).

This concludes the discussion of the different, abstract ways to detect external changes and to react on them. The next step in the control loop of Figure 1-2 is to change the cluster objects or to change the external world following the spec. We'll look at it now.

Changing Cluster Objects or the External World

In this phase, the controller changes the state of the objects it is supervising. For example, the ReplicaSet controller in the controller manager (*http://bit.ly/2WUAEVy*) is supervising pods. On each event (edge-triggered), it will observe the current state of its pods and compare that with the desired state (level-driven).

Since the act of changing the resource state is domain- or task-specific, we can provide little guidance. Instead, we'll keep looking at the ReplicaSet controller we introduced earlier. ReplicaSets are used in deployments, and the bottom line of the respective controller is: maintain a user-defined number of identical pod replicas. That is, if there are fewer pods than the user specified—for example, because a pod died or the replica value has been increased—the controller will launch new pods. If, however, there are too many pods, it will select some for termination. The entire business logic of the controller is available via the *replica_set.go* package (*http://bit.ly/2L4eKxa*), and the following excerpt of the Go code deals with the state change (edited for clarity):

```
// manageReplicas checks and updates replicas for the given ReplicaSet.
// It does NOT modify <filteredPods>.
// It will requeue the replica set in case of an error while creating/deleting pods.
```

```go
func (rsc *ReplicaSetController) manageReplicas(
        filteredPods []*v1.Pod, rs *apps.ReplicaSet,
) error {
    diff := len(filteredPods) - int(*(rs.Spec.Replicas))
    rsKey, err := controller.KeyFunc(rs)
    if err != nil {
        utilruntime.HandleError(
          fmt.Errorf("Couldn't get key for %v %#v: %v", rsc.Kind, rs, err),
        )
        return nil
    }
    if diff < 0 {
        diff *= -1
        if diff > rsc.burstReplicas {
            diff = rsc.burstReplicas
        }
        rsc.expectations.ExpectCreations(rsKey, diff)
        klog.V(2).Infof("Too few replicas for %v %s/%s, need %d, creating %d",
          rsc.Kind, rs.Namespace, rs.Name, *(rs.Spec.Replicas), diff,
        )
        successfulCreations, err := slowStartBatch(
          diff,
          controller.SlowStartInitialBatchSize,
          func() error {
                ref := metav1.NewControllerRef(rs, rsc.GroupVersionKind)
                err := rsc.podControl.CreatePodsWithControllerRef(
                  rs.Namespace, &rs.Spec.Template, rs, ref,
                )
                if err != nil && errors.IsTimeout(err) {
                  return nil
                }
                return err
          },
        )
        if skippedPods := diff - successfulCreations; skippedPods > 0 {
            klog.V(2).Infof("Slow-start failure. Skipping creation of %d pods," +
              " decrementing expectations for %v %v/%v",
              skippedPods, rsc.Kind, rs.Namespace, rs.Name,
            )
            for i := 0; i < skippedPods; i++ {
                rsc.expectations.CreationObserved(rsKey)
            }
        }
        return err
    } else if diff > 0 {
        if diff > rsc.burstReplicas {
            diff = rsc.burstReplicas
        }
        klog.V(2).Infof("Too many replicas for %v %s/%s, need %d, deleting %d",
          rsc.Kind, rs.Namespace, rs.Name, *(rs.Spec.Replicas), diff,
        )

        podsToDelete := getPodsToDelete(filteredPods, diff)
        rsc.expectations.ExpectDeletions(rsKey, getPodKeys(podsToDelete))
        errCh := make(chan error, diff)
        var wg sync.WaitGroup
        wg.Add(diff)
        for _, pod := range podsToDelete {
            go func(targetPod *v1.Pod) {
```

```
            defer wg.Done()
            if err := rsc.podControl.DeletePod(
              rs.Namespace,
              targetPod.Name,
              rs,
            ); err != nil {
                podKey := controller.PodKey(targetPod)
                klog.V(2).Infof("Failed to delete %v, decrementing " +
                "expectations for %v %s/%s",
                podKey, rsc.Kind, rs.Namespace, rs.Name,
                )
                rsc.expectations.DeletionObserved(rsKey, podKey)
                errCh <- err
            }
        }(pod)
    }
    wg.Wait()

    select {
    case err := <-errCh:
        if err != nil {
            return err
        }
    default:
    }
}
return nil
}
```

You can see that the controller computes the difference between specification and current state in the line `diff := len(filteredPods) - int(*(rs.Spec.Replicas))` and then implements two cases depending on that:

- `diff < 0`: Too few replicas; more pods must be created.
- `diff > 0`: Too many replicas; pods must be deleted.

It also implements a strategy to choose pods where it is least harmful to delete them in `getPodsToDelete`.

Changing the resource state does not, however, necessarily mean that the resources themselves have to be part of the Kubernetes cluster. In other words, a controller can change the state of resources that are located outside of Kubernetes, such as a cloud storage service. For example, the AWS Service Operator (*http://bit.ly/2ItJcif*) allows you to manage AWS resources. Among other things, it allows you to manage S3 buckets—that is, the S3 controller is supervising a resource (the S3 bucket) that exists outside of Kubernetes, and the state changes reflect concrete phases in its lifecycle: an S3 bucket is created and at some point deleted.

This should convince you that with a custom controller you can manage not only core resources, like pods, and custom resources, like our cnat example, but even compute or store resources that exist outside of Kubernetes. This makes controllers very flexible and powerful integration mechanisms, providing a unified way to use resources across platforms and environments.

Optimistic Concurrency

In "The Control Loop" on page 6, we discussed in step 3 that a controller—after updating cluster objects and/or the external world according to the spec—writes the results into the status of the resource that triggered the controller run in step 1.

This and actually any other write (also in step 2) can go wrong. In a distributed system, this controller is probably only one of many that update resources. Concurrent writes can fail because of write conflicts.

To better understand what's happening, let's step back a bit and have a look at Figure 1-4.[2]

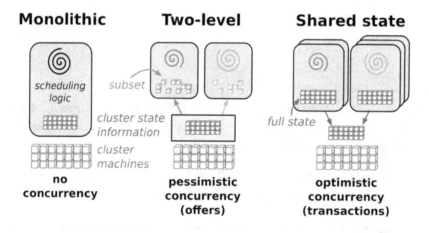

Figure 1-4. Scheduling architectures in distributed systems

The source defines Omega's parallel scheduler architecture as follows:

> Our solution is a new parallel scheduler architecture built around shared state, using lock-free optimistic concurrency control, to achieve both implementation extensibility and performance scalability. This architecture is being used in Omega, Google's next-generation cluster management system.

While Kubernetes inherited a lot of traits and lessons learned from Borg (http://bit.ly/2XNSv5p), this specific, transactional control plane feature comes from Omega: in

---

2 Source: "Omega: Flexible, Scalable Schedulers for Large Compute Clusters" (http://bit.ly/2PjYZ59), by Malte Schwarzkopf et al., Google AI, 2013.

---

order to carry out concurrent operations without locks, the Kubernetes API server uses optimistic concurrency.

This means, in a nutshell, that if and when the API server detects concurrent write attempts, it rejects the latter of the two write operations. It is then up to the client (controller, scheduler, kubectl, etc.) to handle a conflict and potentially retry the write operation.

The following demonstrates the idea of optimistic concurrency in Kubernetes:

```
var err error
for retries := 0; retries < 10; retries++ {
    foo, err = client.Get("foo", metav1.GetOptions{})
    if err != nil {
        break
    }

    <update-the-world-and-foo>

    _, err = client.Update(foo)
    if err != nil && errors.IsConflict(err) {
        continue
    } else if err != nil {
        break
    }
}
```

The code shows a retry loop that gets the latest object foo in each iteration, then tries to update the world and foo's status to match foo's spec. The changes done before the Update call are optimistic.

The returned object foo from the client.Get call contains a *resource version* (part of the embedded ObjectMeta struct—see "ObjectMeta" on page 50 for details), which will tell etcd on the write operation behind the client.Update call that another actor in the cluster wrote the foo object in the meantime. If that's the case, our retry loop will get a *resource version conflict error*. This means that the optimistic concurrency logic failed. In other words, the client.Update call is also optimistic.

The resource version is actually the etcd key/value version. The resource version of each object is a string in Kubernetes that contains an integer. This integer comes directly from etcd. etcd maintains a counter that increases each time the value of a key (which holds the object's serialization) is modified.

Throughout the API machinery code the resource version is (more or less consequently) handled like an arbitrary string, but with some ordering on it. The fact that integers are stored is just an implementation detail of the current etcd storage backend.

Let's look at a concrete example. Imagine your client is not the only actor in the cluster that modifies a pod. There is another actor, namely the kubelet, that constantly modifies some fields because a container is constantly crashing. Now your controller reads the pod object's latest state like so:

```
kind: Pod
metadata:
  name: foo
  resourceVersion: 57
spec:
  ...
status:
  ...
```

Now assume the controller needs several seconds with its updates to the world. Seven seconds later, it tries to update the pod it read—for example, it sets an annotation. Meanwhile, the kubelet has noticed yet another container restart and updated the pod's status to reflect that; that is, resourceVersion has increased to 58.

The object your controller sends in the update request has resourceVersion: 57. The API server tries to set the etcd key for the pod with that value. etcd notices that the resource versions do not match and reports back that 57 conflicts with 58. The update fails.

The bottom line of this example is that for your controller, you are responsible for implementing a retry strategy and for adapting if an optimistic operation failed. You never know who else might be manipulating state, whether other custom controllers or core controllers such as the deployment controller.

The essence of this is: *conflict errors are totally normal in controllers. Always expect them and handle them gracefully.*

It's important to point out that optimistic concurrency is a perfect fit for level-based logic, because by using level-based logic you can just rerun the control loop (see "Edge- Versus Level-Driven Triggers" on page 9). Another run of that loop will automatically undo optimistic changes from the previous failed optimistic attempt, and it will try to update the world to the latest state.

Let's move on to a specific case of custom controllers (along with custom resources): the operator.

Operators

Operators as a concept in Kubernetes were introduced by CoreOS in 2016. In his seminal blog post, "Introducing Operators: Putting Operational Knowledge into Software" (*http://bit.ly/2ZC4Rui*), CoreOS CTO Brandon Philips defined operators as follows:

A Site Reliability Engineer (SRE) is a person [who] operates an application by writing software. They are an engineer, a developer, who knows how to develop software specifically for a particular application domain. The resulting piece of software has an application's operational domain knowledge programmed into it.

[...]

We call this new class of software Operators. An Operator is an application-specific controller that extends the Kubernetes API to create, configure, and manage instances of complex stateful applications on behalf of a Kubernetes user. It builds upon the basic Kubernetes resource and controller concepts but includes domain or application-specific knowledge to automate common tasks.

In the context of this book, we will use operators as Philips describes them and, more formally, require that the following three conditions hold (see also Figure 1-5):

- There's some domain-specific operational knowledge you'd like to automate.

- The best practices for this operational knowledge are known and can be made explicit—for example, in the case of a Cassandra operator, when and how to re-balance nodes, or in the case of an operator for a service mesh, how to create a route.

- The artifacts shipped in the context of the operator are:

  — A set of *custom resource definitions* (CRDs) capturing the domain-specific schema and custom resources following the CRDs that, on the instance level, represent the domain of interest.

  — A custom controller, supervising the custom resources, potentially along with core resources. For example, the custom controller might spin up a pod.

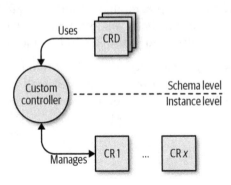

Figure 1-5. The concept of an operator

Operators have come a long way (*http://bit.ly/2x5TSNw*) from the conceptual work and prototyping in 2016 to the launch of OperatorHub.io (*https://operatorhub.io*) by Red Hat (which acquired CoreOS in 2018 and continued to build out the idea) in early 2019. See Figure 1-6 for a screenshot of the hub in mid-2019 sporting some 17 operators, ready to be used.

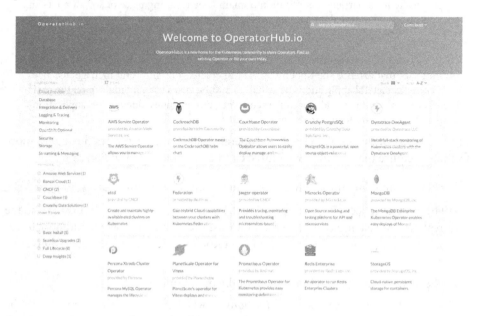

Figure 1-6. OperatorHub.io screenshot

Summary

In this first chapter we defined the scope of our book and what we expect from you. We explained what we mean by programming Kubernetes and defined Kubernetes-native apps in the context of this book. As preparation for later examples, we also provided a high-level introduction to controllers and operators.

So, now that you know what to expect from the book and how you can benefit from it, let's jump into the deep end. In the next chapter, we'll take a closer look at the Kubernetes API, the API server's inner workings, and how you can interact with the API using command-line tools such as `curl`.

## CHAPTER 2

Kubernetes API Basics

In this chapter we walk you through the Kubernetes API basics. This includes a deep dive into the API server's inner workings, the API itself, and how you can interact with the API from the command line. We will introduce you to Kubernetes API concepts such as resources and kinds, as well as grouping and versioning.

The API Server

Kubernetes is made up of a bunch of nodes (machines in the cluster) with different roles, as shown in Figure 2-1: the control plane on the master node(s) consists of the API server, controller manager, and scheduler. The API server is the central management entity and the only component that talks directly with the distributed storage component etcd.

The API server has the following core responsibilities:

- To serve the Kubernetes API. This API is used cluster-internally by the master components, the worker nodes, and your Kubernetes-native apps, as well as externally by clients such as kubectl.
- To proxy cluster components, such as the Kubernetes dashboard, or to stream logs, service ports, or serve kubectl exec sessions.

Serving the API means:

- Reading state: getting single objects, listing them, and streaming changes
- Manipulating state: creating, updating, and deleting objects

State is persisted via etcd.

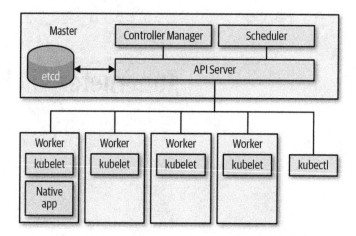

Figure 2-1. Kubernetes architecture overview

The heart of Kubernetes is its API server. But how does the API server work? We'll first treat the API server as a black box and take a closer look at its HTTP interface, then we'll move on to the inner workings of the API server.

The HTTP Interface of the API Server

From a client's perspective, the API server exposes a RESTful HTTP API with JSON or *protocol buffer* (*http://bit.ly/1HhFC5L*) (*protobuf* for short) payload, which is used mainly for cluster-internal communication, for performance reasons.

The API server HTTP interface handles HTTP requests to query and manipulate Kubernetes resources using the following HTTP verbs (*https://mzl.la/2WX21hL*) (or HTTP methods):

- The HTTP GET verb is used for retrieving the data with a specific resource (such as a certain pod) or a collection or list of resources (for example, all pods in a namespace).

- The HTTP POST verb is used for creating a resource, such as a service or a deployment.

- The HTTP PUT verb is used for updating an existing resource—for example, changing the container image of a pod.

- The HTTP PATCH verb is used for partial updates of existing resources. Read "Use a JSON merge patch to update a Deployment" (*http://bit.ly/2Xpbi6I*) in the Kubernetes documentation to learn more about the available strategies and implications here.

- The HTTP `DELETE` verb is used for destroying a resource in a nonrecoverable manner.

If you look at, say, the Kubernetes 1.14 API reference (*http://bit.ly/2IVevBG*), you can see the different HTTP verbs in action. For example, to list pods in the current name-space with the CLI command equivalent of `kubectl -n THENAMESPACE get pods`, you would issue `GET /api/v1/namespaces/THENAMESPACE/pods` (see Figure 2-2).

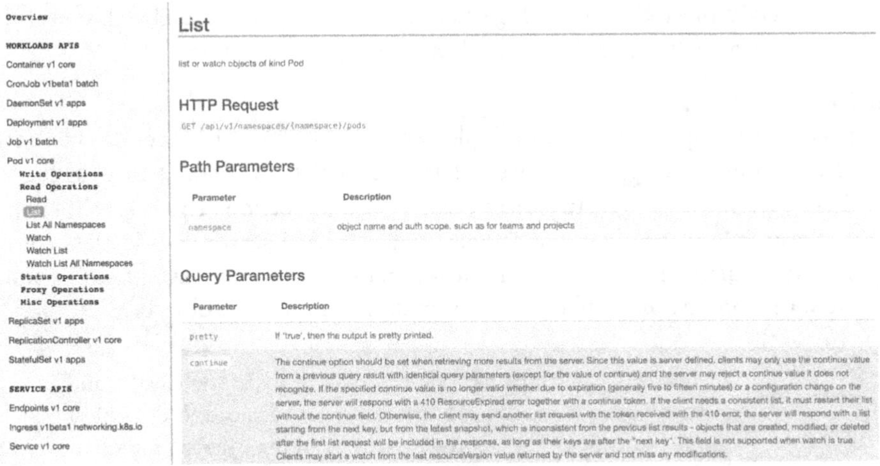

Figure 2-2. API server HTTP interface in action: listing pods in a given namespace

For an introduction on how the API server HTTP interface is invoked from a Go program, see "The Client Library" on page 35.

API Terminology

Before we get into the API business, let's first define the terms used in the context of the Kubernetes API server:

Kind

The type of an entity. Each object has a field `Kind` (lowercase `kind` in JSON, capi-talized `Kind` in Golang), which tells a client such as `kubectl` that it represents, for example, a pod. There are three categories of kinds:

- Objects represent *a persistent entity in the system*—for example, `Pod` or `End points`. Objects have names, and many of them live in namespaces.

- Lists are collections of one or more kinds of entities. Lists have a limited set of common metadata. Examples include `PodLists` or `NodeLists`. When you do a **kubectl get pods**, that's exactly what you get.

- Special-purpose kinds are used for specific actions on objects and for non-persistent entities such as /binding or /scale. For discovery, Kubernetes uses APIGroup and APIResource; for error results, it uses Status.

In Kubernetes programs, a kind directly corresponds with a Golang type. Thus, as Golang types, kinds are singular and begin with a capital letter.

API group

A collection of Kinds that are logically related. For example, all batch objects like Job or ScheduledJob are in the batch API group.

Version

Each API group can exist in multiple versions, and most of them do. For example, a group first appears as v1alpha1 and is then promoted to v1beta1 and finally graduates to v1. An object created in one version (e.g., v1beta1) can be retrieved in each of the supported versions. The API server does lossless conversion to return objects in the requested version. From the cluster user's point of view, versions are just different representations of the same objects.

> There is no such thing as "one object is in v1 in the cluster, and another object is in v1beta1 in the cluster." Instead, every object can be returned as a v1 representation or in the v1beta1 representation, as the cluster user desires.

Resource

A usually lowercase, plural word (e.g., pods) identifying a set of HTTP endpoints (paths) exposing the CRUD (create, read, update, delete) semantics of a certain object type in the system. Common paths are:

- The root, such as .../*pods*, which lists all instances of that type
- A path for individual named resources, such as .../*pods/nginx*

Typically, each of these endpoints returns and receives one kind (a PodList in the first case, and a Pod in the second). But in other situations (e.g., in case of errors), a Status kind object is returned.

In addition to the main resource with full CRUD semantics, a resource can have further endpoints to perform specific actions (e.g., .../*pod/nginx/port-forward*, .../*pod/nginx/exec*, or .../*pod/nginx/logs*). We call these *subresources* (see "Subresources" on page 81). These usually implement custom protocols instead of REST —for example, some kind of streaming connection via WebSockets or imperative APIs.

Resources and kinds are often mixed up. Note the clear distinction:

- Resources correspond to HTTP paths.
- Kinds are the types of objects returned by and received by these endpoints, as well as persisted into etcd.

Resources are always part of an API group and a version, collectively referred to as *GroupVersionResource* (or GVR). A GVR uniquely defines an HTTP path. A concrete path, for example, in the default namespace would be */apis/batch/v1/namespaces/default/jobs*. Figure 2-3 shows an example GVR for a namespaced resource, a Job.

Figure 2-3. Kubernetes API—GroupVersionResource (GVR)

In contrast to the jobs GVR example, cluster-wide resources such as nodes or namespaces themselves do not have the *$NAMESPACE* part in the path. For example, a nodes GVR example might look as follows: */api/v1/nodes*. Note that namespaces show up in other resources' HTTP paths but are also a resource themselves, accessible at */api/v1/namespaces*.

Similarly to GVRs, each kind lives in an API group, is versioned, and is identified via a *GroupVersionKind* (GVK).

Cohabitation—Kinds Living in Multiple API Groups

Kinds of the same name may coexist not only in different *versions*, but also in different API groups, simultaneously. For example, Deployment started as an alpha kind in the extensions group and was eventually promoted to a stable version in its own group, apps.k8s.io. We call this *cohabitation*. While not common in Kubernetes, there are a handful of them:

- Ingress, NetworkPolicy in extensions and networking.k8s.io
- Deployment, DaemonSet, ReplicaSet in extensions and apps
- Event in the core group and events.k8s.io

GVKs and GVRs are related. GVKs are served under HTTP paths identified by GVRs. The process of mapping a GVK to a GVR is called REST mapping. We will see

`RESTMappers` that implement REST mapping in Golang in "REST Mapping" on page 63.

From a global point of view, the API resource space logically forms a tree with top-level nodes including */api*, */apis*, and some nonhierarchical endpoints such as */healthz* or */metrics*. An example rendering of this API space is shown in Figure 2-4. Note that the exact shape and paths depend on the Kubernetes version, with an increasing tendency to stabilize over the years.

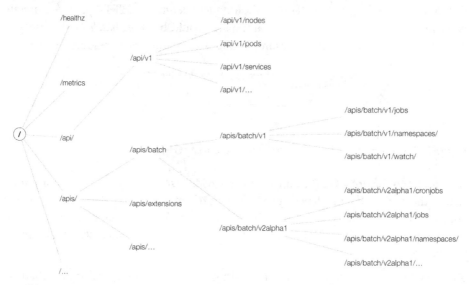

Figure 2-4. An example Kubernetes API space

Kubernetes API Versioning

For extensibility reasons, Kubernetes supports multiple API versions at different API paths, such as */api/v1* or */apis/extensions/v1beta1*. Different API versions imply different levels of stability and support:

- *Alpha* level (e.g., `v1alpha1`) is usually disabled by default; support for a feature may be dropped at any time without notice and should be used only in short-lived testing clusters.

- *Beta* level (e.g., `v2beta3`) is enabled by default, meaning that the code is well tested; however, the semantics of objects may change in incompatible ways in a subsequent beta or stable release.

- *Stable* (generally available, or GA) level (e.g., `v1`) will appear in released software for many subsequent versions.

Let's look at how the HTTP API space is constructed: at the top level we distinguish between the core group—that is, everything below */api/v1*—and the named groups in paths of the form */apis/$NAME/$VERSION*.

The core group is located under /api/v1 and not, as one would expect, under */apis/core/v1*, for historic reasons. The core group existed before the concept of an API group was introduced.

There is a third type of HTTP paths—ones that are not resource aligned—that the API server exposes: cluster-wide entities such as */metrics*, */logs*, or */healthz*. In addition, the API server supports watches; that is, rather than polling resources at set intervals, you can add a ?watch=true to certain requests and the API server changes into a watch modus (*http://bit.ly/2x5PnTl*).

Declarative State Management

Most API objects make a distinction between the specification of the *desired state* of the resource and the *status* of the object at the current time. A *specification*, or spec for short, is a complete description of the desired state of a resource and is typically persisted in stable storage, usually etcd.

Why do we say "usually etcd"? Well, there are Kubernetes distros and offerings, such as k3s (*https://k3s.io*) or Microsoft's AKS, that have replaced or are working on replacing etcd with something else. Thanks to the modular architecture of the Kubernetes control plane, this works just fine.

Let's talk a little more about spec (desired state) versus status (observed state) in the context of the API server.

The spec describes your desired state for the resource, something you need to provide via a command-line tool such as kubectl or programmatically via your Go code. The status describes the observed or actual state of the resource and is managed by the control plane, either by core components such as the controller manager or by your own custom controller (see "Controllers and Operators" on page 5). For example, in a deployment you might specify that you want 20 replicas of the application to be running at all times. The deployment controller, part of the controller manager in the control plane, reads the deployment spec you provided and creates a replica set, which then takes care of managing the replicas: it creates the respective number of pods, which eventually (via the kubelet) results in containers being launched on worker nodes. If any replica fails, the deployment controller would make this known to you in the status. This is what we call *declarative state management*—that is, declaring the desired state and letting Kubernetes take care of the rest.

We will see declarative state management in action in the next section, as we start to explore the API from the command line.

Using the API from the Command Line

In this section we'll be using `kubectl` and `curl` to demonstrate the use of the Kubernetes API. If you're not familiar with these CLI tools, now is a good time to install them and try them out.

For starters, let's have a look at the desired and observed state of a resource. We will be using a control plane component that is likely available in every cluster, the CoreDNS plug-in (old Kubernetes versions were using `kube-dns` instead) in the `kube-system` namespace (this output is heavily edited to highlight the important parts):

```
$ kubectl -n kube-system get deploy/coredns -o=yaml
apiVersion: apps/v1
kind: Deployment
metadata:
  name: coredns
  namespace: kube-system
  ...
spec:
  template:
    spec:
      containers:
      - name: coredns
        image: 602401143452.dkr.ecr.us-east-2.amazonaws.com/eks/coredns:v1.2.2
  ...
status:
  replicas: 2
  conditions:
  - type: Available
    status: "True"
    lastUpdateTime: "2019-04-01T16:42:10Z"
  ...
```

As you can see from this `kubectl` command, in the `spec` section of the deployment you'd define characteristics such as which container image to use and how many replicas you want to run in parallel, and in the `status` section you'd learn how many replicas at the current point in time are actually running.

To carry out CLI-related operations, we will, for the remainder of this chapter, be using batch operations as the running example. Let's start by executing the following command in a terminal:

```
$ kubectl proxy --port=8080
Starting to serve on 127.0.0.1:8080
```

This command proxies the Kubernetes API to our local machine and also takes care of the authentication and authorization bits. It allows us to directly issue requests via HTTP and receive JSON payloads in return. Let's do that by launching a second terminal session where we query v1:

```
$ curl http://127.0.0.1:8080/apis/batch/v1
{
  "kind": "APIResourceList",
  "apiVersion": "v1",
  "groupVersion": "batch/v1",
  "resources": [
    {
      "name": "jobs",
      "singularName": "",
      "namespaced": true,
      "kind": "Job",
      "verbs": [
        "create",
        "delete",
        "deletecollection",
        "get",
        "list",
        "patch",
        "update",
        "watch"
      ],
      "categories": [
        "all"
      ]
    },
    {
      "name": "jobs/status",
      "singularName": "",
      "namespaced": true,
      "kind": "Job",
      "verbs": [
        "get",
        "patch",
        "update"
      ]
    }
  ]
}
```

You don't have to use curl along with the kubectl proxy command to get direct HTTP API access to the Kubernetes API. You can instead use the kubectl get --raw command: for example, replace curl http://127.0.0.1:8080/apis/batch/v1 with kubectl get --raw /apis/batch/v1.

Compare this with the v1beta1 version, noting that you can get a list of supported versions for the batch API group when looking at *http://127.0.0.1:8080/apis/batch* v1beta1:

```
$ curl http://127.0.0.1:8080/apis/batch/v1beta1
{
  "kind": "APIResourceList",
  "apiVersion": "v1",
  "groupVersion": "batch/v1beta1",
  "resources": [
    {
      "name": "cronjobs",
      "singularName": "",
      "namespaced": true,
      "kind": "CronJob",
      "verbs": [
        "create",
        "delete",
        "deletecollection",
        "get",
        "list",
        "patch",
        "update",
        "watch"
      ],
      "shortNames": [
        "cj"
      ],
      "categories": [
        "all"
      ]
    },
    {
      "name": "cronjobs/status",
      "singularName": "",
      "namespaced": true,
      "kind": "CronJob",
      "verbs": [
        "get",
        "patch",
        "update"
      ]
    }
  ]
}
```

As you can see, the v1beta1 version also contains the cronjobs resource with the kind CronJob. At the time of this writing, cron jobs have not been promoted to v1.

If you want to get an idea of what API resources are supported in your cluster, including their kinds, whether or not they are namespaced, and their short names (primarily for kubectl on the command line), you can use the following command:

```
$ kubectl api-resources
NAME              SHORTNAMES  APIGROUP  NAMESPACED  KIND
bindings                                true        Binding
componentstatuses cs                    false       ComponentStatus
configmaps        cm                    true        ConfigMap
endpoints         ep                    true        Endpoints
events            ev                    true        Event
limitranges       limits                true        LimitRange
namespaces        ns                    false       Namespace
```

```
nodes                      no              false   Node
persistentvolumeclaims     pvc             true    PersistentVolumeClaim
persistentvolumes          pv              false   PersistentVolume
pods                       po              true    Pod
podtemplates                               true    PodTemplate
replicationcontrollers     rc              true    ReplicationController
resourcequotas             quota           true    ResourceQuota
secrets                                    true    Secret
serviceaccounts            sa              true    ServiceAccount
services                   svc             true    Service
controllerrevisions              apps      true    ControllerRevision
daemonsets                 ds    apps      true    DaemonSet
deployments                deploy apps     true    Deployment
...
```

The following is a related command that can be very useful to determine the different resource versions supported in your cluster:

```
$ kubectl api-versions
admissionregistration.k8s.io/v1beta1
apiextensions.k8s.io/v1beta1
apiregistration.k8s.io/v1
apiregistration.k8s.io/v1beta1
appmesh.k8s.aws/v1alpha1
appmesh.k8s.aws/v1beta1
apps/v1
apps/v1beta1
apps/v1beta2
authentication.k8s.io/v1
authentication.k8s.io/v1beta1
authorization.k8s.io/v1
authorization.k8s.io/v1beta1
autoscaling/v1
autoscaling/v2beta1
autoscaling/v2beta2
batch/v1
batch/v1beta1
certificates.k8s.io/v1beta1
coordination.k8s.io/v1beta1
crd.k8s.amazonaws.com/v1alpha1
events.k8s.io/v1beta1
extensions/v1beta1
networking.k8s.io/v1
policy/v1beta1
rbac.authorization.k8s.io/v1
rbac.authorization.k8s.io/v1beta1
scheduling.k8s.io/v1beta1
storage.k8s.io/v1
storage.k8s.io/v1beta1
v1
```

How the API Server Processes Requests

Now that you have an understanding of the external-facing HTTP interface, let's focus on the inner workings of the API server. Figure 2-5 shows a high-level overview of the request processing in the API server.

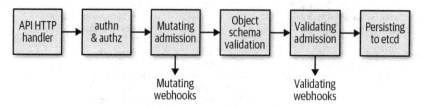

Figure 2-5. Kubernetes API server request processing overview

So, what actually happens now when an HTTP request hits the Kubernetes API? On a high level, the following interactions take place:

1. The HTTP request is processed by a chain of filters registered in `DefaultBuild HandlerChain()`. This chain is defined in *k8s.io/apiserver/pkg/server/config.go* (*http://bit.ly/2x9t27e*) and discussed in detail shortly. It applies a series of filter operations on said request. Either the filter passes and attaches respective information to the context—to be precise, `ctx.RequestInfo`, with `ctx` being the context (*https://golang.org/pkg/context*) in Go (e.g., the authenticated user)—or, if a request does not pass a filter, it returns an appropriate HTTP response code stating the reason (e.g., a `401` response (*https://httpstatuses.com/401*) if the user authentication failed).

2. Next, depending on the HTTP path, the multiplexer in *k8s.io/apiserver/pkg/ server/handler.go* (*http://bit.ly/2WUd0c6*) routes the HTTP request to the respective handler.

3. A handler is registered for each API group—see *k8s.io/apiserver/pkg/endpoints/ groupversion.go* (*http://bit.ly/2IvvSKA*) and *k8s.io/apiserver/pkg/endpoints/installer.go* (*http://bit.ly/2Y1eySV*) for details. It takes the HTTP request as well as the context (for example, user and access rights) and retrieves as well as delivers the requested object from `etcd` storage.

Let's now take a closer look at the chain of filters that `DefaultBuildHandlerChain()` in *server/config.go* (*http://bit.ly/2LWUUnQ*) sets up, and what happens in each of them:

```
func DefaultBuildHandlerChain(apiHandler http.Handler, c *Config) http.Handler {
    h := WithAuthorization(apiHandler, c.Authorization.Authorizer, c.Serializer)
    h = WithMaxInFlightLimit(h, c.MaxRequestsInFlight,
        c.MaxMutatingRequestsInFlight, c.LongRunningFunc)
    h = WithImpersonation(h, c.Authorization.Authorizer, c.Serializer)
    h = WithAudit(h, c.AuditBackend, c.AuditPolicyChecker, LongRunningFunc)
    ...
    h = WithAuthentication(h, c.Authentication.Authenticator, failed, ...)
    h = WithCORS(h, c.CorsAllowedOriginList, nil, nil, nil, "true")
    h = WithTimeoutForNonLongRunningRequests(h, LongRunningFunc, RequestTimeout)
    h = WithWaitGroup(h, c.LongRunningFunc, c.HandlerChainWaitGroup)
    h = WithRequestInfo(h, c.RequestInfoResolver)
```

```
    h = WithPanicRecovery(h)
    return h
}
```

All packages are in *k8s.io/apiserver/pkg* (*http://bit.ly/2LUzTdx*). To review more specifically:

WithPanicRecovery()

Takes care of recovery and log panics. Defined in *server/filters/wrap.go* (*http://bit.ly/2N0zfNB*).

WithRequestInfo()

Attaches a RequestInfo to the context. Defined in *endpoints/filters/requestinfo.go* (*http://bit.ly/2KvKjQH*).

WithWaitGroup()

Adds all non-long-running requests to a wait group; used for graceful shutdown. Defined in *server/filters/waitgroup.go* (*http://bit.ly/2ItnsD6*).

WithTimeoutForNonLongRunningRequests()

Times out non-long-running requests (like most GET, PUT, POST, and DELETE requests), in contrast to long-running requests such as watches and proxy requests. Defined in *server/filters/timeout.go* (*http://bit.ly/2KrKk8r*).

WithCORS()

Provides a CORS (*https://enable-cors.org*) implementation. CORS, short for cross-origin resource sharing, is a mechanism that allows JavaScript embedded in an HTML page to make XMLHttpRequests to a domain different from the one that the JavaScript originated in. Defined in *server/filters/cors.go* (*http://bit.ly/2L2A6uJ*).

WithAuthentication()

Attempts to authenticate the given request as a human or machine user and stores the user info in the provided context. On success, the Authorization HTTP header is removed from the request. If the authentication fails, it returns an HTTP 401 status code. Defined in *endpoints/filters/authentication.go* (*http://bit.ly/2Fjzr4b*).

WithAudit()

Decorates the handler with audit logging information for all incoming requests. The audit log entries contain information such as the source IP of the request, user invoking the operation, and namespace of the request. Defined in *admission/audit.go* (*http://bit.ly/2XpQN9U*).

`WithImpersonation()`

> Handles user impersonation by checking requests that attempt to change the user (similar to `sudo`). Defined in *endpoints/filters/impersonation.go* (*http://bit.ly/2L2UETP*).

`WithMaxInFlightLimit()`

> Limits the number of in-flight requests. Defined in *server/filters/maxinflight.go* (*http://bit.ly/2IY4unl*).

`WithAuthorization()`

> Checks permissions by invoking authorization modules and passes all authorized requests on to a multiplexer, which dispatches the request to the right handler. If the user doesn't have sufficient rights, it returns an HTTP 403 status code. Kubernetes nowadays uses role-based access control (RBAC). Defined in *endpoints/filters/authorization.go* (*http://bit.ly/31M2NSA*).

After this generic handler chain is passed (the first box in Figure 2-5), the actual request processing starts (i.e., the semantics of the request handler is executed):

- Requests for */*, */version*, */apis*, */healthz*, and other nonRESTful APIs are directly handled.

- Requests for RESTful resources go into the request pipeline consisting of:

admission

> Incoming objects go through an admission chain. That chain has some 20 different admission plug-ins.[1] Each plug-in can be part of the mutating phase (see the third box in Figure 2-5), part of the validating phase (see the fourth box in the figure), or both.
>
> In the mutating phase, the incoming request payload can be changed; for example, the image pull policy is set to `Always`, `IfNotPresent`, or `Never` depending on the admission configuration.
>
> The second admission phase is purely for validation; for example, security settings in pods are verified, or the existence of a namespace is verified before creating objects in that namespace.

---

1 In a Kubernetes 1.14 cluster, these are (in this order): `AlwaysAdmit`, `NamespaceAutoProvision`, `Name spaceLifecycle`, `NamespaceExists`, `SecurityContextDeny`, `LimitPodHardAntiAffinityTopology`, `PodPre set`, `LimitRanger`, `ServiceAccount`, `NodeRestriction`, `TaintNodesByCondition`, `AlwaysPullImages`, `ImagePolicyWebhook`, `PodSecurityPolicy`, `PodNodeSelector`, `Priority`, `DefaultTolerationSeconds`, `PodTolerationRestriction`, `DenyEscalatingExec`, `DenyExecOnPrivileged`, `EventRateLimit`, `ExtendedRe sourceToleration`, `PersistentVolumeLabel`, `DefaultStorageClass`, `StorageObjectInUseProtection`, `Own erReferencesPermissionEnforcement`, `PersistentVolumeClaimResize`, `MutatingAdmissionWebhook`, `ValidatingAdmissionWebhook`, `ResourceQuota`, and `AlwaysDeny`.

validation

Incoming objects are checked against a large validation logic, which exists for each object type in the system. For example, string formats are checked to verify that only valid DNS-compatible characters are used in service names, or that all container names in a pod are unique.

etcd-*backed CRUD logic*

Here the different verbs we saw in "The HTTP Interface of the API Server" on page 20 are implemented; for example, the update logic reads the object from etcd, checks that no other user has modified the object in the sense of "Optimistic Concurrency" on page 14, and, if not, writes the request object to etcd.

We will look into all these steps in greater detail in the following chapters; for example:

Custom resources

Validation in "Validating Custom Resources" on page 76, admission in "Admission Webhooks" on page 226, and general CRUD semantics in Chapter 4

Golang native resource

Validation in "Validation" on page 179, admission in "Admission" on page 189, and the implementation of CRUD semantics in "Registry and Strategy" on page 181

Summary

In this chapter we first discussed the Kubernetes API server as a black box and had a look at its HTTP interface. Then you learned how to interact with that black box on the command line, and finally we opened up the black box and explored its inner workings. By now you should know how the API server works internally, and how to interact with it using the CLI tool kubectl for resource exploration and manipulation.

It's now time to leave the manual interaction on the command line behind us and get started with programmatic API server access using Go: meet client-go, the core of the Kubernetes "standard library."

## CHAPTER 3

Basics of client-go

We'll now focus on the Kubernetes programming interface in Go. You'll learn how to access the Kubernetes API of the well-known native types like pods, services, and deployment. In later chapters, these techniques will be extended to user-defined types. Here, though, we first concentrate on all API objects that are shipped with every Kubernetes cluster.

The Repositories

The Kubernetes project provides a number of third-party consumable Git repositories under the *kubernetes* organization on GitHub. You'll need to import all of these with the domain alias *k8s.io/...* (not *github.com/kubernetes/...*) into your project. We'll present the most important of these repositories in the following sections.

The Client Library

The Kubernetes programming interface in Go mainly consists of the *k8s.io/client-go* library (for brevity we will just call it `client-go` going forward). *client-go* is a typical web service client library that supports all API types that are officially part of Kubernetes. It can be used to execute the usual REST verbs:

- *Create*
- *Get*
- *List*
- *Update*
- *Delete*

- *Patch*

Each of these REST verbs are implemented using the "The HTTP Interface of the API Server" on page 20. Furthermore, the verb `Watch` is supported, which is special for Kubernetes-like APIs, and one of the main differentiators compared to other APIs.

`client-go` (*http://bit.ly/2RryyLM*) is available on GitHub (see Figure 3-1), and used in Go code with the *k8s.io/client-go* package name. It is shipped in parallel to Kubernetes itself; that is, for each Kubernetes `1.x.y` release, there is a `client-go` release with a matching tag `kubernetes-1.x.y`.

Figure 3-1. The client-go repository on GitHub

In addition, there is a semantic versioning scheme. For example, `client-go` 9.0.0 matches the Kubernetes 1.12 release, `client-go` 10.0.0 matches Kubernetes 1.13, and so on. There may be more fine-grained releases in the future. Besides the client code for Kubernetes API objects, `client-go` also contains a lot of generic library code. This is also used for user-defined API objects in Chapter 4. See Figure 3-1 for a list of packages.

While all packages have their use, most of your code that speaks to Kubernetes APIs will use *tools/clientcmd/* to set up a client from a `kubeconfig` file and *kubernetes/* for the actual Kubernetes API clients. We will see code doing this very soon. Before that, let's finish a quick walk through with other relevant repositories and packages.

Kubernetes API Types

As we have seen, `client-go` holds the client interfaces. The Kubernetes API Go types for objects like pods, services, and deployments are located in their own repository (*http://bit.ly/2ZA6dWH*). It is accessed as `k8s.io/api` in Go code.

Pods are part of the legacy API group (often also called the "core" group) version `v1`. Hence, the `Pod` Go type is found in *k8s.io/api/core/v1*, and similarly for all other API types in Kubernetes. See Figure 3-2 for a list of packages, most of which correspond to Kubernetes API groups and their versions.

The actual Go types are contained in a *types.go* file (e.g., *k8s.io/api/core/v1/types.go*). In addition, there are other files, most of them automatically generated by a code generator.

core/v1
- Pod
- Services
- ReplicaSet
~ ...

Figure 3-2. The API repository on GitHub

API Machinery

Last but not least, there is a third repository called API Machinery (*http://bit.ly/2xAZiR2*), which is used as k8s.io/apimachinery in Go. It includes all the generic building blocks to implement a Kubernetes-like API. API Machinery is not restricted to container management, so, for example, it could be used to build APIs for an online shop or any other business-specific domain.

Nevertheless, you'll meet a lot of API Machinery packages in Kubernetes-native Go code. An important one is *k8s.io/apimachinery/pkg/apis/meta/v1*. It contains many of the generic API types such as ObjectMeta, TypeMeta, GetOptions, and ListOptions (see Figure 3-3).

pkg/apis/meta/v1
- ObjectMeta
- TypeMeta
- ListOptions
- DeleteOptions
- GetOptions
- Status
- Event
- ...

Figure 3-3. The API Machinery repository on GitHub

Creating and Using a Client

Now we know all the building blocks to create a Kubernetes client object, which means we can access resources in a Kubernetes cluster. Assuming you have access to a cluster in your local environment (i.e., kubectl is properly set up and credentials are configured), the following code illustrates how you can use client-go in a Go project:

```
import (
    metav1 "k8s.io/apimachinery/pkg/apis/meta/v1"
    "k8s.io/client-go/tools/clientcmd"
    "k8s.io/client-go/kubernetes"
)

kubeconfig = flag.String("kubeconfig", "~/.kube/config", "kubeconfig file")
flag.Parse()
config, err := clientcmd.BuildConfigFromFlags("", *kubeconfig)
clientset, err := kubernetes.NewForConfig(config)

pod, err := clientset.CoreV1().Pods("book").Get("example", metav1.GetOptions{})
```

The code imports the meta/v1 package to get access to metav1.GetOptions. Furthermore, it imports clientcmd from client-go in order to read and parse the kubeconfig (i.e., the client configuration with server name, credentials, etc.). Then it imports the `client-go kubernetes` package with the client sets for Kubernetes resources.

The default location for the kubeconfig file is in *.kube/config* in the user's home directory. This is also where `kubectl` gets the credentials for the Kubernetes clusters.

That kubeconfig is then read and parsed using `clientcmd.BuildConfigFromFlags`. We omitted the mandatory error handling throughout this code, but the `err` variable would normally contain, for example, the syntax error if a kubeconfig is not well formed. As syntax errors are common in Go code, such an error ought to be checked for properly, like so:

```
config, err := clientcmd.BuildConfigFromFlags("", *kubeconfig)
if err != nil {
    fmt.Printf("The kubeconfig cannot be loaded: %v\n", err
    os.Exit(1)
}
```

From `clientcmd.BuildConfigFromFlags` we get a `rest.Config`, which you can find in the *k8s.io/client-go/rest* package). This is passed to `kubernetes.NewForConfig` in order to create the actual Kubernetes *client set*. It's called a *client set* because it contains multiple clients for all native Kubernetes resources.

When running a binary inside of a pod in a cluster, the `kubelet` will automatically mount a service account into the container at */var/run/secrets/kubernetes.io/serviceaccount*. It replaces the kubeconfig file just mentioned and can easily be turned into a `rest.Config` via the `rest.InClusterConfig()` method. You'll often find the following combination of `rest.InClusterConfig()` and `clientcmd.BuildConfigFrom Flags()`, including support for the `KUBECONFIG` environment variable:

```
config, err := rest.InClusterConfig()
if err != nil {
    // fallback to kubeconfig
    kubeconfig := filepath.Join("~", ".kube", "config")
    if envvar := os.Getenv("KUBECONFIG"); len(envvar) >0 {
        kubeconfig = envvar
    }
    config, err = clientcmd.BuildConfigFromFlags("", kubeconfig)
    if err != nil {
        fmt.Printf("The kubeconfig cannot be loaded: %v\n", err
        os.Exit(1)
    }
}
```

In the following example code we select the core group in `v1` with `client set.CoreV1()` and then access the pod `"example"` in the `"book"` namespace:

```
pod, err := clientset.CoreV1().Pods("book").Get("example", metav1.GetOptions{})
```

Note that only the last function call, Get, actually accesses the server. Both CoreV1 and Pods select the client and set the namespace only for the following Get call (this is often called the *builder pattern*, in this case to build a request).

The Get call sends an HTTP GET request to */api/v1/namespaces/book/pods/example* on the server, which is set in the kubeconfig. If the Kubernetes API server answers with HTTP code 200, the body of the response will carry the encoded pod objects, either as JSON—which is the default wire format of client-go—or as protocol buffers.

You can enable protobuf for native Kubernetes resource clients by modifying the REST config before creating a client from it:

```
cfg, err := clientcmd.BuildConfigFromFlags("", *kubeconfig)
cfg.AcceptContentTypes = "application/vnd.kubernetes.protobuf,
                          application/json"
cfg.ContentType = "application/vnd.kubernetes.protobuf"
clientset, err := kubernetes.NewForConfig(cfg)
```

Note that the custom resources presented in Chapter 4 do not support protocol buffers.

Versioning and Compatibility

Kubernetes APIs are versioned. We have seen in the previous section that pods are in v1 of the core group. The core group actually exists in only one version today. There are other groups, though—for example, the apps group, which exists in v1, v1beta2, and v1beta1 (as of this writing). If you look into the *k8s.io/api/apps* (*http://bit.ly/ 2L1Nyio*) package, you will find all the API objects of these versions. In the *k8s.io/ client-go/kubernetes/typed/apps* (*http://bit.ly/2x45Uab*) package, you'll see the client implementations for all of these versions.

All of this is only the client side. It does not say anything about the Kubernetes cluster and its API server. Using a client with a version of an API group that the API server does not support will fail. Clients are hardcoded to a version, and the application developer has to select the right API group version in order to speak to the cluster at hand. See "API Versions and Compatibility Guarantees" on page 44 for more on API group compatibility guarantees.

A second aspect of compatibility is the meta API features of the API server that client-go is speaking to. For example, there are option structs for CRUD verbs, like CreateOptions, GetOptions, UpdateOptions, and DeleteOptions. Another important one is ObjectMeta (discussed in detail in "ObjectMeta" on page 50), which is part of every kind. All of these are frequently extended with new features; we usually call them *API machinery features*. In the Go documentation of their fields, comments specify when features are considered alpha or beta. The same API compatibility guarantees apply as for any other API fields.

In the example that follows, the `DeleteOptions` struct is defined in the package *k8s.io/apimachinery/pkg/apis/meta/v1/types.go* (*http://bit.ly/2MZ9flL*):

```
// DeleteOptions may be provided when deleting an API object.
type DeleteOptions struct {
    TypeMeta `json:",inline"`

    GracePeriodSeconds *int64 `json:"gracePeriodSeconds,omitempty"`
    Preconditions *Preconditions `json:"preconditions,omitempty"`
    OrphanDependents *bool `json:"orphanDependents,omitempty"`
    PropagationPolicy *DeletionPropagation `json:"propagationPolicy,omitempty"`

    // When present, indicates that modifications should not be
    // persisted. An invalid or unrecognized dryRun directive will
    // result in an error response and no further processing of the
    // request. Valid values are:
    // - All: all dry run stages will be processed
    // +optional
    DryRun []string `json:"dryRun,omitempty" protobuf:"bytes,5,rep,name=dryRun"`
}
```

The last field, `DryRun`, was added in Kubernetes 1.12 as alpha and in 1.13 as beta (enabled by default). It is not understood by the API server in earlier versions. Depending on the feature, passing such an option might simply be ignored or even rejected. So it is important to have a `client-go` version that is not too far off from the cluster version.

> The reference for which fields are available in which quality level is the sources in *k8s.io/api*, which are accessible, for example, for Kubernetes 1.13 in the `release-1.13` branch (*http://bit.ly/2Yrhjgq*). Alpha fields are marked as such in their description.
>
> There is generated API documentation (*http://bit.ly/2YrfiB2*) for easier consumption. It is the same information, though, as in *k8s.io/api*.
>
> Last but not least, many alpha and beta features have corresponding feature gates (*http://bit.ly/2RP5nmi*) (check here for the primary source (*http://bit.ly/2FPZPTT*)). Features are tracked in issues (*http://bit.ly/2YuHYcd*).

The formally guaranteed support matrix between cluster and `client-go` versions is published in the `client-go` README (*http://bit.ly/2RryyLM*) (see Table 3-1).

Table 3-1. client-go compatibility with Kubernetes versions

	Kubernetes 1.9	Kubernetes 1.10	Kubernetes 1.11	Kubernetes 1.12	Kubernetes 1.13	Kubernetes 1.14	Kubernetes 1.15
client-go 6.0	✓	+−	+−	+−	+−	+−	+−
client-go 7.0	+−	✓	+−	+−	+−	+−	+−
client-go 8.0	+−	+−	✓	+−	+−	+−	+−
client-go 9.0	+−	+−	+−	✓	+−	+−	+−
client-go 10.0	+−	+−	+−	+−	✓	+−	+−
client-go 11.0	+−	+−	+−	+−	+−	✓	+−
client-go 12.0	+−	+−	+−	+−	+−	+−	✓
client-go HEAD	+−	+−	+−	+−	+−	+−	+−

- ✓: both `client-go` and the Kubernetes version have the same features and the same API group versions.
- +: `client-go` has features or API group versions that may be absent from the Kubernetes cluster. This may be because of added functionality in `client-go` or because Kubernetes removed old, deprecated functionality. However, everything they have in common (i.e., most APIs) will work.
- −: `client-go` is knowingly incompatible with the Kubernetes cluster.

The takeaway from Table 3-1 is that the `client-go` library is supported with its corresponding cluster version. In case of version skew, developers have to carefully consider which features and which API groups they use and whether these are supported in the cluster version the application speaks to.

In Table 3-1, the `client-go` versions are listed. We briefly mentioned in "The Client Library" on page 35 that `client-go` uses semantic versioning (semver) formally, though by increasing the major version of `client-go` each time the minor version of Kubernetes (the 13 in 1.13.2) is increased. With `client-go` 1.0 being released for Kubernetes 1.4, we are now at `client-go` 12.0 (at the time of this writing) for Kubernetes 1.15.

This semver applies only to client-go itself, not to API Machinery or the API repository. Instead, the latter are tagged using Kubernetes versions, as seen in Figure 3-4. See "Vendoring" on page 66 to see what this means for vendoring *k8s.io/client-go*, *k8s.io/apimachinery*, and *k8s.io/api* in your project.

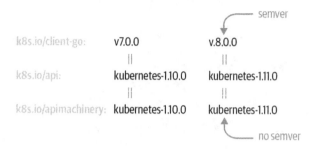

Figure 3-4. client-go versioning

API Versions and Compatibility Guarantees

As seen in the previous section, the selection of the right API group versions may be crucial if you target different cluster versions with your code. Kubernetes versions all API groups. A common Kubernetes-style versioning scheme is used, which consists of alpha, beta, and GA (general availability) versions.

The pattern is:

- v1alpha1, v1alpha2, v2alpha1, and so on are called *alpha versions* and considered unstable. This means:
  - They might go away or change at any time, in any incompatible way.
  - Data might be dropped, get lost, or become inaccessible from Kubernetes version to version.
  - They are often disabled by default, if the administrator does not opt in manually.
- v1beta1, v1beta2, v2beta1, and so on, are called *beta versions*. They are on the way to stability, which means:
  - They will still exist for at least one Kubernetes release in parallel to the corresponding stable API version.
  - They will usually not change in incompatible ways, but there is no strict guarantee of that.
  - Objects stored in a beta version will not be dropped or become inaccessible.

— Beta versions are often enabled in clusters by default. But this might depend on the Kubernetes distribution or cloud provider used.

- v1, v2, and so on are stable, generally available APIs; that is:

  — They will stay.

  — They will be compatible.

 Kubernetes has a formal deprecation policy (*http://bit.ly/2FOrKU8*) behind these rules of thumb. You can find many more details about which APIs constructs are considered compatible at the Kubernetes community GitHub (*http://bit.ly/2XKPWAX*).

In connection to API group versions, there are two important points to keep in mind:

- API group versions apply to API resources as a whole, like the format of pods or services. In addition to API group versions, API resources might have single fields that are versioned orthogonally; for example, fields in stable APIs might be marked as alpha quality in their Go inline code documentation. The same rules as those just listed for API groups will apply to those fields. For example:

  — An alpha field in a stable API could become incompatible, lose data, or go away at any time. For example, the `ObjectMeta.Initializers` field, which was never promoted beyond alpha, will go away in the near future (it is deprecated in 1.14):

    ```
    // DEPRECATED - initializers are an alpha field and will be removed
    // in v1.15.
    Initializers *Initializers `json:"initializers,omitempty"
    ```

  — It usually will be disabled by default and must be enabled with an API server feature gate, like so:

    ```
    type JobSpec struct {
        ...
        // This field is alpha-level and is only honored by servers that
        // enable the TTLAfterFinished feature.
        TTLSecondsAfterFinished *int32 `json:"ttlSecondsAfterFinished,omitempty"
    }
    ```

  — The behavior of the API server will differ from field to field. Some alpha fields will be rejected and some will be ignored if the corresponding feature gate is not enabled. This is documented in the field description (see `TTLSecondsAf terFinished` in the previous example).

- Furthermore, API group versions play a role in accessing the API. Between different versions of the same resource, there is an on-the-fly conversion done by the API server. That is, you can access objects created in one version (e.g., v1beta1) in any of the other supported versions (e.g., v1) without any further work in your application. This is very convenient for building backward- and forward-compatible applications.

— Each object stored in etcd is stored in a specific version. By default, this is called the *storage version* of that resource. While the storage version can change from Kubernetes version to version, the object stored in etcd will not automatically be updated as of this writing. Hence, the cluster administrator has to make sure migration happens in time when Kubernetes clusters are updated, before old version support is dropped. There is no generic migration mechanism for that, and migration differs from Kubernetes distribution to distribution.

— For the application developer, though, this operational work should not matter at all. On-the-fly conversion will make sure the application has a unified picture of the objects in the cluster. The application will not even notice which storage version is in use. Storage versioning will be transparent to the written Go code.

Kubernetes Objects in Go

In "Creating and Using a Client" on page 39, we saw how to create a client for the core group in order to access pods in a Kubernetes cluster. In the following, we want to look in more detail at what a pod—or any other Kubernetes resource, for that matter—is in the world of Go.

Kubernetes resources—or more precisely the objects—that are instances of a kind[1] and are served as a resource by the API server are represented as structs. Depending on the kind in question, their fields of course differ. But on the other hand, they share a common structure.

From the type system point of view, Kubernetes objects fulfill a Go interface called runtime.Object from the package *k8s.io/apimachinery/pkg/runtime*, which actually is very simple:

```
// Object interface must be supported by all API types registered with Scheme.
// Since objects in a scheme are expected to be serialized to the wire, the
// interface an Object must provide to the Scheme allows serializers to set
// the kind, version, and group the object is represented as. An Object may
// choose to return a no-op ObjectKindAccessor in cases where it is not
// expected to be serialized.
type Object interface {
    GetObjectKind() schema.ObjectKind
```

---

1 See "API Terminology" on page 21.

```
    DeepCopyObject() Object
}
```

Here, `schema.ObjectKind` (from the *k8s.io/apimachinery/pkg/runtime/schema* package) is another simple interface:

```
// All objects that are serialized from a Scheme encode their type information.
// This interface is used by serialization to set type information from the
// Scheme onto the serialized version of an object. For objects that cannot
// be serialized or have unique requirements, this interface may be a no-op.
type ObjectKind interface {
    // SetGroupVersionKind sets or clears the intended serialized kind of an
    // object. Passing kind nil should clear the current setting.
    SetGroupVersionKind(kind GroupVersionKind)
    // GroupVersionKind returns the stored group, version, and kind of an
    // object, or nil if the object does not expose or provide these fields.
    GroupVersionKind() GroupVersionKind
}
```

In other words, a Kubernetes object in Go is a data structure that can:

- Return *and* set the GroupVersionKind
- Be *deep-copied*

A *deep copy* is a clone of the data structure such that it does not share any memory with the original object. It is used wherever code has to mutate an object without modifying the original. See "Global Tags" on page 98 about code generation for details on how deep copy is implemented in Kubernetes.

Put simply, an object stores its type and allows cloning.

TypeMeta

While `runtime.Object` is only an interface, we want to know how it is actually implemented. Kubernetes objects from *k8s.io/api* implement the type getter and setter of `schema.ObjectKind` by embedding the `metav1.TypeMeta` struct from the package *k8s.io/apimachinery/meta/v1*:

```
// TypeMeta describes an individual object in an API response or request
// with strings representing the type of the object and its API schema version.
// Structures that are versioned or persisted should inline TypeMeta.
//
// +k8s:deepcopy-gen=false
type TypeMeta struct {
    // Kind is a string value representing the REST resource this object
    // represents. Servers may infer this from the endpoint the client submits
    // requests to.
    // Cannot be updated.
    // In CamelCase.
    // +optional
    Kind string `json:"kind,omitempty" protobuf:"bytes,1,opt,name=kind"`

    // APIVersion defines the versioned schema of this representation of an
    // object. Servers should convert recognized schemas to the latest internal
```

```
    // value, and may reject unrecognized values.
    // +optional
    APIVersion string `json:"apiVersion,omitempty"`
}
```

With this, a pod declaration in Go looks like this:

```
// Pod is a collection of containers that can run on a host. This resource is
// created by clients and scheduled onto hosts.
type Pod struct {
    metav1.TypeMeta `json:",inline"`
    // Standard object's metadata.
    // +optional
    metav1.ObjectMeta `json:"metadata,omitempty"`

    // Specification of the desired behavior of the pod.
    // +optional
    Spec PodSpec `json:"spec,omitempty"`

    // Most recently observed status of the pod.
    // This data may not be up to date.
    // Populated by the system.
    // Read-only.
    // +optional
    Status PodStatus `json:"status,omitempty"`
}
```

As you can see, `TypeMeta` is embedded. Moreover, the pod type has JSON tags that also declare `TypeMeta` as being inlined.

> This ",inline" tag is actually superfluous with the Golang JSON en/decoders: embedded structs are automatically inlined.
>
> This is different in the YAML en/decoder *go-yaml/yaml* (*http://bit.ly/2ZuPZy2*), which was used in very early Kubernetes code in parallel to JSON. We inherited the inline tag from that time (*http://bit.ly/2IUGwcC*), but today it is merely documentation without any effect.
>
> The YAML serializers foudn in *k8s.io/apimachinery/pkg/runtime/serializer/yaml* use the *sigs.k8s.io/yaml* marshal and unmarshal functions. And these in turn encode and decode YAML via `interface{}`, and use the JSON encoder into and decoder from Golang API structs.

This matches the YAML representation of a pod, which all Kubernetes users know:[2]

```
apiVersion: v1
kind: Pod
metadata:
```

---

2 `kubectl explain pod` lets you query the API server for the schema of an object, including field documentation.

```
    namespace: default
    name: example
spec:
  containers:
  - name: hello
    image: debian:latest
    command:
    - /bin/sh
    args:
    - -c
    - echo "hello world"; sleep 10000
```

The version is stored in `TypeMeta.APIVersion`, the kind in `TypeMeta.Kind`.

The Core Group Is Different for Historic Reasons

Pods and many other types that were added to Kubernetes very early on are part of the *core group*—often also called the *legacy group*—which is represented by the empty string. Hence, `apiVersion` is just set to "v1."

Eventually API groups were added to Kubernetes, and the group name, separated by a slash, was prepended to `apiVersion`. In the case of `apps`, the version would be `apps/v1`. Hence, the `apiVersion` field is actually misnamed; it stores the API group name and the version string. This is for historic reasons because `apiVersion` was defined when only the core group—and none of these other API groups—existed.

When running the example in "Creating and Using a Client" on page 39 to get a pod from the cluster, notice that the pod object returned by the client does not actually have the kind and the version set. The convention in `client-go`–based applications is that these fields are empty in memory, and they are filled with the actual values on the wire only when they're marshaled to JSON or protobuf. This is done automatically by the client, however, or, more precisely, by a versioning serializer.

Behind the Scenes: How Do Go Type, Packages, Kinds, and Group Names Relate?

You might be wondering how the client knows the kind and the API group to fill in the `TypeMeta` field. Although this question sounds trivial at first, it is not:

- It looks like the kind is just the Go type name, which could be derived from an object via reflection. This is mostly true—maybe in 99% of the cases—but there are exceptions (in Chapter 4 you will learn about custom resources where this does not work).

- It looks like the group is just the Go package name (types for the `apps` API group are declared in *k8s.io/api/apps*). This often matches, but not in all cases: the core group has the empty group name string, as we have seen. The types for the group

In other words, client-go–based applications check the Golang type of objects to determine the object at hand. This might differ in other frameworks, like the Operator SDK (see "The Operator SDK" on page 123).

ObjectMeta

In addition to TypeMeta, most top-level objects have a field of type metav1.Object Meta, again from the *k8s.io/apimachinery/pkg/meta/v1* package:

```
type ObjectMeta struct {
    Name string `json:"name,omitempty"`
    Namespace string `json:"namespace,omitempty"`
    UID types.UID `json:"uid,omitempty"`
    ResourceVersion string `json:"resourceVersion,omitempty"`
    CreationTimestamp Time `json:"creationTimestamp,omitempty"`
    DeletionTimestamp *Time `json:"deletionTimestamp,omitempty"`
    Labels map[string]string `json:"labels,omitempty"`
    Annotations map[string]string `json:"annotations,omitempty"`
    ...
}
```

In JSON or YAML these fields are under *metadata*. For example, for the previous pod, metav1.ObjectMeta stores:

```
metadata:
  namespace: default
  name: example
```

In general, it contains all metalevel information like name, namespace, resource version (not to be confused with the API group version), several timestamps, and the well-known labels and annotations is part of ObjectMeta. See "Anatomy of a type" on page 88 for a deeper discussion of ObjectMeta fields.

The resource version was discussed earlier in "Optimistic Concurrency" on page 14. It is hardly ever read or written from client-go code. But it is one of the fields in Kubernetes that makes the whole system work. resourceVersion is part of Object Meta because each object with embedded ObjectMeta corresponds to a key in etcd where the resourceVersion value originated.

spec and status

Finally, nearly every top-level object has a spec and a status section. This convention comes from the declarative nature of the Kubernetes API: spec is the user desire, and `status` is the outcome of that desire, usually filled by a controller in the system. See "Controllers and Operators" on page 5 for a detailed discussion of controllers in Kubernetes.

There are only a few exceptions to the `spec` and `status` convention in the system—for example, endpoints in the core group, or RBAC objects like `ClusterRole`.

Client Sets

In the introductory example in "Creating and Using a Client" on page 39, we saw that `kubernetes.NewForConfig(config)` gives us a *client set*. A client set gives access to clients for multiple API groups and resources. In the case of `kubernetes.NewForConfig(config)` from *k8s.io/client-go/kubernetes*, we get access to all API groups and resources defined in *k8s.io/api*. This is, with a few exceptions—such as `APIServices` (for aggregated API servers) and `CustomResourceDefinition` (see Chapter 4)—the whole set of resources served by the Kubernetes API server.

In Chapter 5, we will explain how these client sets are actually generated from the API types (*k8s.io/api*, in this case). Third-party projects with custom APIs use more than just the Kubernetes client sets. What all of the client sets have in common is a REST config (e.g., returned by `clientcmd.BuildConfigFromFlags("", *kubeconfig)`, like in the example).

The client set main interface in *k8s.io/client-go/kubernetes/typed* for Kubernetes-native resources looks like this:

```
type Interface interface {
    Discovery() discovery.DiscoveryInterface
    AppsV1() appsv1.AppsV1Interface
    AppsV1beta1() appsv1beta1.AppsV1beta1Interface
    AppsV1beta2() appsv1beta2.AppsV1beta2Interface
    AuthenticationV1() authenticationv1.AuthenticationV1Interface
    AuthenticationV1beta1() authenticationv1beta1.AuthenticationV1beta1Interface
    AuthorizationV1() authorizationv1.AuthorizationV1Interface
    AuthorizationV1beta1() authorizationv1beta1.AuthorizationV1beta1Interface

    ...
}
```

There used to be unversioned methods in this interface—for example, just `Apps() appsv1.AppsV1Interface`—but they were deprecated as of Kubernetes 1.14–based `client-go` 11.0. As mentioned before, it is seen as a good practice to be very explicit about the version of an API group that an application uses.

Every client set also gives access to the discovery client (it will be used by the RESTMappers; see "REST Mapping" on page 63 and "Using the API from the Command Line" on page 26).

Behind each GroupVersion method (e.g., AppsV1beta1), we find the resources of the API group—for example:

```
type AppsV1beta1Interface interface {
    RESTClient() rest.Interface
    ControllerRevisionsGetter
    DeploymentsGetter
    StatefulSetsGetter
}
```

with RESTClient being a generic *REST client*, and one interface per resource, as in:

```
// DeploymentsGetter has a method to return a DeploymentInterface.
// A group's client should implement this interface.
type DeploymentsGetter interface {
    Deployments(namespace string) DeploymentInterface
}

// DeploymentInterface has methods to work with Deployment resources.
type DeploymentInterface interface {
    Create(*v1beta1.Deployment) (*v1beta1.Deployment, error)
    Update(*v1beta1.Deployment) (*v1beta1.Deployment, error)
    UpdateStatus(*v1beta1.Deployment) (*v1beta1.Deployment, error)
    Delete(name string, options *v1.DeleteOptions) error
    DeleteCollection(options *v1.DeleteOptions, listOptions v1.ListOptions) error
```

```
    Get(name string, options v1.GetOptions) (*v1beta1.Deployment, error)
    List(opts v1.ListOptions) (*v1beta1.DeploymentList, error)
    Watch(opts v1.ListOptions) (watch.Interface, error)
    Patch(name string, pt types.PatchType, data []byte, subresources ...string)
        (result *v1beta1.Deployment, err error)
    DeploymentExpansion
}
```

Depending on the scope of the resource—that is, whether it is cluster or namespace scoped—the accessor (here `DeploymentGetter`) may or may not have a `namespace` argument.

The `DeploymentInterface` gives access to all the supported verbs of the resource. Most of them are self-explanatory, but those requiring additional commentary are described next.

Status Subresources: UpdateStatus

Deployments have a so-called *status subresource*. This means that `UpdateStatus` uses an additional HTTP endpoint suffixed with `/status`. While updates on the */apis/apps/v1beta1/namespaces/ns/deployments/name* endpoint can change only the spec of the deployment, the endpoint */apis/apps/v1beta1/namespaces/ns/deployments/name/status* can change only the status of the object. This is useful in order to set different permissions for spec updates (done by a human) and status updates (done by a controller).

By default the `client-gen` (see "client-gen Tags" on page 102) generates the `UpdateStatus()` method. The existence of the method does not guarantee that the resource actually supports the subresource. This will be important when we're working with CRDs in "Subresources" on page 81.

Listings and Deletions

`DeleteCollection` allows us to delete multiple objects of a namespace at once. The `ListOptions` parameter allows us to define which objects should be deleted using a *field* or *label selector*:

```
type ListOptions struct {
    ...

    // A selector to restrict the list of returned objects by their labels.
    // Defaults to everything.
    // +optional
    LabelSelector string `json:"labelSelector,omitempty"`
    // A selector to restrict the list of returned objects by their fields.
    // Defaults to everything.
    // +optional
    FieldSelector string `json:"fieldSelector,omitempty"`

    ...
}
```

Watches

Watch gives an event interface for all changes (adds, removes, and updates) to objects. The returned watch.Interface from *k8s.io/apimachinery/pkg/watch* looks like this:

```
// Interface can be implemented by anything that knows how to watch and
// report changes.
type Interface interface {
    // Stops watching. Will close the channel returned by ResultChan(). Releases
    // any resources used by the watch.
    Stop()

    // Returns a chan which will receive all the events. If an error occurs
    // or Stop() is called, this channel will be closed, in which case the
    // watch should be completely cleaned up.
    ResultChan() <-chan Event
}
```

The result channel of the watch interface returns three kinds of events:

```
// EventType defines the possible types of events.
type EventType string

const (
    Added    EventType = "ADDED"
    Modified EventType = "MODIFIED"
    Deleted  EventType = "DELETED"
    Error    EventType = "ERROR"
)

// Event represents a single event to a watched resource.
// +k8s:deepcopy-gen=true
type Event struct {
    Type EventType

    // Object is:
    //  * If Type is Added or Modified: the new state of the object.
    //  * If Type is Deleted: the state of the object immediately before
    //      deletion.
    //  * If Type is Error: *api.Status is recommended; other types may
    //      make sense depending on context.
    Object runtime.Object
}
```

While it is tempting to use this interface directly, in practice it is actually discouraged in favor of informers (see "Informers and Caching" on page 56). Informers are a combination of this event interface and an in-memory cache with indexed lookup. This is by far the most common use case for watches. Under the hood informers first call List on the client to get the set of all objects (as a baseline for the cache) and then Watch to update the cache. They handle error conditions correctly—that is, recover from network issues or other cluster problems.

Client Expansion

DeploymentExpansion is actually an empty interface. It is used to add custom client behavior, but it's hardly used in Kubernetes nowadays. Instead, the client generator allows us to add custom methods in a declarative way (see "client-gen Tags" on page 102).

Note again that all of those methods in DeploymentInterface neither expect valid information in the TypeMeta fields Kind and APIVersion, nor set those fields on Get() and List() (see also "TypeMeta" on page 47). These fields are filled with real values only on the wire.

Client Options

It is worth looking at the different options we can set when creating a client set. In the note before "Versioning and Compatibility" on page 41, we saw that we can switch to the protobuf wire format for native Kubernetes types. Protobuf is more efficient than JSON (both spacewise and for the CPU load of the client and server) and therefore preferable.

For debugging purposes and readability of metrics, it is often helpful to differentiate between different clients accessing the API server. To do so, we can set the *user agent* field in the REST config. The default value is binary/version (os/arch) kubernetes/commit; for example, kubectl will use a user agent like kubectl/v1.14.0 (darwin/amd64) kubernetes/d654b49. If that pattern does not suffice for the setup, it can be customized like so:

```
cfg, err := clientcmd.BuildConfigFromFlags("", *kubeconfig)
cfg.AcceptContentTypes = "application/vnd.kubernetes.protobuf,application/json"
cfg.UserAgent = fmt.Sprintf(
    "book-example/v1.0 (%s/%s) kubernetes/v1.0",
    runtime.GOOS, runtime.GOARCH
)
clientset, err := kubernetes.NewForConfig(cfg)
```

Other values often overridden in the REST config are those for client-side *rate limiting* and *timeouts*:

```
// Config holds the common attributes that can be passed to a Kubernetes
// client on initialization.
type Config struct {

    ...

    // QPS indicates the maximum QPS to the master from this client.
    // If it's zero, the created RESTClient will use DefaultQPS: 5
    QPS float32

    // Maximum burst for throttle.
    // If it's zero, the created RESTClient will use DefaultBurst: 10.
    Burst int
```

```
// The maximum length of time to wait before giving up on a server request.
// A value of zero means no timeout.
Timeout time.Duration

    ...
}
```

The QPS value defaults to 5 requests per second, with a burst of 10.

The timeout has no default value, at least not in the client REST config. By default the Kubernetes API server will timeout every request that is not a *long-running* request after 60 seconds. A long-running request can be a watch request or unbounded requests to subresources like */exec*, */portforward*, or */proxy*.

Graceful Shutdown and Being Resilient to Connection Errors

Requests are split into long-running and non-long-running. Watches are long-running, while GET, LIST, UPDATE, and the like are non-long-running. Many subresources (e.g., for log streaming, exec, port-forward) are long-running as well.

When the Kubernetes API server is restarted (e.g., during an update), it waits for up to 60 seconds to gracefully shut down. During that time, it finishes non-long-running requests and then terminates. When it terminates, long-running requests like ongoing watch connections are cut off.

Non-long-running requests are bounded by 60 seconds anyway (and then they timeout). Hence, from the client point of view, the shutdown is graceful.

In general, application code should always be prepared for requests that are not successful and should respond in such a way that they are not fatal for the application. In the world of distributed systems, those connection errors are normal and nothing to worry about. But special attention is required to carefully handle error conditions and recover from them.

Error handling is especially important for watches. Watches are long-running, but they can fail at any time. The informers described in the next section provide a resilient implementation around watches and handle errors gracefully—that is, they recover from disconnects with a new connection. Application code usually will not notice.

Informers and Caching

The client interface in "Client Sets" on page 51 includes the Watch verb, which offers an event interface that reacts to changes (adds, removes, updates) of objects. Informers give a higher-level programming interface for the most common use case for watches: in-memory caching and fast, indexed lookup of objects by name or other properties in-memory.

A controller that accesses the API server every time it needs an object creates a high load on the system. In-memory caching using informers is the solution to this problem. Moreover, informers can react to changes of objects nearly in real-time instead of requiring polling requests.

Figure 3-5 shows the conceptional pattern of informers; specifically, they:

- Get input from the API server as events.
- Offer a client-like interface called Lister to get and list objects from the in-memory cache.
- Register event handlers for adds, removes, and updates.
- Implement the in-memory cache using a *store*.

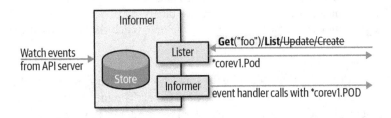

Figure 3-5. Informers

Informers also have advanced error behavior: when the long-running watch connection breaks down, they recover from it by trying another watch request, picking up the event stream without losing any events. If the outage is long, and the API server lost events because etcd purged them from its database before the new watch request was successful, the informer will relist all objects.

Next to *relists*, there is a configurable *resync period* for reconciliation between the in-memory cache and the business logic: the registered event handlers will be called for all objects each time this period has passed. Common values are in minutes (e.g., 10 or 30 minutes).

 The resync is purely in-memory and *does not trigger a call to the server*. This used to be different but was eventually changed (*http:// bit.ly/2FmeMge*) because the error behavior of the watch mechanism had been improved enough to make relists unnecessary.

All this advanced and battle-proven error behavior is a good reason for using informers instead of rolling out custom logic using the client Watch() method directly. Informers are used everywhere in Kubernetes itself and are one of the main architectural concepts in the Kubernetes API design.

While informers are preferred over polling, they create load on the API server. One binary should instantiate only one informer per GroupVersionResource. To make sharing of informers easy, we can instantiate an informer by using the *shared informer factory*.

The shared informer factory allows informers to be shared for the same resource in an application. In other words, different control loops can use the same watch connection to the API server under the hood. For example, the kube-controller-manager, one of the main Kubernetes cluster components (see "The API Server" on page 19), has a larger, two-digit number of controllers. But for each resource (e.g., pods), there is only one informer in the process.

 Always use a shared informer factory to instantiate informers. Don't try to instantiate informers manually. The overhead is minimal, and a nontrivial controller binary that does not use shared informers probably is opening multiple watch connections for the same resource somewhere.

Starting with a REST config (see "Creating and Using a Client" on page 39), it is easy to create a shared informer factory using a client set. The informers are generated by a code generator and shipped as part of client-go for the standard Kubernetes resources in *k8s.io/client-go/informers*:

```
import (
    ...
    "k8s.io/client-go/informers"
)
...
clientset, err := kubernetes.NewForConfig(config)
informerFactory := informers.NewSharedInformerFactory(clientset, time.Second*30)
podInformer := informerFactory.Core().V1().Pods()
podInformer.Informer().AddEventHandler(cache.ResourceEventHandlerFuncs{
    AddFunc: func(new interface{}) {...},
    UpdateFunc: func(old, new interface{}) {...},
    DeleteFunc: func(obj interface{}) {...},
})
informerFactory.Start(wait.NeverStop)
informerFactory.WaitForCacheSync(wait.NeverStop)
pod, err := podInformer.Lister().Pods("programming-kubernetes").Get("client-go")
```

The example shows how to get a shared informer for pods.

You can see that informers allow for the addition of event handlers for the three cases *add*, *update*, and *delete*. These are usually used to trigger the business logic of a controller—that is, to process a certain object again (see "Controllers and Operators" on page 5). Often those handlers just add the modified object into a work queue.

Also note that many event handlers can be added. The whole shared informer factory concept exists only because this is so common in controller binaries with many control loops, each installing event handlers to add objects to their own work queue.

After registering handlers, the shared informer factory has to be started. There are Go routines under the hood that do the actual calls to the API server. The Start method (with a stop channel to control the lifecycle) starts these Go routines, and the WaitFor CacheSync() method makes the code wait for the first List calls to the clients to finish. If the controller logic requires that the cache is filled, this WaitForCacheSync call is essential.

In general, the event interface of the watches behind the scenes leads to a certain lag. In a setup with proper capacity planning, this lag is not huge. Of course, it is good practice to measure this lag using metrics. But the lag exists regardless, so the application logic has be built in such a way that the lag does not harm the behavior of the code.

The lag of informers can lead to races between changes the controller makes with client-go directly on the API server, and the state of the world as known by the informers.

If the controller changes an object, the informer in the same process has to wait until the corresponding event arrives and the in-memory store is then updated. This process is not instantaneous, and another controller work loop run might be started through another trigger before the previous change has become visible.

The resync interval of 30 seconds in this example leads to a complete set of events being sent to the registered UpdateFunc such that the controller logic is able to reconcile its state with that of the API server. By comparing the ObjectMeta.resourceVer sion field, it is possible to distinguish a real update from a resync.

Choosing a good resync interval depends on the context. For example, 30 seconds is pretty short. In many situations several minutes, or even 30 minutes, is a good choice. In the worst case, 30 minutes means that it takes 30 minutes until a bug in the code (e.g., a lost signal due to bad error handling) is repaired via reconciliation.

Also note that the final line in the example calling `Get("client-go")` is purely in-memory; there is no access to the API server. Objects in the in-memory store cannot be modified directly. Instead, the client set must be used for any write access to the resources. The informer will then get events from the API server and update its in-memory store.

Never Mutate Objects from Informers

It is very important to remember that any object passed from the listers to the event handlers is owned by the informers. If you mutate it in any way, you risk introducing hard-to-debug cache coherency issues into your application. Always do a deep copy (see "Kubernetes Objects in Go" on page 46) before changing an object.

In general: before mutating an object, always ask yourself who owns this object or the data structures in it. As a rule of thumb:

- Informers and listers own objects they return. Hence, consumers have to deep-copy before mutation.
- Clients return fresh objects, which the caller owns.
- Conversions return shared objects. If the caller does own the input object, it does not own the output.

The informer constructor `NewSharedInformerFactory` in the example caches all objects of a resource in all namespaces in the store. If this is too much for the application, there is an alternative constructor with more flexibility:

```
// NewFilteredSharedInformerFactory constructs a new instance of
// sharedInformerFactory. Listers obtained via this sharedInformerFactory will be
// subject to the same filters as specified here.
func NewFilteredSharedInformerFactory(
    client versioned.Interface, defaultResync time.Duration,
    namespace string,
    tweakListOptions internalinterfaces.TweakListOptionsFunc
) SharedInformerFactor

type TweakListOptionsFunc func(*v1.ListOptions)
```

It allows us to specify a namespace and to pass a `TweakListOptionsFunc`, which may mutate the `ListOptions` struct used to list and watch objects using the `List` and `Watch` calls of the client. It can be used to set *label* or *field selectors*, for example.

Informers are one of the building blocks of controllers. In Chapter 6 we will see what a typical `client-go`-based controller looks like. After the clients and informers, the third main building block is the work queue. Let's look at it now.

Work Queue

A work queue is a data structure. You can add elements and take elements out of the queue, in an order predefined by the queue. Formally, this kind of queue is called a *priority queue*. `client-go` provides a powerful implementation for the purpose of building controllers in *k8s.io/client-go/util/workqueue* (*http://bit.ly/2IV0JPz*).

More precisely, the package contains a number of variants for different purposes. The base interface implemented by all variants looks like this:

```
type Interface interface {
    Add(item interface{})
    Len() int
    Get() (item interface{}, shutdown bool)
    Done(item interface{})
    ShutDown()
    ShuttingDown() bool
}
```

Here `Add(item)` adds an item, `Len()` gives the length, and `Get()` returns an item with the highest priority (and it blocks until one is available). Every item returned by `Get()` needs a `Done(item)` call when the controller has finished processing it. Meanwhile, a repeated `Add(item)` will only mark the item as dirty such that it is readded when `Done(item)` has been called.

The following queue types are derived from this generic interface:

- `DelayingInterface` can add an item at a later time. This makes it easier to requeue items after failures without ending up in a hot-loop:

  ```
  type DelayingInterface interface {
      Interface
      // AddAfter adds an item to the workqueue after the
      // indicated duration has passed.
      AddAfter(item interface{}, duration time.Duration)
  }
  ```

- `RateLimitingInterface` rate-limits items being added to the queue. It extends the `DelayingInterface`:

  ```
  type RateLimitingInterface interface {
      DelayingInterface

      // AddRateLimited adds an item to the workqueue after the rate
  ```

```
    // limiter says it's OK.
    AddRateLimited(item interface{})

    // Forget indicates that an item is finished being retried.
    // It doesn't matter whether it's for perm failing or success;
    // we'll stop the rate limiter from tracking it. This only clears
    // the `rateLimiter`; you still have to call `Done` on the queue.
    Forget(item interface{})

    // NumRequeues returns back how many times the item was requeued.
    NumRequeues(item interface{}) int
}
```

Most interesting here is the `Forget(item)` method: it resets the back-off of the given item. Usually, it will be called when an item has been processed successfully.

The rate limiting algorithm can be passed to the constructor `NewRateLimiting Queue`. There are several rate limiters defined in the same package, such as the `BucketRateLimiter`, the `ItemExponentialFailureRateLimiter`, the `ItemFast SlowRateLimiter`, and the `MaxOfRateLimiter`. For more details, you can refer to the package documentation. Most controllers will just use the `DefaultControl lerRateLimiter() *RateLimiter` functions, which gives:

— An exponential back-off starting at 5 ms and going up to 1,000 seconds, doubling the delay on each error

— A maximal rate of 10 items per second and 100 items burst

Depending on the context, you might want to customize the values. A 1,000 seconds maximal back-off per item is a lot for certain controller applications.

API Machinery in Depth

The API Machinery repository implements the basics of the Kubernetes type system. But what is this type system exactly? What is a type to begin with?

The term *type* actually does not exist in the terminology of API Machinery. Instead, it refers to *kinds*.

Kinds

Kinds are divided into API groups and are versioned, as we already have seen in "API Terminology" on page 21. Therefore, a core term in the API Machinery repository is GroupVersionKind, or *GVK* for short.

In Go, each GVK corresponds to one Go type. In contrast, a Go type can belong to multiple GVKs.

Kinds do not formally map one-to-one to HTTP paths. Many kinds have HTTP REST endpoints that are used to access objects of the given kind. But there are also kinds without any HTTP endpoint (e.g., *admission.k8s.io/v1beta1.AdmissionReview* (*http://bit.ly/2XJXBQD*), which is used to call out to a webhook). There are also kinds that are returned from many endpoints—for example, *meta.k8s.io/v1.Status* (*http:// bit.ly/31Ktjvz*), which is returned by all endpoints to report a nonobject status like an error.

By convention, kinds are formatted in CamelCase (*http://bit.ly/31IqMSC*) like words and are usually singular. Depending on the context, their concrete format differs. For CustomResourceDefinition kinds, it must be a DNS path label (RFC 1035).

Resources

In parallel to kinds, as we saw in "API Terminology" on page 21, there is the concept of a *resource*. Resources are again grouped and versioned, leading to the term *Group-VersionResource*, or *GVR* for short.

Each GVR corresponds to one HTTP (base) path. GVRs are used to identify REST endpoints of the Kubernetes API. For example, the GVR *apps/v1.deployments* maps to */apis/apps/v1/namespaces/namespace/deployments*.

Client libraries use this mapping to construct the HTTP path to access a GVR.

Knowing Whether a Resource Is Namespaced or Cluster-Scoped

You have to know whether a GVR is namespaced or cluster-scoped in order to know the HTTP path. Deployments, for example, are namespaced and therefore get the namespace as part of their HTTP path. Other GVRs, such as *rbac.authorization.k8s.io/v1.clusterroles*, are cluster-scoped; for example, cluster roles can be accessed at *apis/rbac.authorization.k8s.io/v1/clusterroles*.

By convention, resources are lowercase and plural, usually corresponding to the plural words of the parallel kind. They must conform to the DNS path label format (RFC 1025). As resources map directly to HTTP paths, this is not surprising.

REST Mapping

The mapping of a GVK to a GVR is called *REST mapping*.

A RESTMapper is the Golang interface (*http://bit.ly/2Y7wYS8*) that enables us to request the GVR for a GVK:

```
RESTMapping(gk schema.GroupKind, versions ...string) (*RESTMapping, error)
```

where the type RESTMapping on the right looks like this:

```
type RESTMapping struct {
    // Resource is the GroupVersionResource (location) for this endpoint.
    Resource schema.GroupVersionResource.

    // GroupVersionKind is the GroupVersionKind (data format) to submit
    // to this endpoint.
    GroupVersionKind schema.GroupVersionKind

    // Scope contains the information needed to deal with REST Resources
    // that are in a resource hierarchy.
    Scope RESTScope
}
```

In addition, a `RESTMapper` provides a number of convenience functions:

```
// KindFor takes a partial resource and returns the single match.
// Returns an error if there are multiple matches.
KindFor(resource schema.GroupVersionResource) (schema.GroupVersionKind, error)

// KindsFor takes a partial resource and returns the list of potential
// kinds in priority order.
KindsFor(resource schema.GroupVersionResource) ([]schema.GroupVersionKind, error)

// ResourceFor takes a partial resource and returns the single match.
// Returns an error if there are multiple matches.
ResourceFor(input schema.GroupVersionResource) (schema.GroupVersionResource, error)

// ResourcesFor takes a partial resource and returns the list of potential
// resource in priority order.
ResourcesFor(input schema.GroupVersionResource) ([]schema.GroupVersionResource, error)

// RESTMappings returns all resource mappings for the provided group kind
// if no version search is provided. Otherwise identifies a preferred resource
// mapping for the provided version(s).
RESTMappings(gk schema.GroupKind, versions ...string) ([]*RESTMapping, error)
```

Here, a partial GVR means that not all fields are set. For example, imagine you type **kubectl get pods**. In that case, the group and the version are missing. A RESTMap per with enough information might still manage to map it to the v1 Pods kind.

For the preceding deployment example, a `RESTMapper` that knows about deployments (more about what this means in a bit) will map *apps/v1.Deployment* (*http://bit.ly/2IujaLU*) to *apps/v1.deployments* as a namespaced resource.

There are multiple different implementations of the `RESTMapper` interface. The most important one for client applications is the discovery-based `DeferredDiscoveryREST Mapper` (*http://bit.ly/2XroxUq*) in the package *k8s.io/client-go/restmapper*: it uses discovery information from the Kubernetes API server to dynamically build up the REST mapping. It will also work with non-core resources like custom resources.

Scheme

The final core concept we want to present here in the context of the Kubernetes type system is the *scheme (http://bit.ly/2N1PGJB)* in the package *k8s.io/apimachinery/pkg/ runtime.*

A scheme connects the world of Golang with the implementation-independent world of GVKs. The main feature of a scheme is the mapping of Golang types to possible GVKs:

```
func (s *Scheme) ObjectKinds(obj Object) ([]schema.GroupVersionKind, bool, error)
```

As we saw in "Kubernetes Objects in Go" on page 46, an object can return its group and kind via the GetObjectKind() schema.ObjectKind method. However, these values are empty most of the time and are therefore pretty useless for identification.

Instead, the scheme takes the Golang type of the given object via reflection and maps it to the registered GVK(s) of that Golang type. For that to work, of course, the Golang types have to be registered into the scheme like this:

```
scheme.AddKnownTypes(schema.GroupVersionKind{"", "v1", "Pod"}, &Pod{})
```

The scheme is used not only to register the Golang types and their GVK, but also to store a list of conversion functions and defaulters (see Figure 3-6). We'll discuss conversions and defaulters in more detail in Chapter 8. It is the data source to implement encoders and decoders as well.

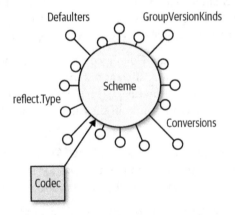

Figure 3-6. The scheme, connecting Golang data types with the GVK, conversions, and defaulters

For Kubernetes core types there is a predefined scheme in the client-go client set (*http://bit.ly/2FkXDn2*) in the package *k8s.io/client-go/kubernetes/scheme*, with all the types preregistered. Actually, every client set generated by the client-gen code generator (see Chapter 5) has the subpackage scheme with all types in all groups and versions in the client set.

With the scheme we conclude our deep dive into API Machinery concepts. If you only remember one thing about these concepts, let it be Figure 3-7.

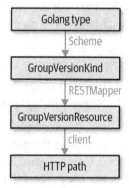

Figure 3-7. From Golang types to GVKs to GVRs to an HTTP path—API Machinery in a nutshell

Vendoring

We have seen in this chapter that *k8s.io/client-go*, *k8s.io/api*, and *k8s.io/apimachinery* are central to Kubernetes programming in Golang. Golang uses *vendoring* to include these libraries in a third-party application source code repository.

Vendoring is a moving target in the Golang community. At the time of this writing, several vendoring tools are common, such as *godeps*, *dep*, and *glide*. At the same time, Go 1.12 is getting support for Go modules, which will probably become the standard vendoring method in the Go community in the future, but is not ready in the Kubernetes ecosystem at this time.

Most projects nowadays use either dep or glide. Kubernetes itself in *github.com/kubernetes/kubernetes* made the jump to Go modules for the 1.15 development cycle. The following comments are relevant for all of these vendoring tools.

The source of truth for supported dependency versions in each of the *k8s.io/** repositories is the shipped *Godeps/Godeps.json* file. It is important to stress that any other dependency selection can break the functionality of the library.

See "The Client Library" on page 35 for more on the published tags of *k8s.io/client-go*, *k8s.io/api*, and *k8s.io/apimachinery* and which tags are compatible with each other.

glide

Projects using `glide` can use its ability to read the *Godeps/Godeps.json* file on any dependency change. This has proven to work pretty reliably: the developer has only to declare the right *k8s.io/client-go* version, and `glide` will select the right version of *k8s.io/apimachinery*, *k8s.io/api*, and other dependencies.

For some projects on GitHub, the *glide.yaml* file might look like this:

```
package: github.com/book/example
import:
- package: k8s.io/client-go
  version: v10.0.0
...
```

With that, `glide install -v` will download *k8s.io/client-go* and its dependencies into the local *vendor/* package. Here, `-v` means to drop *vendor/* packages from vendored libraries. This is required for our purposes.

If you update to a new version of `client-go` by editing *glide.yaml*, `glide update -v` will download the new dependencies, again in the right versions.

dep

`dep` is often considered more powerful and advanced than `glide`. For a long time it was seen as the successor to `glide` in the ecosystem and seemed destined to be *the* Go vendoring tool. At the time of this writing, its future is not clear, and Go modules seem to be the path forward.

In the context of `client-go`, it is very important to be aware of a couple of restrictions of `dep`:

- `dep` does read *Godeps/Godeps.json* on the first run of `dep init`.
- `dep` does not read *Godeps/Godeps.json* on later `dep ensure -update` calls.

This means that the resolution for dependencies of `client-go` is most probably wrong when the `client-go` version is updated in *Godep.toml*. This is unfortunate, because it requires the developer to explicitly and usually manually declare *all* dependencies.

A working and consistent *Godep.toml* file looks like this:

```
[[constraint]]
  name = "k8s.io/api"
  version = "kubernetes-1.13.0"

[[constraint]]
  name = "k8s.io/apimachinery"
  version = "kubernetes-1.13.0"
```

```
[[constraint]]
  name = "k8s.io/client-go"
  version = "10.0.0"

[prune]
  go-tests = true
  unused-packages = true

# the following overrides are necessary to enforce
# the given version, even though our
# code does not import the packages directly.
[[override]]
  name = "k8s.io/api"
  version = "kubernetes-1.13.0"

[[override]]
  name = "k8s.io/apimachinery"
  version = "kubernetes-1.13.0"

[[override]]
  name = "k8s.io/client-go"
  version = "10.0.0"
```

Not only does *Gopkg.toml* declare explicit versions for both *k8s.io/apimachinery* and *k8s.io/api*, it also has overrides for them. This is necessary for when the project is started without explicit imports of packages from those two repositories. In that case, without these overrides dep would ignore the constraints in the beginning, and the developer would get wrong dependencies from the beginning.

Even the *Gopkg.toml* file shown here is technically not correct because it is incomplete, as it does not declare dependencies *on all* other libraries required by client-go. In the past, an upstream library broke compilation of client-go. So be prepared for this to happen if you use dep for dependency management.

Go Modules

Go modules are the future of dependency management in Golang. They were introduced in Go 1.11 with preliminary support (*http://bit.ly/2FmBp3Y*) and were further stabilized in 1.12. A number of commands, like go run and go get, work with Go modules by setting the GO111MODULE=on environment variable. In Go 1.13 this will be the default setting.

Go modules are driven by a *go.mod* file in the root of a project. Here is an excerpt of the *go.mod* file for our *github.com/programming-kubernetes/pizza-apiserver* project in Chapter 8:

```
module github.com/programming-kubernetes/pizza-apiserver

require (
```

```
    ...
    k8s.io/api v0.0.0-20190222213804-5cb15d344471 // indirect
    k8s.io/apimachinery v0.0.0-20190221213512-86fb29eff628
    k8s.io/apiserver v0.0.0-20190319190228-a4358799e4fe
    k8s.io/client-go v2.0.0-alpha.0.0.20190307161346-7621a5ebb88b+incompatible
    k8s.io/klog v0.2.1-0.20190311220638-291f19f84ceb
    k8s.io/kube-openapi v0.0.0-20190320154901-c59034cc13d5 // indirect
    k8s.io/utils v0.0.0-20190308190857-21c4ce38f2a7 // indirect
    sigs.k8s.io/yaml v1.1.0 // indirect
)
```

client-go v11.0.0—matching Kubernetes 1.14—and older versions do not have explicit support for Go modules. Still, it is possible to use Go modules with the Kubernetes libraries, as you see in the preceding example.

As long as client-go and the other Kubernetes repositories do not ship a *go.mod* file, though (at least until Kubernetes 1.15), the right versions must be selected manually. That is, you'll need a complete list of all dependencies matching the revisions of dependencies of the *Godeps/Godeps.json* in client-go.

Also note the not-very-readable revisions in the previous example. They are pseudo-versions derived from existing tags, or using v0.0.0 as the prefix if there are no tags. Even worse, you can reference tagged versions in that file, but the Go module commands will replace those on the next run with the pseudo-versions.

With client-go v12.0.0—matching Kubernetes 1.15—we ship a *go.mod* file and deprecate support for all other vendoring tools (see the corresponding proposal document (*http://bit.ly/2IZ9MPg*)). The shipped *go.mod* file includes all dependencies, and your project *go.mod* file no longer has to list all transitive dependencies manually. In later releases, it's also possible that the tagging scheme will be changed to fix the ugly pseudo-revisions and replace them with proper semver tags. But at the time of this writing, this is still not fully implemented or decided.

Summary

In this chapter our focus was on the Kubernetes programming interface in Go. We discussed accessing the Kubernetes API of well-known core types—that is, the API objects that are shipped with every Kubernetes cluster.

With this we've covered the basics of the Kubernetes API and its representation in Go. Now we're ready to move on to the topic of custom resources, one of the pillars of operators.

## CHAPTER 4

Using Custom Resources

In this chapter we introduce you to custom resources (CR), one of the central extension mechanisms used throughout the Kubernetes ecosystem.

Custom resources are used for small, in-house configuration objects without any corresponding controller logic—purely declaratively defined. But custom resources also play a central role for many serious development projects on top of Kubernetes that want to offer a Kubernetes-native API experience. Examples are service meshes such as Istio, Linkerd 2.0, and AWS App Mesh, all of which have custom resources at their heart.

Remember "A Motivational Example" from Chapter 1? At its core, it has a CR that looks like this:

```
apiVersion: cnat.programming-kubernetes.info/v1alpha1
kind: At
metadata:
  name: example-at
spec:
  schedule: "2019-07-03T02:00:00Z"
status:
  phase: "pending"
```

Custom resources are available in every Kubernetes cluster since version 1.7. They are stored in the same etcd instance as the main Kubernetes API resources and served by the same Kubernetes API server. As shown in Figure 4-1, requests fall back to the apiextensions-apiserver, which serves the resources defined via CRDs, if they are neither of the following:

- Handled by aggregated API servers (see Chapter 8).
- Native Kubernetes resources.

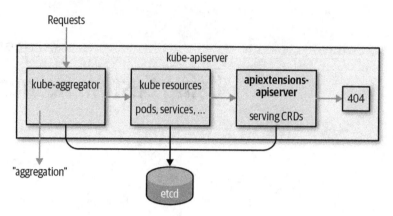

Figure 4-1. The API Extensions API server inside the Kubernetes API server

A CustomResourceDefinition (CRD) is a Kubernetes resource itself. It describes the available CRs in the cluster. For the preceding example CR, the corresponding CRD looks like this:

```
apiVersion: apiextensions.k8s.io/v1beta1
kind: CustomResourceDefinition
metadata:
  name: ats.cnat.programming-kubernetes.info
  spec:
  group: cnat.programming-kubernetes.info
  names:
    kind: At
    listKind: AtList
    plural: ats
    singular: at
  scope: Namespaced
  subresources:
    status: {}
  version: v1alpha1
  versions:
  - name: v1alpha1
    served: true
    storage: true
```

The name of the CRD—in this case, `ats.cnat.programming-kubernetes.info`—must match the plural name followed by the group name. It defines the kind `At` CR in the API group `cnat.programming-kubernetes.info` as a namespaced resource called `ats`.

If this CRD is created in a cluster, `kubectl` will automatically detect the resource, and the user can access it via:

```
$ kubectl get ats
NAME                                      CREATED AT
ats.cnat.programming-kubernetes.info      2019-04-01T14:03:33Z
```

Discovery Information

Behind the scenes, `kubectl` uses discovery information from the API server to find out about the new resources. Let's look a bit deeper into this discovery mechanism.

After increasing the verbosity level of `kubectl`, we can actually see how it learns about the new resource type:

```
$ kubectl get ats -v=7
... GET https://XXX.eks.amazonaws.com/apis/cnat.programming-kubernetes.info/
                                v1alpha1/namespaces/cnat/ats?limit=500
... Request Headers:
... Accept: application/json;as=Table;v=v1beta1;g=meta.k8s.io,application/json
    User-Agent: kubectl/v1.14.0 (darwin/amd64) kubernetes/641856d
... Response Status: 200 OK in 607 milliseconds
NAME         AGE
example-at   43s
```

The discovery steps in detail are:

1. Initially, `kubectl` does not know about `ats`.

2. Hence, kubectl asks the API server about all existing API groups via the */apis* discovery endpoint.

3. Next, kubectl asks the API server about resources in all existing API groups via the */apis/group version* group discovery endpoints.

4. Then, kubectl translates the given type, `ats`, to a triple of:

    - Group (here `cnat.programming-kubernetes.info`)

    - Version (here `v1alpha1`)

    - Resource (here `ats`).

The discovery endpoints provide all the necessary information to do the translation in the last step:

```
$ http localhost:8080/apis/
{
  "groups": [{
    "name": "at.cnat.programming-kubernetes.info",
    "preferredVersion": {
      "groupVersion": "cnat.programming-kubernetes.info/v1",
      "version": "v1alpha1"
    },
    "versions": [{
      "groupVersion": "cnat.programming-kubernetes.info/v1alpha1",
      "version": "v1alpha1"
    }]
  }, ...]
}

$ http localhost:8080/apis/cnat.programming-kubernetes.info/v1alpha1
```

```
{
  "apiVersion": "v1",
  "groupVersion": "cnat.programming-kubernetes.info/v1alpha1",
  "kind": "APIResourceList",
  "resources": [{
    "kind": "At",
    "name": "ats",
    "namespaced": true,
    "verbs": ["create", "delete", "deletecollection",
      "get", "list", "patch", "update", "watch"
    ]
  }, ...]
}
```

This is all implemented by the discovery RESTMapper. We also saw this very common type of RESTMapper in "REST Mapping" on page 63.

 The kubectl CLI also maintains a cache of resource types in ~/.kubectl so that it does not have to re-retrieve the discovery information on every access. This cache is invalidated every 10 minutes. Hence, a change in the CRD might show up in the CLI of the respective user up to 10 minutes later.

Type Definitions

Now let's look at the CRD and the offered features in more detail: as in the cnat example, CRDs are Kubernetes resources in the apiextensions.k8s.io/v1beta1 API group provided by the apiextensions-apiserver inside the Kubernetes API server process.

The schema of CRDs looks like this:

```
apiVersion: apiextensions.k8s.io/v1beta1
kind: CustomResourceDefinition
metadata:
  name: name
spec:
  group: group name
  version: version name
  names:
    kind: uppercase name
    plural: lowercase plural name
    singular: lowercase singular name # defaulted to be lowercase kind
    shortNames: list of strings as short names # optional
    listKind: uppercase list kind # defaulted to be kindList
    categories: list of category membership like "all" # optional
  validation: # optional
    openAPIV3Schema: OpenAPI schema # optional
  subresources: # optional
    status: {} # to enable the status subresource (optional)
    scale: # optional
      specReplicasPath: JSON path for the replica number in the spec of the
                        custom resource
      statusReplicasPath: JSON path for the replica number in the status of
```

```
                            the custom resource
        labelSelectorPath: JSON path of the Scale.Status.Selector field in the
                            scale resource
    versions: # defaulted to the Spec.Version field
    - name: version name
      served: boolean whether the version is served by the API server # defaults to false
      storage: boolean whether this version is the version used to store object
    - ...
```

Many of the fields are optional or are defaulted. We will explain the fields in more detail in the following sections.

After creating a CRD object, the `apiextensions-apiserver` inside of `kube-apiserver` will check the names and determine whether they conflict with other resources or whether they are consistent in themselves. After a few moments it will report the result in the status of the CRD, for example:

```
apiVersion: apiextensions.k8s.io/v1beta1
kind: CustomResourceDefinition
metadata:
  name: ats.cnat.programming-kubernetes.info
spec:
  group: cnat.programming-kubernetes.info
  names:
    kind: At
    listKind: AtList
    plural: ats
    singular: at
  scope: Namespaced
  subresources:
    status: {}
  validation:
    openAPIV3Schema:
      type: object
      properties:
        apiVersion:
          type: string
        kind:
          type: string
        metadata:
          type: object
        spec:
          properties:
            schedule:
              type: string
          type: object
        status:
          type: object
  version: v1alpha1
  versions:
  - name: v1alpha1
    served: true
    storage: true
status:
    acceptedNames:
      kind: At
      listKind: AtList
      plural: ats
```

```
        singular: at
    conditions:
    - lastTransitionTime: "2019-03-17T09:44:21Z"
      message: no conflicts found
      reason: NoConflicts
      status: "True"
      type: NamesAccepted
    - lastTransitionTime: null
      message: the initial names have been accepted
      reason: InitialNamesAccepted
      status: "True"
      type: Established
    storedVersions:
    - v1alpha1
```

You can see that the missing name fields in the spec are defaulted and reflected in the status as accepted names. Moreover, the following conditions are set:

- `NamesAccepted` describes whether the given names in the spec are consistent and free of conflicts.

- `Established` describes that the API server serves the given resource under the names in `status.acceptedNames`.

Note that certain fields can be changed long after the CRD has been created. For example, you can add short names or columns. In this case, a CRD can be established —that is, served with the old names—although the spec names have conflicts. Hence the `NamesAccepted` condition would be false and the spec names and accepted names would differ.

Advanced Features of Custom Resources

In this section we discuss advanced features of custom resources, such as validation or subresources.

Validating Custom Resources

CRs can be validated by the API server during creation and updates. This is done based on the OpenAPI v3 schema (*http://bit.ly/2RqtN5i*) specified in the `validation` fields in the CRD spec.

When a request creates or mutates a CR, the JSON object in the spec is validated against this spec, and in case of errors the conflicting field is returned to the user in an HTTP code 400 response. Figure 4-2 shows where validation takes places in the request handler inside the `apiextensions-apiserver`.

More complex validations can be implemented in validating admission webhooks— that is, in a Turing-complete programming language. Figure 4-2 shows that these webhooks are called directly after the OpenAPI-based validations described in this section. In "Admission Webhooks" on page 226, we will see how admission webhooks are implemented and deployed. There, we'll look into validations that take other resources into account and therefore go far beyond OpenAPI v3 validation. Luckily, for many use cases OpenAPI v3 schemas are sufficient.

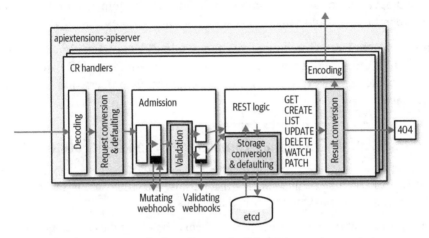

Figure 4-2. Validation step in the handler stack of the apiextensions-apiserver

The OpenAPI schema language is based on the JSON Schema standard (*http://bit.ly/ 2J7aIT7*), which uses JSON/YAML itself to express a schema. Here's an example:

```
type: object
properties:
  apiVersion:
    type: string
  kind:
    type: string
  metadata:
    type: object
  spec:
    type: object
    properties:
      schedule:
        type: string
        pattern: "^\d{4}-([0]\d|1[0-2])-([0-2]\d|3[01])..."
      command:
        type: string
    required:
    - schedule
    - command
  status:
    type: object
    properties:
      phase:
        type: string
required:
- metadata
- apiVersion
```

```
- kind
- spec
```

This schema specifies that the value is actually a JSON object;[1] that is, it is a string map and not a slice or a value like a number. Moreover, it has (aside from `metadata`, `kind`, and `apiVersion`, which are implicitly defined for custom resources) two additional properties: `spec` and `status`.

Each is a JSON object as well. `spec` has the required fields `schedule` and `command`, both of which are strings. `schedule` has to match a pattern for an ISO date (sketched here with some regular expressions). The optional `status` property has a string field called `phase`.

OpenAPI v3 Schemas, Completeness, and Their Future

OpenAPI v3 schemas used to be optional in CRDs. Until Kubernetes 1.14, they were used only for server-side validation. For that purpose they could also be incomplete—in other words, they might not specify all the fields.

Starting with Kubernetes 1.15, the CRD schemas will be published as part of the Kubernetes API server OpenAPI spec. This is used especially by `kubectl` for client-side validation. Client-side validation complains about unknown fields. For example, when the user types `foo:bar` in an object and the OpenAPI schema does not specify `foo`, `kubectl` will reject the object. Hence, it is good practice to pass a complete OpenAPI schema.

Finally, in the future custom resource instances will be pruned (*http://bit.ly/ 2WY8lKY*). This means that—similarly to native Kubernetes resource–like pods— unknown (unspecified) fields will not be persisted. This is important not only for data consistency, but also for security. This is another reason why OpenAPI schemas for CRDs should be complete.

For a complete reference, see the OpenAPI v3 schema documentation (*http://bit.ly/ 2RqtN5i*).

Creating OpenAPI schemata manually can be tedious. Luckily, work is underway to make this much easier via code generation: the Kubebuilder project—see "Kubebuilder" on page 113—has developed `crd-gen` in *sig.k8s.io/controller-tools* (*http:// bit.ly/2J00kvi*), and this is being extended step by step so that it's usable in other contexts. The generator `crd-schema-gen` (*http://bit.ly/31N0eQf*) is a fork of `crd-gen` in this direction.

---

1 Do not confuse Kubernetes and JSON objects here. The latter is just another term for a string map, used in the context of JSON and in OpenAPI.

Short Names and Categories

Like native resources, custom resources might have long resource names. They are great on the API level but tedious to type in the CLI. CRs can have short names as well, like the native resource daemonsets, which can be queried with kubectl get ds. These short names are also known as aliases, and each resource can have any number of them.

To view all of the available short names, use the kubectl api-resources command like so:

```
$ kubectl api-resources
NAME                    SHORTNAMES  APIGROUP NAMESPACED  KIND
bindings                                     true        Binding
componentstatuses       cs                   false       ComponentStatus
configmaps              cm                   true        ConfigMap
endpoints               ep                   true        Endpoints
events                  ev                   true        Event
limitranges             limits               true        LimitRange
namespaces              ns                   false       Namespace
nodes                   no                   false       Node
persistentvolumeclaims  pvc                  true        PersistentVolumeClaim
persistentvolumes       pv                   false       PersistentVolume
pods                    po                   true        Pod
statefulsets            sts         apps     true        StatefulSet
...
```

Again, kubectl learns about short names via discovery information (see "Discovery Information" on page 73). Here is an example:

```
apiVersion: apiextensions.k8s.io/v1beta1
kind: CustomResourceDefinition
metadata:
  name: ats.cnat.programming-kubernetes.info
spec:
  ...
  shortNames:
  - at
```

After that, a kubectl get at will list all cnat CRs in the namespace.

Further, CRs—as with any other resource—can be part of categories. The most common use is the all category, as in kubectl get all. It lists all user-facing resources in a cluster, like pods and services.

The CRs defined in the cluster can join a category or create their own category via the categories field:

```
apiVersion: apiextensions.k8s.io/v1beta1
kind: CustomResourceDefinition
metadata:
  name: ats.cnat.programming-kubernetes.info
spec:
  ...
```

```
categories:
- all
```

With this, `kubectl get all` will also list the `cnat` CR in the namespace.

Printer Columns

The `kubectl` CLI tool uses server-side printing to render the output of `kubectl get`. This means that it queries the API server for the columns to display and the values in each row.

Custom resources support server-side printer columns as well, via `additionalPrinterColumns`. They are called "additional" because the first column is always the name of the object. These columns are defined like this:

```
apiVersion: apiextensions.k8s.io/v1beta1
kind: CustomResourceDefinition
metadata:
  name: ats.cnat.programming-kubernetes.info
spec:
  additionalPrinterColumns: (optional)
  - name: kubectl column name
    type: OpenAPI type for the column
    format: OpenAPI format for the column (optional)
    description: human-readable description of the column (optional)
    priority: integer, always zero supported by kubectl
    JSONPath: JSON path inside the CR for the displayed value
```

The `name` field is the column name, the `type` is an OpenAPI type as defined in the data types (*http://bit.ly/2N0DSY4*) section of the specification, and the `format` (as defined in the same document) is optional and might be interpreted by `kubectl` or other clients.

Further, `description` is an optional human-readable string, used for documentation purposes. The `priority` controls in which verbosity mode of `kubectl` the column is displayed. At the time of this writing (with Kubernetes 1.14), only zero is supported, and all columns with higher priority are hidden.

Finally, `JSONPath` defines which values are to be displayed. It is a simple JSON path inside of the CR. Here, "simple" means that it supports object field syntax like `.spec.foo.bar`, but not more complex JSON paths that loop over arrays or similar.

With this, the example CRD from the introduction could be extended with `additionalPrinterColumns` like this:

```
additionalPrinterColumns: #(optional)
- name: schedule
  type: string
  JSONPath: .spec.schedule
- name: command
  type: string
```

```
    JSONPath: .spec.command
- name: phase
  type: string
  JSONPath: .status.phase
```

Then `kubectl` would render a `cnat` resource as follows:

```
$ kubectl get ats
NAME   SCHEDULER              COMMAND            PHASE
foo    2019-07-03T02:00:00Z   echo "hello world" Pending
```

Next up, we have a look at subresources.

Subresources

We briefly mentioned subresources in "Status Subresources: UpdateStatus" on page 53. Subresources are special HTTP endpoints, using a suffix appended to the HTTP path of the normal resource. For example, the pod standard HTTP path is */api/v1/ namespace/namespace/pods/name*. Pods have a number of subresources, such as */logs, / portforward, /exec*, and */status*. The corresponding subresource HTTP paths are:

- */api/v1/namespace/namespace/pods/name/logs*
- */api/v1/namespace/namespace/pods/name/portforward*
- */api/v1/namespace/namespace/pods/name/exec*
- */api/v1/namespace/namespace/pods/name/status*

The subresource endpoints use a different protocol than the main resource endpoint.

At the time of this writing, custom resources support two subresources: */scale* and */status*. Both are opt-in—that is, they must be explicitly enabled in the CRD.

Status subresource

The */status* subresource is used to split the user-provided specification of a CR instance from the controller-provided status. The main motivation for this is privilege separation:

- The user usually should not write status fields.
- The controller should not write specification fields.

The RBAC mechanism for access control does not allow rules at that level of detail. Those rules are always per resource. The */status* subresource solves this by providing two endpoints that are resources on their own. Each can be controlled with RBAC rules independently. This is often called a *spec-status split*. Here's an example of such a rule for the `ats` resource, which applies only to the */status* subresource (while `"ats"` would match the main resource):

```
apiVersion: rbac.authorization.k8s.io/v1
kind: Role
metadata: ...
rules:
- apiGroups: [""]
  resources: ["ats/status"]
  verbs: ["update", "patch"]
```

Resources (including custom resources) that have a /*status* subresource have changed semantics, also for the main resource endpoint:

- They ignore changes to the status on the main HTTP endpoint during create (the status is just dropped during a create) and updates.

- Likewise, the /*status* subresource endpoint ignores changes outside of the status of the payload. A create operation on the /*status* endpoint is not possible.

- Whenever something outside of `metadata` and outside of `status` changes (this especially means changes in the spec), the main resource endpoint will increase the `metadata.generation` value. This can be used as a trigger for a controller indicating that the user desire has changed.

Note that usually both `spec` and `status` are sent in update requests, but technically you could leave out the respective other part in a request payload.

Also note that the /*status* endpoint will ignore everything outside of the status, including metadata changes like labels or annotations.

The spec-status split of a custom resource is enabled as follows:

```
apiVersion: apiextensions.k8s.io/v1beta1
kind: CustomResourceDefinition
spec:
  subresources:
    status: {}
  ...
```

Note here that the `status` field in that YAML fragment is assigned the empty object. This is the way to set a field that has no other properties. Just writing

```
subresources:
  status:
```

will result in a validation error because in YAML the result is a `null` value for `status`.

Enabling the spec-status split is a breaking change for an API. Old controllers will write to the main endpoint. They won't notice that the status is always ignored from the point where the split is activated. Likewise, a new controller can't write to the new /*status* endpoint until the split is activated.

In Kubernetes 1.13 and later, subresources can be configured per version. This allows us to introduce the */status* subresource without a breaking change:

```
apiVersion: apiextensions.k8s.io/v1beta1
kind: CustomResourceDefinition
spec:
  ...
  versions:
  - name: v1alpha1
    served: true
    storage: true
  - name: v1beta1
    served: true
    subresources:
      status: {}
```

This enables the */status* subresource for `v1beta1`, but not for `v1alpha1`.

 The optimistic concurrency semantics (see "Optimistic Concurrency" on page 14) are the same as for the main resource endpoints; that is, `status` and `spec` share the same resource version counter and */status* updates can conflict due to writes to the main resource, and vice versa. In other words, there is no split of `spec` and `status` on the storage layer.

Scale subresource

The second subresource available for custom resources is */scale*. The */scale* subresource is a (projective)[2] view on the resource, allowing us to view and to modify replica values only. This subresource is well known for resources like deployments and replica sets in Kubernetes, which obviously can be scaled up and down.

The `kubectl scale` command makes use of the */scale* subresource; for example, the following will modify the specified replica value in the given instance:

```
$ kubectl scale --replicas=3 your-custom-resource -v=7
I0429 21:17:53.138353   66743 round_trippers.go:383] PUT
https://host/apis/group/v1/your-custom-resource/scale

apiVersion: apiextensions.k8s.io/v1beta1
kind: CustomResourceDefinition
spec:
  subresources:
    scale:
      specReplicasPath: .spec.replicas
      statusReplicasPath: .status.replicas
      labelSelectorPath: .status.labelSelector
  ...
```

---

2 "Projective" here means that the `scale` object is a projection of the main resource in the sense that it shows only certain fields and hides everything else.

With this, an update of the replica value is written to spec.replicas and returned from there during a GET.

The label selector cannot be changed through the /status subresource, only read. Its purpose is to give a controller the information to count the corresponding objects. For example, the ReplicaSet controller counts the corresponding pods that satisfy this selector.

The label selector is optional. If your custom resource semantics do not fit label selectors, just don't specify the JSON path for one.

In the previous example of kubectl scale --replicas=3 ... the value 3 is written to spec.replicas. Any other simple JSON path can be used, of course; for example, spec.instances or spec.size would be a sensible field name, depending on the context.

The Replica Integer Value Versus the Controller That Creates and Deletes Replicas

We only speak about reading and setting the replica integer value in the custom resource. The actual semantics behind that—for example, the creation and deletion of instances of the actual replicas—must be implemented by a custom controller (see "Controllers and Operators" on page 5).

The kind of the object read from or written to the endpoint is Scale from the autoscaling/v1 API group. Here is what it looks like:

```
type Scale struct {
    metav1.TypeMeta `json:",inline"`
    // Standard object metadata; More info: https://git.k8s.io/
    // community/contributors/devel/api-conventions.md#metadata.
    // +optional
    metav1.ObjectMeta `json:"metadata,omitempty"`

    // defines the behavior of the scale. More info: https://git.k8s.io/community/
    // contributors/devel/api-conventions.md#spec-and-status.
    // +optional
    Spec ScaleSpec `json:"spec,omitempty"`

    // current status of the scale. More info: https://git.k8s.io/community/
    // contributors/devel/api-conventions.md#spec-and-status. Read-only.
    // +optional
    Status ScaleStatus `json:"status,omitempty"`
}

// ScaleSpec describes the attributes of a scale subresource.
type ScaleSpec struct {
    // desired number of instances for the scaled object.
    // +optional
    Replicas int32 `json:"replicas,omitempty"`
```

```
    }

    // ScaleStatus represents the current status of a scale subresource.
    type ScaleStatus struct {
        // actual number of observed instances of the scaled object.
        Replicas int32 `json:"replicas"`

        // label query over pods that should match the replicas count. This is the
        // same as the label selector but in the string format to avoid
        // introspection by clients. The string will be in the same
        // format as the query-param syntax. More info about label selectors:
        // http://kubernetes.io/docs/user-guide/labels#label-selectors.
        // +optional
        Selector string `json:"selector,omitempty"`
    }
```

An instance will look like this:

```
metadata:
  name: cr-name
  namespace: cr-namespace
  uid: cr-uid
  resourceVersion: cr-resource-version
  creationTimestamp: cr-creation-timestamp
spec:
  replicas: 3
  status:
    replicas: 2
    selector: "environment = production"
```

Note that the optimistic concurrency semantics are the same for the main resource and for the *scale* subresource. That is, main resource writes can conflict with *scale* writes, and vice versa.

A Developer's View on Custom Resources

Custom resources can be accessed from Golang using a number of clients. We will concentrate on:

- Using the client-go dynamic client (see "Dynamic Client" on page 86)
- Using a typed client:
  - As provided by kubernetes-sigs/controller-runtime (*http://bit.ly/2ZFtDKd*) and used by the Operator SDK and Kubebuilder (see "controller-runtime Client of Operator SDK and Kubebuilder" on page 92)
  - As generated by client-gen, like that in *k8s.io/client-go/kubernetes* (*http://bit.ly/2FnmGWA*) (see "Typed client created via client-gen" on page 90)

The choice of which client to use depends mainly on the context of the code to be written, especially the complexity of implemented logic and the requirements (e.g., to be dynamic and to support GVKs unknown at compile time).

The preceding list of clients:

- Decreases in the flexibility to handle unknown GVKs.
- Increases in type safety.
- Increases in the completeness of features of the Kubernetes API they provide.

Dynamic Client

The dynamic client in *k8s.io/client-go/dynamic* (*http://bit.ly/2Y6eeSK*) is totally agnostic to known GVKs. It does not even use any Go types other than *unstructured.Unstructured* (*http://bit.ly/2WYZ6oS*), which wraps just `json.Unmarshal` and its output.

The dynamic client makes use of neither a scheme nor a RESTMapper. This means that the developer has to provide all the knowledge about types manually by providing a resource (see "Resources" on page 63) in the form of a GVR:

```
schema.GroupVersionResource{
    Group: "apps",
    Version: "v1",
    Resource: "deployments",
}
```

If a REST client config is available (see "Creating and Using a Client" on page 39), the dynamic client can be created in one line:

```
client, err := NewForConfig(cfg)
```

The REST access to a given GVR is just as simple:

```
client.Resource(gvr).
    Namespace(namespace).Get("foo", metav1.GetOptions{})
```

This gives you the deployment `foo` in the given namespace.

 You must know the scope of the resource (i.e., whether it is namespaced or cluster-scoped). Cluster-scoped resources just leave out the `Namespace(namespace)` call.

The input and output of the dynamic client is an `*unstructured.Unstructured`—that is, an object that contains the same data structure that `json.Unmarshal` would output on unmarshaling:

- Objects are represented by `map[string]interface{}`.
- Arrays are represented by `[]interface{}`.

- Primitive types are `string`, `bool`, `float64`, or `int64`.

The method `UnstructuredContent()` provides access to this data structure inside of an unstructured object (we can also just access `Unstructured.Object`). There are helpers in the same package to make retrieval of fields easy and manipulation of the object possible—for example:

```
name, found, err := unstructured.NestedString(u.Object, "metadata", "name")
```

which returns the name of the deployment—`"foo"` in this case. `found` is true if the field was actually found (not only empty, but actually existing). `err` reports if the type of an existing field is unexpected (i.e., not a string in this case). Other helpers are the generic ones, once with a deep copy of the result and once without:

```
func NestedFieldCopy(obj map[string]interface{}, fields ...string)
    (interface{}, bool, error)
func NestedFieldNoCopy(obj map[string]interface{}, fields ...string)
    (interface{}, bool, error)
```

There are other typed variants that do a type-cast and return an error if that fails:

```
func NestedBool(obj map[string]interface{}, fields ...string) (bool, bool, error)
func NestedFloat64(obj map[string]interface{}, fields ...string)
    (float64, bool, error)
func NestedInt64(obj map[string]interface{}, fields ...string) (int64, bool, error)
func NestedStringSlice(obj map[string]interface{}, fields ...string)
    ([]string, bool, error)
func NestedSlice(obj map[string]interface{}, fields ...string)
    ([]interface{}, bool, error)
func NestedStringMap(obj map[string]interface{}, fields ...string)
    (map[string]string, bool, error)
```

And finally a generic setter:

```
func SetNestedField(obj, value, path...)
```

The dynamic client is used in Kubernetes itself for controllers that are generic, like the garbage collection controller, which deletes objects whose parents have disappeared. The garbage collection controller works with any resource in the system and hence makes extensive use of the dynamic client.

Typed Clients

Typed clients do not use `map[string]interface{}`-like generic data structures but instead use real Golang types, which are different and specific for each GVK. They are much easier to use, have considerably increased type safety, and make code much more concise and readable. On the downside, they are less flexible because the processed types have to be known at compile time, and those clients are generated, and this adds complexity.

Before going into two implementations of typed clients, let's look into the representation of kinds in the Golang type system (see "API Machinery in Depth" on page 62 for the theory behind the Kubernetes type system).

Anatomy of a type

Kinds are represented as Golang structs. Usually the struct is named as the kind (though technically it doesn't have to be) and is placed in a package corresponding to the group and version of the GVK at hand. A common convention is to place the GVK *group/version.Kind* into a Go package:

```
pkg/apis/group/version
```

and define a Golang struct *Kind* in the file *types.go*.

Every Golang type corresponding to a GVK embeds the `TypeMeta` struct from the package *k8s.io/apimachinery/pkg/apis/meta/v1* (*http://bit.ly/2Y5HdWT*). `TypeMeta` just consists of the `Kind` and `ApiVersion` fields:

```
type TypeMeta struct {
    // +optional
    APIVersion string `json:"apiVersion,omitempty" yaml:"apiVersion,omitempty"`
    // +optional
    Kind string `json:"kind,omitempty" yaml:"kind,omitempty"`
}
```

In addition, every top-level kind—that is, one that has its own endpoint and therefore one (or more) corresponding GVRs (see "REST Mapping" on page 63)—has to store a name, a namespace for namespaced resources, and a pretty long number of further metalevel fields. All these are stored in a struct called `ObjectMeta` in the package *k8s.io/apimachinery/pkg/apis/meta/v1* (*http://bit.ly/2XSt8eo*):

```
type ObjectMeta struct {
    Name string `json:"name,omitempty"`
    Namespace string `json:"namespace,omitempty"`
    UID types.UID `json:"uid,omitempty"`
    ResourceVersion string `json:"resourceVersion,omitempty"`
    CreationTimestamp Time `json:"creationTimestamp,omitempty"`
    DeletionTimestamp *Time `json:"deletionTimestamp,omitempty"`
    Labels map[string]string `json:"labels,omitempty"`
    Annotations map[string]string `json:"annotations,omitempty"`
    ...
}
```

There are a number of additional fields. We highly recommend you read through the extensive inline documentation (*http://bit.ly/2IutNyh*), because it gives a good picture of the core functionality of Kubernetes objects.

Kubernetes top-level types (i.e., those that have an embedded `TypeMeta`, and an embedded `ObjectMeta`, and—in this case—are persisted into `etcd`) look very similar to each other in the sense that they usually have a `spec` and a `status`. See this example of a deployment from *k8s.io/kubernetes/apps/v1/types.go* (*http://bit.ly/2RroTFb*):

```
type Deployment struct {
    metav1.TypeMeta `json:",inline"`
    metav1.ObjectMeta `json:"metadata,omitempty"`

    Spec DeploymentSpec `json:"spec,omitempty"`
    Status DeploymentStatus `json:"status,omitempty"`
}
```

While the actual content of the types for `spec` and `status` differs significantly between different types, this split into `spec` and `status` is a common theme or even a convention in Kubernetes, though it's not technically required. Hence, it is good practice to follow this structure of CRDs as well. Some CRD features even require this structure; for example, the */status* subresource for custom resources (see "Status subresource" on page 81)—when enabled—always applies to the `status` substructure only of the custom resource instance. It cannot be renamed.

Golang package structure

As we have seen, the Golang types are traditionally placed in a file called *types.go* in the package *pkg/apis/group/version*. In addition to that file, there are a couple more files we want to go through now. Some of them are manually written by the developer, while some are generated with code generators. See Chapter 5 for details.

The *doc.go* file describes the API's purpose and includes a number of package-global code generation tags:

```
// Package v1alpha1 contains the cnat v1alpha1 API group
//
// +k8s:deepcopy-gen=package
// +groupName=cnat.programming-kubernetes.info
package v1alpha1
```

Next, *register.go* includes helpers to register the custom resource Golang types into a scheme (see "Scheme" on page 65):

```
package version

import (
    metav1 "k8s.io/apimachinery/pkg/apis/meta/v1"
    "k8s.io/apimachinery/pkg/runtime"
    "k8s.io/apimachinery/pkg/runtime/schema"

    group "repo/pkg/apis/group"
)

// SchemeGroupVersion is group version used to register these objects
var SchemeGroupVersion = schema.GroupVersion{
    Group: group.GroupName,
    Version: "version",
}

// Kind takes an unqualified kind and returns back a Group qualified GroupKind
func Kind(kind string) schema.GroupKind {
    return SchemeGroupVersion.WithKind(kind).GroupKind()
```

```
    }

    // Resource takes an unqualified resource and returns a Group
    // qualified GroupResource
    func Resource(resource string) schema.GroupResource {
        return SchemeGroupVersion.WithResource(resource).GroupResource()
    }

    var (
        SchemeBuilder = runtime.NewSchemeBuilder(addKnownTypes)
        AddToScheme   = SchemeBuilder.AddToScheme
    )

    // Adds the list of known types to Scheme.
    func addKnownTypes(scheme *runtime.Scheme) error {
        scheme.AddKnownTypes(SchemeGroupVersion,
            &SomeKind{},
            &SomeKindList{},
        )
        metav1.AddToGroupVersion(scheme, SchemeGroupVersion)
        return nil
    }
```

Then, *zz_generated.deepcopy.go* defines deep-copy methods on the custom resource Golang top-level types (i.e., SomeKind and SomeKindList in the preceding example code). In addition, all substructs (like those for the spec and status) become deep-copyable as well.

Because the example uses the tag +k8s:deepcopy-gen=package in *doc.go*, the deep-copy generation is on an opt-out basis; that is, DeepCopy methods are generated for every type in the package that does not opt out with +k8s:deepcopy-gen=false. See Chapter 5 and especially "deepcopy-gen Tags" on page 100 for more details.

Typed client created via client-gen

With the API package *pkg/apis/group/version* in place, the client generator client-gen creates a typed client (see Chapter 5 for details, especially "client-gen Tags" on page 102), in *pkg/generated/clientset/versioned* by default (pkg/client/clientset/versioned in old versions of the generator). More precisely, the generated top-level object is a client set. It subsumes a number of API groups, versions, and resources.

The top-level file (*http://bit.ly/2GdcikH*) looks like the following:

```
    // Code generated by client-gen. DO NOT EDIT.

    package versioned

    import (
        discovery "k8s.io/client-go/discovery"
        rest "k8s.io/client-go/rest"
        flowcontrol "k8s.io/client-go/util/flowcontrol"

        cnatv1alpha1 ".../cnat/cnat-client-go/pkg/generated/clientset/versioned/
    )
```

```
type Interface interface {
    Discovery() discovery.DiscoveryInterface
    CnatV1alpha1() cnatv1alpha1.CnatV1alpha1Interface
}

// Clientset contains the clients for groups. Each group has exactly one
// version included in a Clientset.
type Clientset struct {
    *discovery.DiscoveryClient
    cnatV1alpha1 *cnatv1alpha1.CnatV1alpha1Client
}

// CnatV1alpha1 retrieves the CnatV1alpha1Client
func (c *Clientset) CnatV1alpha1() cnatv1alpha1.CnatV1alpha1Interface {
    return c.cnatV1alpha1
}

// Discovery retrieves the DiscoveryClient
func (c *Clientset) Discovery() discovery.DiscoveryInterface {
    ...
}

// NewForConfig creates a new Clientset for the given config.
func NewForConfig(c *rest.Config) (*Clientset, error) {
    ...
}
```

The client set is represented by the interface `Interface` and gives access to the API group client interface for each version—for example, `CnatV1alpha1Interface` in this sample code:

```
type CnatV1alpha1Interface interface {
    RESTClient() rest.Interface
    AtsGetter
}

// AtsGetter has a method to return a AtInterface.
// A group's client should implement this interface.
type AtsGetter interface {
    Ats(namespace string) AtInterface
}

// AtInterface has methods to work with At resources.
type AtInterface interface {
    Create(*v1alpha1.At) (*v1alpha1.At, error)
    Update(*v1alpha1.At) (*v1alpha1.At, error)
    UpdateStatus(*v1alpha1.At) (*v1alpha1.At, error)
    Delete(name string, options *v1.DeleteOptions) error
    DeleteCollection(options *v1.DeleteOptions, listOptions v1.ListOptions) error
    Get(name string, options v1.GetOptions) (*v1alpha1.At, error)
    List(opts v1.ListOptions) (*v1alpha1.AtList, error)
    Watch(opts v1.ListOptions) (watch.Interface, error)
    Patch(name string, pt types.PatchType, data []byte, subresources ...string)
        (result *v1alpha1.At, err error)
    AtExpansion
}
```

An instance of a client set can be created with the `NewForConfig` helper function. This is analogous to the clients for core Kubernetes resources discussed in "Creating and Using a Client" on page 39:

```
import (
    metav1 "k8s.io/apimachinery/pkg/apis/meta/v1"
    "k8s.io/client-go/tools/clientcmd"

    client "github.com/.../cnat/cnat-client-go/pkg/generated/clientset/versioned"
)

kubeconfig = flag.String("kubeconfig", "~/.kube/config", "kubeconfig file")
flag.Parse()
config, err := clientcmd.BuildConfigFromFlags("", *kubeconfig)
clientset, err := client.NewForConfig(config)

ats := clientset.CnatV1alpha1Interface().Ats("default")
book, err := ats.Get("kubernetes-programming", metav1.GetOptions{})
```

As you can see, the code generation machinery allows us to program logic for custom resources in the very same way as for core Kubernetes resources. Higher-level tools like informers are also available; see `informer-gen` in Chapter 5.

controller-runtime Client of Operator SDK and Kubebuilder

For the sake of completeness, we want to take a quick look at the third client, which is listed as the second option in "A Developer's View on Custom Resources" on page 85. The `controller-runtime` project provides the basis for the operator solutions Operator SDK and Kubebuilder presented in Chapter 6. It includes a client that uses the Go types presented in "Anatomy of a type" on page 88.

In contrast to the `client-gen`–generated client of the previous "Typed client created via client-gen" on page 90, and similarly to the "Dynamic Client" on page 86, this client is one instance, capable of handling any kind that is registered in a given scheme.

It uses discovery information from the API server to map the kinds to HTTP paths. Note that Chapter 6 will go into greater detail on how this client is used as part of those two operator solutions.

Here is a quick example of how to use `controller-runtime`:

```
import (
    "flag"

    corev1 "k8s.io/api/core/v1"
    metav1 "k8s.io/apimachinery/pkg/apis/meta/v1"
    "k8s.io/client-go/kubernetes/scheme"
    "k8s.io/client-go/tools/clientcmd"

    runtimeclient "sigs.k8s.io/controller-runtime/pkg/client"
)

kubeconfig = flag.String("kubeconfig", "~/.kube/config", "kubeconfig file path")
```

```
flag.Parse()
config, err := clientcmd.BuildConfigFromFlags("", *kubeconfig)

cl, _ := runtimeclient.New(config, client.Options{
    Scheme: scheme.Scheme,
})
podList := &corev1.PodList{}
err := cl.List(context.TODO(), client.InNamespace("default"), podList)
```

The client object's `List()` method accepts any `runtime.Object` registered in the given scheme, which in this case is the one borrowed from `client-go` with all standard Kubernetes kinds being registered. Internally, the client uses the given scheme to map the Golang type `*corev1.PodList` to a GVK. In a second step, the `List()` method uses discovery information to get the GVR for pods, which is `schema.Group VersionResource{"", "v1", "pods"}`, and therefore accesses /api/v1/namespace/default/pods to get the list of pods in the passed namespace.

The same logic can be used with custom resources. The main difference is to use a custom scheme that contains the passed Go type:

```
import (
    "flag"

    corev1 "k8s.io/api/core/v1"
    metav1 "k8s.io/apimachinery/pkg/apis/meta/v1"
    "k8s.io/client-go/kubernetes/scheme"
    "k8s.io/client-go/tools/clientcmd"

    runtimeclient "sigs.k8s.io/controller-runtime/pkg/client"
    cnatv1alpha1 "github.com/.../cnat/cnat-kubebuilder/pkg/apis/cnat/v1alpha1"
)

kubeconfig = flag.String("kubeconfig", "~/.kube/config", "kubeconfig file")
flag.Parse()
config, err := clientcmd.BuildConfigFromFlags("", *kubeconfig)

crScheme := runtime.NewScheme()
cnatv1alpha1.AddToScheme(crScheme)

cl, _ := runtimeclient.New(config, client.Options{
    Scheme: crScheme,
})
list := &cnatv1alpha1.AtList{}
err := cl.List(context.TODO(), client.InNamespace("default"), list)
```

Note how the invocation of the `List()` command does not change at all.

Imagine you write an operator that accesses many different kinds using this client. With the typed client of "Typed client created via client-gen" on page 90, you would have to pass many different clients into the operator, making the plumbing code pretty complex. In contrast, the `controller-runtime` client presented here is just one object for all kinds, assuming all of them are in one scheme.

All three types of clients have their uses, with advantages and disadvantages depending on the context in which they are used. In generic controllers that handle unknown objects, only the dynamic client can be used. In controllers where type safety helps a lot to enforce code correctness, the generated clients are a good fit. The Kubernetes project itself has so many contributors that stability of the code is very important, even when it is extended and rewritten by so many people. If convenience and high velocity with minimal plumbing is important, the `controller-runtime` client is a good fit.

Summary

We introduced you to custom resources, the central extension mechanisms used in the Kubernetes ecosystem, in this chapter. By now you should have a good understanding of their features and limitations as well as the available clients.

Let's now move on to code generation for managing said resources.

## CHAPTER 5

Automating Code Generation

In this chapter you'll learn how to use the Kubernetes code generators in Go projects to write custom resources in a natural way. Code generators are used a lot in the implementation of native Kubernetes resources, and we'll use the very same generators here.

Why Code Generation

Go is a simple language by design. It lacks higher-level or even metaprogramming-like mechanisms to express algorithms on different data types in a generic (i.e., type-independent) way. The "Go way" is to use external code generation instead.

Very early in the Kubernetes development process, more and more code had to be rewritten as more resources were added to the system. Code generation made the maintenance of this code much easier. Very early on, the Gengo library (*http://bit.ly/2L9kwNJ*) was created, and eventually, based on Gengo, *k8s.io/code-generator* (*http://bit.ly/2Kw8I8U*) was developed as an externally usable collection of generators. We will use these generators in the following sections for CRs.

Calling the Generators

Usually, the code generators are called in mostly the same way in every controller project. Only packages, group names, and API versions differ. Calling the script *k8s.io/code-generator/generate-groups.sh* or a bash script like *hack/update-codegen.sh* is the easiest way to add code generation to CR Go types from the build system (see the book's GitHub repository (*http://bit.ly/2J0s2YL*)).

Note that some projects call the generator binaries directly due to very special requirements and often historic reasons. For the use case of building a controller for

CRs, it is much easier to just call the *generate-groups.sh* script from the *k8s.io/code-generator* repository:

```
$ vendor/k8s.io/code-generator/generate-groups.sh all \
    github.com/programming-kubernetes/cnat/cnat-client-go/pkg/generated \
    github.com/programming-kubernetes/cnat/cnat-client-go/pkg/apis \
    cnat:v1alpha1 \
    --output-base "${GOPATH}/src" \
    --go-header-file "hack/boilerplate.go.txt"
```

Here, `all` means to call all four standard code generators for CRs:

`deepcopy-gen`

Generates `func (t *T) DeepCopy() *T` and `func (t *T) DeepCopyInto(*T)` methods.

`client-gen`

Creates typed client sets.

`informer-gen`

Creates informers for CRs that offer an event-based interface to react to changes of CRs on the server.

`lister-gen`

Creates listers for CRs that offer a read-only caching layer for `GET` and `LIST` requests.

The last two are the basis for building controllers (see "Controllers and Operators" on page 5). These four code generators make up a powerful basis for building full-featured, production-ready controllers using the same mechanisms and packages that the Kubernetes upstream controllers are using.

> There are some more generators in *k8s.io/code-generator*, mostly for other contexts. For example, if you build your own aggregated API server (see Chapter 8), you will work with internal types in addition to versioned types, and you have to define defaulting functions. Then these two generators, which you can access by calling the *generate-internal-groups.sh* (*http://bit.ly/2L9kSE3*) script from *k8s.io/code-generator*, will become relevant:
>
> `conversion-gen`
>
> Creates functions for converting between internal and external types.
>
> `defaulter-gen`
>
> Takes care of defaulting certain fields.

Now let's look in detail at the parameters to `generate-groups.sh`:

- The second parameter is the target package name for the generated clients, listers, and informers.
- The third parameter is the base package for the API group.
- The fourth parameter is a space-separated list of API groups with their versions.
- `--output-base` is passed as a flag to all generators to define the base directory where the given packages are found.
- `--go-header-file` enables us to put copyright headers into generated code.

Some generators, like `deepcopy-gen`, create files directly inside the API group packages. Those files follow a standard naming scheme with a *zz_generated.* prefix such that it is easy to exclude them from version control systems (e.g., via *.gitignore* file), though most projects decide to check generated files in because the Go tooling around code generators is not well developed.[1]

If the project follows the pattern of *k8s.io/sample-controller* (*http://bit.ly/2UppsTN*)— the `sample-controller` is a blueprint project replicating the patterns established by the many controllers built in Kubernetes itself—then the code generation starts with:

```
$ hack/update-codegen.sh
```

The `cnat` example in the `sample-controller+client-go` variant in "Following sample-controller" on page 106 goes this route.

Usually, in addition to the `hack/update-codegen.sh` (*http://bit.ly/2J0s2YL*) script, there is a second script called `hack/verify-codegen.sh` (*http://bit.ly/2IXUWsy*).

This script calls the `hack/update-codegen.sh` script and checks whether anything changed, and then it terminates with a nonzero return code if any of the generated files is not up-to-date.

This is very helpful in a continuous integration (CI) script: if a developer modified the files by accident or if the files are just outdated, CI will notice and complain.

Controlling the Generators with Tags

While some of the code-generator behavior is controlled via command-line flags as described earlier (especially the packages to process), a lot more properties are

---

1 The Go tools do not run the generation automatically when needed and lack a way to define dependencies between source and generated files.

controlled via *tags* in your Go files. A tag is a specially formatted Go comment in the following form:

```
// +some-tag
// +some-other-tag=value
```

There are two kind of tags:

- Global tags above the `package` line in a file called *doc.go*
- Local tags above a type declaration (e.g., above a struct definition)

Depending on the tags in question, the position of the comment might be important.

Follow Examples (including Comment Blocks) Precisely

There are a number of tags that must be in a comment directly above a type (or the package line for a global tag), while others must be separated from the type (or the package line) with at least one empty line in between them. For example:

```
// +second-comment-block-tag

// +first-comment-block-tag
type Foo struct {
}
```

The reason for this distinction is historic: the API documentation generators in Kubernetes used not to know about code generation tags and instead exported only the first comment block. Therefore, tags in that block would have showed up in API HTML documents.

The code generator tag parsing logic is not always very consistent, and often the error handling is far from perfect. While this is improved with each version, be prepared to follow existing examples very precisely—for example, an empty line might matter.

Global Tags

Global tags are written into a package's *doc.go*. A typical *pkg/apis/group/version/doc.go* file looks like this:

```
// +k8s:deepcopy-gen=package

// Package v1 is the v1alpha1 version of the API.
// +groupName=cnat.programming-kubernetes.info
package v1alpha1
```

The first line of this file tells `deepcopy-gen` to create deep-copy methods by default for every type in that package. If you have types where deep copy is not necessary, not desired, or even not possible, you can opt out for them with the local tag `// +k8s:deepcopy-gen=false`. If you do not enable package-wide deep copy, you have to opt in to deep copy for each desired type via `// +k8s:deepcopy-gen=true`.

The second tag, `// +groupName=example.com`, defines the fully qualified API group name. This tag is necessary if the Go parent package name does not match the group name.

The file shown here actually comes from the cnat `client-go` example *pkg/apis/cnat/v1alpha1/doc.go* file (*http://bit.ly/2L6M9ad*) (see "Following sample-controller" on page 106). There, `cnat` is the parent package, but `cnat.programming-kubernetes.info` is the group name.

With the `// +groupName` tag, the client generator (see "Typed client created via client-gen" on page 90) will generate a client using the correct HTTP path */apis/foo.project.example.com*. Besides `+groupName` there is also `+groupGoName`, which defines a custom Go identifier (for variable and type names) to be used instead of the parent package name. For example, the generators will use the uppercase parent package name for identifies by default, which in our example is `Cnat`. A better identifier would be `CNAt` for "Cloud Native At." With `// +groupGoName=CNAt` we could use that instead of `Cnat` (though we don't do that in this example—we've stayed with `Cnat`), and the `client-gen` result would look like the following:

```
type Interface interface {
    Discovery() discovery.DiscoveryInterface
    CNatV1() atv1alpha1.CNatV1alpha1Interface
}
```

Local Tags

Local tags are written either directly above an API type or in the second comment block above it. Here are the main types in the *types.go* file of the cnat example (*http://bit.ly/31QosJw*):

```
// AtSpec defines the desired state of At
type AtSpec struct {
    // Schedule is the desired time the command is supposed to be executed.
    // Note: the format used here is UTC time https://www.utctime.net
    Schedule string `json:"schedule,omitempty"`
    // Command is the desired command (executed in a Bash shell) to be executed.
    Command string `json:"command,omitempty"`
    // Important: Run "make" to regenerate code after modifying this file
}

// AtStatus defines the observed state of At
type AtStatus struct {
    // Phase represents the state of the schedule: until the command is executed
    // it is PENDING, afterwards it is DONE.
    Phase string `json:"phase,omitempty"`
    // Important: Run "make" to regenerate code after modifying this file
}
```

```
// +genclient
// +k8s:deepcopy-gen:interfaces=k8s.io/apimachinery/pkg/runtime.Object

// At runs a command at a given schedule.
type At struct {
    metav1.TypeMeta   `json:",inline"`
    metav1.ObjectMeta `json:"metadata,omitempty"`

    Spec   AtSpec   `json:"spec,omitempty"`
    Status AtStatus `json:"status,omitempty"`
}

// +k8s:deepcopy-gen:interfaces=k8s.io/apimachinery/pkg/runtime.Object

// AtList contains a list of At
type AtList struct {
    metav1.TypeMeta `json:",inline"`
    metav1.ListMeta `json:"metadata,omitempty"`
    Items           []At `json:"items"`
}
```

In the following sections we'll walk through the tags of this example.

> In this example, the API documentation is in the first comment block, while we put the tags into the second comment block. This helps to keep the tags out of the API documentation, if you use some tool to extract the Go doc comments for that purpose.

deepcopy-gen Tags

Deep-copy method generation is usually enabled for all types by default via the global `// +k8s:deepcopy-gen=package` tag (see "Global Tags" on page 98)—that is, with possible opt-out. However, in the preceding example file (and actually the whole package), all API types need deep-copy methods. Hence, we don't have to opt out locally.

If we had a helper struct in the API types package (this is usually discouraged to keep API packages clean), we would have to disable deep-copy generation. For example:

```
// +k8s:deepcopy-gen=false
//
// Helper is a helper struct, not an API type.
type Helper struct {
    ...
}
```

runtime.Object and DeepCopyObject

There is a special deep-copy tag that needs more explanation:

```
// +k8s:deepcopy-gen:interfaces=k8s.io/apimachinery/pkg/runtime.Object
```

In "Kubernetes Objects in Go" on page 46 we saw that runtime.Objects have to implement the DeepCopyObject() runtime.Object method. The reason is that generic code within Kubernetes has to be able to create deep copies of objects. This method allows that.

Historical Background

Prior to 1.8, the scheme (see "Scheme" on page 65) was also keeping references to type-specific deep-copy functions, and it had a reflection-based deep-copy implementation. Both mechanisms were the reason for a number of nontrivial and hard-to-discover bugs. Therefore, Kubernetes switched to static deep copy with the DeepCopyObject method in the runtime.Object interface.

The DeepCopyObject() method does nothing other than calling the generated Deep Copy method. The signature of the latter varies from type to type (DeepCopy() *T depends on T). The signature of the former is always DeepCopyObject() run time.Object:

```
func (in *T) DeepCopyObject() runtime.Object {
    if c := in.DeepCopy(); c != nil {
        return c
    } else {
        return nil
    }
}
```

Put the local tag // +k8s:deepcopy-gen:interfaces=k8s.io/apimachi nery/pkg/runtime.Object above your top-level API types to generate this method with deepcopy-gen. This tells deepcopy-gen to create such a method for run time.Object, called DeepCopyObject().

In the previous example, both At and AtList are top-level types because they are used as runtime.Objects.

As a rule of thumb, top-level types are those that have metav1.Type Meta embedded.

It happens that other interfaces need a way to be deep-copied. This is usually the case if, for example, API types have a field of interface type Foo:

```
type SomeAPIType struct {
    Foo Foo `json:"foo"`
}
```

As we have seen, API types must be deep-copyable, and hence the field Foo must be deep-copied too. How could you do that in a generic way (without type-casts) without adding DeepCopyFoo() Foo to the Foo interface?

```
type Foo interface {
    ...
    DeepCopyFoo() Foo
}
```

In that case the same tag can be used:

```
// +k8s:deepcopy-gen:interfaces=<package>.Foo
type FooImplementation struct {
    ...
}
```

There are a few examples beyond runtime.Object in the Kubernetes source where this tag is actually used:

```
// +k8s:deepcopy-gen:interfaces=.../pkg/registry/rbac/reconciliation.RuleOwner
// +k8s:deepcopy-gen:interfaces=.../pkg/registry/rbac/reconciliation.RoleBinding
```

client-gen Tags

Finally, there are a number of tags to control client-gen, one of which we saw in the earlier example for At and AtList:

```
// +genclient
```

It tells client-gen to create a client for this type (this is always opt-in). Note that you don't have to and indeed *must not* put it above the List type of the API objects.

In our cnat example, we use the */status* subresource and update the status of the CRs with the UpdateStatus method of the client (see "Status subresource" on page 81). There are instances of CRs without a status or without a spec-status split. In those cases, the following tag avoids the generation of that UpdateStatus() method:

```
// +genclient:noStatus
```

Without this tag, client-gen will blindly generate the UpdateSta tus() method. It is important to understand, however, that the spec-status split works only if the */status* subresource is actually enabled in the CustomResourceDefinition manifest (see "Subre-sources" on page 81).

The existence of the method alone in the client has no effect. Requests to it without the change in the manifest will even fail.

The client generator has to choose the right HTTP path, either with or without a namespace. For cluster-wide resources, you have to use the tag:

```
// +genclient:nonNamespaced
```

The default is to generate a namespaced client. Again, this has to match the scope setting in the CRD manifest. For special-purpose clients, you might also want to control in detail which HTTP methods are offered. You can do this by using a couple of tags, for example:

```
// +genclient:noVerbs
// +genclient:onlyVerbs=create,delete
// +genclient:skipVerbs=get,list,create,update,patch,delete,watch
// +genclient:method=Create,verb=create,
// result=k8s.io/apimachinery/pkg/apis/meta/v1.Status
```

The first three should be pretty self-explanatory, but the last one warrants some explanation.

The type this tag is written above will be create-only and will not return the API type itself, but a `metav1.Status`. For CRs this does not make much sense, but for user-provided API servers written in Go (see Chapter 8) those resources can exist, and they do in practice.

One common case for the `// +genclient:method=` tag is the addition of a method to scale a resource. In "Scale subresource" on page 83 we describe how the /scale subresource can be enabled for CRs. The following tags create the corresponding client methods:

```
// +genclient:method=GetScale,verb=get,subresource=scale,\
//     result=k8s.io/api/autoscaling/v1.Scale
// +genclient:method=UpdateScale,verb=update,subresource=scale,\
//     input=k8s.io/api/autoscaling/v1.Scale,result=k8s.io/api/autoscaling/v1.Scale
```

The first tag creates the getter `GetScale`. The second creates the setter `UpdateScale`.

All CR /scale subresources receive and output the `Scale` type from the autoscaling/v1 group. In the Kubernetes API there are resources that use other types for historic reasons.

informer-gen and lister-gen

Both `informer-gen` and `lister-gen` process the `// +genclient` tag of `client-gen`. There is nothing else to configure. Each type that opted in to client generation gets informers and listers automatically that match the client (if the whole suite of generators is called via the k8s.io/code-generator/generate-group.sh script).

The documentation of the Kubernetes generators has a lot of room for improvement and will certainly be refined slowly over time. For more information about the different generators, it is often helpful to look at examples inside Kubernetes itself—for example, k8s.io/api (http://bit.ly/2ZA6dWH) and OpenShift API types (http://bit.ly/2KxpKnc). Both repositories have many advanced use cases.

Moreover, don't hesitate to look into the generators themselves. `deepcopy-gen` has some documentation available inside its *main.go* (*http://bit.ly/2x9HmN4*) file. `client-gen` has some documentation available in the Kubernetes contributor documentation (*http://bit.ly/2WYNlns*). `informer-gen` and `lister-gen` currently don't have further documentation, but *generate-groups.sh* shows how each is invoked (*http://bit.ly/31MeSHp*).

Summary

In this chapter we showed you how to use the Kubernetes code generators for CRs. With that out of the way, we now move on to higher-level abstraction tooling—that is, solutions for writing custom controllers and operators that enable you to focus on the business logic.

## CHAPTER 6

Solutions for Writing Operators

So far we've had a look at custom controllers and operators on a conceptual level in "Controllers and Operators" on page 5 and, in Chapter 5, how to use Kubernetes code generators—a rather low-level way to deal with the topic. In this chapter we'll walk through three solutions for writing custom controllers and operators in detail and discuss some more alternatives.

Using one of the solutions discussed in this chapter should help you to avoid writing a lot of repetitive code and enable you to focus on the business logic, rather than on boilerplate code. It should get you started more quickly and make you more productive.

 Operators in general, and the tools we discuss in this chapter specifically, are still rapidly evolving as of mid-2019. While we do our best, certain commands and/or their outputs you see shown here, may change. Take this into account, and make sure that you always use the latest version of the respective tool, keeping an eye on the respective issue trackers, mailing lists, and Slack channels.

While there are resources available online that compare (*http://bit.ly/2ZC5fZT*) the solutions we discuss here, we will not recommend a specific solution to you. We do, however, encourage you to evaluate and compare them yourself and pick the one that is the best fit for your organization and environment.

Preparation

We will be using cnat (cloud-native at, which we introduced in "A Motivational Example" on page 3) as the running example for the different solutions in this chapter. If you want to follow along, note that we assume you:

1. Have Go version 1.12 or above installed and set up properly.

2. Have access to a Kubernetes cluster in version 1.12 or above—either locally through, for example, kind or k3d, or remotely through your favorite cloud provider—and kubectl configured to access it.

3. git clone our GitHub repository (*http://bit.ly/2N3R6U4*). The complete, functioning source code and the necessary commands shown in the following sections are available there. Note that what we're showing here is how things work from scratch. If you want to see the results rather than carrying out the steps yourself, you're also welcome to clone the repository and run only the commands to install the CRD, install the CR, and launch the custom controller.

With these housekeeping items out of the way, let's jump into writing operators: we will covers, the sample-controller, Kubebuilder, and the Operator SDK in this chapter.

Ready? Let's Go—pun intended!

Following sample-controller

Let's start off by implementing cnat based on the *k8s.io/sample-controller* (*http://bit.ly/2UppsTN*), which uses the client-go library directly (*http://bit.ly/2Yas9HK*). The sample-controller uses the *k8s.io/code-generator* (*http://bit.ly/2Kw8I8U*) to generate a typed client, informers, listers, and deep-copy functions. Whenever the API types change in your custom controller—for example, adding a new field in the custom resource—you have to use the *update-codegen.sh* script (see also its source (*http://bit.ly/2Fq3Td1*) in GitHub) to regenerate the aforementioned source files.

 You might have noticed *k8s.io* being used as the base URL throughout the book. We introduced its usage in Chapter 3; as a reminder, it is really an alias for *kubernetes.io*, and in the context of Go package management it resolves to *github.com/kubernetes*. Note that *k8s.io* does not come with an automatic redirect. So, for example, *k8s.io/sample-controller* really means that you should be looking at *github.com/kubernetes/sample-controller* (*http://bit.ly/2UppsTN*), and so on.

OK, let's implement our cnat (*http://bit.ly/2RpHhON*) operator using client-go, following the sample-controller. (See the corresponding directory in our repo (*http://bit.ly/2N3R6U4*).)

Bootstrapping

To begin, do a **go get k8s.io/sample-controller** to get the source and dependencies onto your system, which should be in *$GOPATH/src/k8s.io/sample-\controller*.

If you start from scratch, copy the content of the *sample-controller* directory into a directory of your choice (for example, we use *cnat-client-go* in our repo), and you can run the following command sequence to build and run the base controller (with the default implementation, not the cnat business logic yet):

```
# build custom controller binary:
$ go build -o cnat-controller .

# launch custom controller locally:
$ ./cnat-controller -kubeconfig=$HOME/.kube/config
```

This command will launch the custom controller and wait for you to register the CRD and create a custom resource. Let's do this now and see what happens. In a second terminal session, enter:

```
$ kubectl apply -f artifacts/examples/crd.yaml
```

Make sure the CRD is properly registered and available like so:

```
$ kubectl get crds
NAME                       CREATED AT
foos.samplecontroller.k8s.io    2019-05-29T12:16:57Z
```

Note that you may see other CRDs here, depending on the Kubernetes distro you're using; however, *foos.samplecontroller.k8s.io* should be listed, at least.

Next, we create the example custom resource *foo.samplecontroller.k8s.io/example-foo* and check if the controller does its job:

```
$ kubectl apply -f artifacts/examples/example-foo.yaml
foo.samplecontroller.k8s.io/example-foo created

$ kubectl get po,rs,deploy,foo
NAME                               READY   STATUS    RESTARTS   AGE
pod/example-foo-5b8c9679d8-xjhdf   1/1     Running   0          67s

NAME                                          DESIRED   CURRENT   READY   AGE
replicaset.extensions/example-foo-5b8c9679d8  1         1         1       67s

NAME                                 READY   UP-TO-DATE   AVAILABLE   AGE
deployment.extensions/example-foo    1/1     1            1           67s

NAME                                   AGE
foo.samplecontroller.k8s.io/example-foo   67s
```

Yay, it works as expected! We can now move on to implementing the actual cnat-specific business logic.

Business Logic

To kick off implementing the business logic, we first rename the existing directory *pkg/apis/samplecontroller* to *pkg/apis/cnat* and then create our own CRD and custom resource as follows:

```
$ cat artifacts/examples/cnat-crd.yaml
apiVersion: apiextensions.k8s.io/v1beta1
kind: CustomResourceDefinition
metadata:
  name: ats.cnat.programming-kubernetes.info
spec:
  group: cnat.programming-kubernetes.info
  version: v1alpha1
  names:
    kind: At
    plural: ats
  scope: Namespaced

$ cat artifacts/examples/cnat-example.yaml
apiVersion: cnat.programming-kubernetes.info/v1alpha1
kind: At
metadata:
  labels:
    controller-tools.k8s.io: "1.0"
  name: example-at
spec:
  schedule: "2019-04-12T10:12:00Z"
  command: "echo YAY"
```

Note that whenever the API types change—for example, when you add a new field to the At CRD—you have to execute the *update-codegen.sh* script, like so:

```
$ ./hack/update-codegen.sh
```

This will automatically generate the following:

- *pkg/apis/cnat/v1alpha1/zz_generated.deepcopy.go*
- *pkg/generated/**

In terms of the business logic, we have two parts to implement in the operator:

- In *types.go* (*http://bit.ly/31QosJw*) we modify the AtSpec struct to include the respective fields, such as schedule and command. Note that you must run update-codegen.sh whenever you change something here in order to regenerate dependent files.

- In *controller.go* (*http://bit.ly/31MM4OS*) we change the NewController() and syncHandler() functions as well as add helper functions, including creating pods and checking schedule time.

In *types.go*, note the three constants representing the three phases of the At resource: up until the scheduled time in PENDING, then RUNNING to completion, and finally in the DONE state:

```
// +genclient
// +k8s:deepcopy-gen:interfaces=k8s.io/apimachinery/pkg/runtime.Object

const (
    PhasePending = "PENDING"
    PhaseRunning = "RUNNING"
    PhaseDone    = "DONE"
)

// AtSpec defines the desired state of At
type AtSpec struct {
    // Schedule is the desired time the command is supposed to be executed.
    // Note: the format used here is UTC time https://www.utctime.net
    Schedule string `json:"schedule,omitempty"`
    // Command is the desired command (executed in a Bash shell) to be
    // executed.
    Command string `json:"command,omitempty"`
}

// AtStatus defines the observed state of At
type AtStatus struct {
    // Phase represents the state of the schedule: until the command is
    // executed it is PENDING, afterwards it is DONE.
    Phase string `json:"phase,omitempty"`
}
```

Note the explicit usage of the build tags +k8s:deepcopy-gen:interfaces (refer to Chapter 5) so that the respective sources are autogenerated.

We are now in the position to implement the business logic of the custom controller. That is, we implement the state transitions between the three phases—from Phase Pending to PhaseRunning to PhaseDone—in controller.go (*http://bit.ly/31MM4OS*).

In "Work Queue" on page 61 we introduced and explained the work queue that client-go provides. We can now put this knowledge to work: in the processNextWor kItem() in *controller.go*—to be more precise, in lines 176 to 186 (*http://bit.ly/2WYDbyi*)—you can find the following (generated) code:

```
if when, err := c.syncHandler(key); err != nil {
    c.workqueue.AddRateLimited(key)
    return fmt.Errorf("error syncing '%s': %s, requeuing", key, err.Error())
} else if when != time.Duration(0) {
    c.workqueue.AddAfter(key, when)
} else {
    // Finally, if no error occurs we Forget this item so it does not
    // get queued again until another change happens.
    c.workqueue.Forget(obj)
}
```

This snippet shows how our (yet-to-be-written) custom syncHandler() function (explained shortly) is invoked and covers these three cases:

1. The first `if` branch requeues the item via the `AddRateLimited()` function call, handling transient errors.

2. The second branch, the `else if`, requeues the item via the `AddAfter()` function call to avoid hot-looping.

3. The last case, the `else`, is where the item has been processed successfully and is discarded via the `Forget()` function call.

Now that we've got a sound understanding of the generic handling, let's move on to the business-logic-specific functionality. Key to it is the aforementioned `syncHandler()` function, where we are implementing the business logic of our custom controller. It has the following signature:

```
// syncHandler compares the actual state with the desired state and attempts
// to converge the two. It then updates the Status block of the At resource
// with the current status of the resource. It returns how long to wait
// until the schedule is due.
func (c *Controller) syncHandler(key string) (time.Duration, error) {
    ...
}
```

This `syncHandler()` function implements the following state transitions:[1]

```
...
// If no phase set, default to pending (the initial phase):
if instance.Status.Phase == "" {
    instance.Status.Phase = cnatv1alpha1.PhasePending
}

// Now let's make the main case distinction: implementing
// the state diagram PENDING -> RUNNING -> DONE
switch instance.Status.Phase {
case cnatv1alpha1.PhasePending:
    klog.Infof("instance %s: phase=PENDING", key)
    // As long as we haven't executed the command yet, we need
    // to check if it's time already to act:
    klog.Infof("instance %s: checking schedule %q", key, instance.Spec.Schedule)
    // Check if it's already time to execute the command with a
    // tolerance of 2 seconds:
    d, err := timeUntilSchedule(instance.Spec.Schedule)
    if err != nil {
        utilruntime.HandleError(fmt.Errorf("schedule parsing failed: %v", err))
        // Error reading the schedule - requeue the request:
        return time.Duration(0), err
    }
    klog.Infof("instance %s: schedule parsing done: diff=%v", key, d)
    if d > 0 {
        // Not yet time to execute the command, wait until the
        // scheduled time
        return d, nil
```

---

[1] We're only showing the relevant sections here; the function itself has a lot of other boilerplate code we're not concerned with for our purposes.

```go
		}
		klog.Infof(
			"instance %s: it's time! Ready to execute: %s", key,
			instance.Spec.Command,
		)
		instance.Status.Phase = cnatv1alpha1.PhaseRunning
	case cnatv1alpha1.PhaseRunning:
		klog.Infof("instance %s: Phase: RUNNING", key)

		pod := newPodForCR(instance)

		// Set At instance as the owner and controller
		owner := metav1.NewControllerRef(
			instance, cnatv1alpha1.SchemeGroupVersion.
			WithKind("At"),
		)
		pod.ObjectMeta.OwnerReferences = append(pod.ObjectMeta.OwnerReferences, *owner)

		// Try to see if the pod already exists and if not
		// (which we expect) then create a one-shot pod as per spec:
		found, err := c.kubeClientset.CoreV1().Pods(pod.Namespace).
			Get(pod.Name, metav1.GetOptions{})
		if err != nil && errors.IsNotFound(err) {
			found, err = c.kubeClientset.CoreV1().Pods(pod.Namespace).Create(pod)
			if err != nil {
				return time.Duration(0), err
			}
			klog.Infof("instance %s: pod launched: name=%s", key, pod.Name)
		} else if err != nil {
			// requeue with error
			return time.Duration(0), err
		} else if found.Status.Phase == corev1.PodFailed ||
			found.Status.Phase == corev1.PodSucceeded {
			klog.Infof(
				"instance %s: container terminated: reason=%q message=%q",
				key, found.Status.Reason, found.Status.Message,
			)
			instance.Status.Phase = cnatv1alpha1.PhaseDone
		} else {
			// Don't requeue because it will happen automatically
			// when the pod status changes.
			return time.Duration(0), nil
		}
	case cnatv1alpha1.PhaseDone:
		klog.Infof("instance %s: phase: DONE", key)
		return time.Duration(0), nil
	default:
		klog.Infof("instance %s: NOP")
		return time.Duration(0), nil
	}

	// Update the At instance, setting the status to the respective phase:
	_, err = c.cnatClientset.CnatV1alpha1().Ats(instance.Namespace).
		UpdateStatus(instance)
	if err != nil {
		return time.Duration(0), err
	}
```

```
// Don't requeue. We should be reconcile because either the pod or
// the CR changes.
return time.Duration(0), nil
```

Further, to set up informers and the controller at large, we implement the following in NewController():

```
// NewController returns a new cnat controller
func NewController(
    kubeClientset kubernetes.Interface,
    cnatClientset clientset.Interface,
    atInformer informers.AtInformer,
    podInformer corev1informer.PodInformer) *Controller {

    // Create event broadcaster
    // Add cnat-controller types to the default Kubernetes Scheme so Events
    // can be logged for cnat-controller types.
    utilruntime.Must(cnatscheme.AddToScheme(scheme.Scheme))
    klog.V(4).Info("Creating event broadcaster")
    eventBroadcaster := record.NewBroadcaster()
    eventBroadcaster.StartLogging(klog.Infof)
    eventBroadcaster.StartRecordingToSink(&typedcorev1.EventSinkImpl{
        Interface: kubeClientset.CoreV1().Events(""),
    })
    source := corev1.EventSource{Component: controllerAgentName}
    recorder := eventBroadcaster.NewRecorder(scheme.Scheme, source)

    rateLimiter := workqueue.DefaultControllerRateLimiter()
    controller := &Controller{
        kubeClientset: kubeClientset,
        cnatClientset: cnatClientset,
        atLister:      atInformer.Lister(),
        atsSynced:     atInformer.Informer().HasSynced,
        podLister:     podInformer.Lister(),
        podsSynced:    podInformer.Informer().HasSynced,
        workqueue:     workqueue.NewNamedRateLimitingQueue(rateLimiter, "Ats"),
        recorder:      recorder,
    }

    klog.Info("Setting up event handlers")
    // Set up an event handler for when At resources change
    atInformer.Informer().AddEventHandler(cache.ResourceEventHandlerFuncs{
        AddFunc: controller.enqueueAt,
        UpdateFunc: func(old, new interface{}) {
            controller.enqueueAt(new)
        },
    })
    // Set up an event handler for when Pod resources change
    podInformer.Informer().AddEventHandler(cache.ResourceEventHandlerFuncs{
        AddFunc: controller.enqueuePod,
        UpdateFunc: func(old, new interface{}) {
            controller.enqueuePod(new)
        },
    })
    return controller
}
```

There are two further helper functions we need in order to make it work: one calculates the time until the schedule, which looks like this:

```
func timeUntilSchedule(schedule string) (time.Duration, error) {
    now := time.Now().UTC()
    layout := "2006-01-02T15:04:05Z"
    s, err := time.Parse(layout, schedule)
    if err != nil {
        return time.Duration(0), err
    }
    return s.Sub(now), nil
}
```

and the other creates a pod with the command to execute, using a busybox container image:

```
func newPodForCR(cr *cnatv1alpha1.At) *corev1.Pod {
    labels := map[string]string{
        "app": cr.Name,
    }
    return &corev1.Pod{
        ObjectMeta: metav1.ObjectMeta{
            Name:      cr.Name + "-pod",
            Namespace: cr.Namespace,
            Labels:    labels,
        },
        Spec: corev1.PodSpec{
            Containers: []corev1.Container{
                {
                    Name:    "busybox",
                    Image:   "busybox",
                    Command: strings.Split(cr.Spec.Command, " "),
                },
            },
            RestartPolicy: corev1.RestartPolicyOnFailure,
        },
    }
}
```

We will be reusing these two helper functions and the basic flow of the business logic as presented here in the syncHandler() function later in this chapter, so make sure you familiarize yourself with their details.

Note that from the point of the At resource, the pod is a secondary resource and the controller must make sure to clean those pods up or otherwise risk orphaned pods.

Now, sample-controller is a good tool to learn how the sausage is made, but usually you want to focus on creating the business logic rather than dealing with the boiler-plate code. For this, there are two related projects you can choose from: Kubebuilder and the Operator SDK. Let's have a look at each and how cnat is implemented with them.

Kubebuilder

Kubebuilder (*http://bit.ly/2I8w9mz*), owned and maintained by the Kubernetes Special Interest Group (SIG) API Machinery, is a tool and set of libraries enabling you to build operators in an easy and efficient manner. The best resource for a deep dive on

Kubebuilder is the online Kubebuilder book (*https://book.kubebuilder.io*), which walks you through its components and usage. We will, however, focus here on implementing our `cnat` (*http://bit.ly/2RpHhON*) operator with Kubebuilder (see the corresponding directory in our Git repository (*http://bit.ly/2Iv6pAS*)).

First, let's make sure all the dependencies—that is, dep (*http://bit.ly/2x9Yrqq*), kustomize (*http://bit.ly/2Y3JeCV*) (see "Kustomize" on page 134), and Kubebuilder itself (*http://bit.ly/32pQmfu*)—are installed:

```
$ dep version
dep:
 version     : v0.5.1
 build date  : 2019-03-11
 git hash    : faa6189
 go version  : go1.12
 go compiler : gc
 platform    : darwin/amd64
 features    : ImportDuringSolve=false

$ kustomize version
Version: {KustomizeVersion:v2.0.3 GitCommit:a6f65144121d1955266b0cd836ce954c04122dc8
          BuildDate:2019-03-18T22:15:21+00:00 GoOs:darwin GoArch:amd64}

$ kubebuilder version
Version: version.Version{
  KubeBuilderVersion:"1.0.8",
  KubernetesVendor:"1.13.1",
  GitCommit:"1adf50ed107f5042d7472ba5ab50d5e1d357169d",
  BuildDate:"2019-01-25T23:14:29Z", GoOs:"unknown", GoArch:"unknown"
}
```

We'll walk you through the steps for writing the `cnat` operator from scratch. First, create a directory of your choice (we use *cnat-kubebuilder* in our repo) that you'll use as the base for all further commands.

 At the time of this writing, Kubebuilder is moving to a new version (v2). Since it's not stable yet, we show the commands and setup for (stable) version v1 (*https://book-v1.book.kubebuilder.io*).

Bootstrapping

To bootstrap the `cnat` operator, we use the `init` command like so (note that this can take several minutes, depending on your environment):

```
$ kubebuilder init \
            --domain programming-kubernetes.info \
            --license apache2 \
            --owner "Programming Kubernetes authors"
Run `dep ensure` to fetch dependencies (Recommended) [y/n]?
y
dep ensure
```

```
Running make...
make
go generate ./pkg/... ./cmd/...
go fmt ./pkg/... ./cmd/...
go vet ./pkg/... ./cmd/...
go run vendor/sigs.k8s.io/controller-tools/cmd/controller-gen/main.go all
CRD manifests generated under 'config/crds'
RBAC manifests generated under 'config/rbac'
go test ./pkg/... ./cmd/... -coverprofile cover.out
?       github.com/mhausenblas/cnat-kubebuilder/pkg/apis        [no test files]
?       github.com/mhausenblas/cnat-kubebuilder/pkg/controller  [no test files]
?       github.com/mhausenblas/cnat-kubebuilder/pkg/webhook     [no test files]
?       github.com/mhausenblas/cnat-kubebuilder/cmd/manager     [no test files]
go build -o bin/manager github.com/mhausenblas/cnat-kubebuilder/cmd/manager
```

On completion of this command, Kubebuilder has scaffolded the operator, effectively generating a bunch of files, from the custom controller to a sample CRD. Your base directory should now look something like the following (excluding the huge *vendor* directory for clarity):

```
$ tree -I vendor
.
├── Dockerfile
├── Gopkg.lock
├── Gopkg.toml
├── Makefile
├── PROJECT
├── bin
│   └── manager
├── cmd
│   └── manager
│       └── main.go
├── config
│   ├── crds
│   ├── default
│   │   ├── kustomization.yaml
│   │   ├── manager_auth_proxy_patch.yaml
│   │   ├── manager_image_patch.yaml
│   │   └── manager_prometheus_metrics_patch.yaml
│   ├── manager
│   │   └── manager.yaml
│   └── rbac
│       ├── auth_proxy_role.yaml
│       ├── auth_proxy_role_binding.yaml
│       ├── auth_proxy_service.yaml
│       ├── rbac_role.yaml
│       └── rbac_role_binding.yaml
├── cover.out
├── hack
│   └── boilerplate.go.txt
└── pkg
    ├── apis
    │   └── apis.go
    ├── controller
    │   └── controller.go
    └── webhook
        └── webhook.go
```

```
13 directories, 22 files
```

Next, we create an API—that is, a custom controller—using the `create api` command (this should be faster than the previous command but still takes a little while):

```
$ kubebuilder create api \
           --group cnat \
           --version v1alpha1 \
           --kind At
Create Resource under pkg/apis [y/n]?
y
Create Controller under pkg/controller [y/n]?
y
Writing scaffold for you to edit...
pkg/apis/cnat/v1alpha1/at_types.go
pkg/apis/cnat/v1alpha1/at_types_test.go
pkg/controller/at/at_controller.go
pkg/controller/at/at_controller_test.go
Running make...
go generate ./pkg/... ./cmd/...
go fmt ./pkg/... ./cmd/...
go vet ./pkg/... ./cmd/...
go run vendor/sigs.k8s.io/controller-tools/cmd/controller-gen/main.go all
CRD manifests generated under 'config/crds'
RBAC manifests generated under 'config/rbac'
go test ./pkg/... ./cmd/... -coverprofile cover.out
?       github.com/mhausenblas/cnat-kubebuilder/pkg/apis         [no test files]
?       github.com/mhausenblas/cnat-kubebuilder/pkg/apis/cnat    [no test files]
ok      github.com/mhausenblas/cnat-kubebuilder/pkg/apis/cnat/v1alpha1  9.011s
?       github.com/mhausenblas/cnat-kubebuilder/pkg/controller   [no test files]
ok      github.com/mhausenblas/cnat-kubebuilder/pkg/controller/at       8.740s
?       github.com/mhausenblas/cnat-kubebuilder/pkg/webhook      [no test files]
?       github.com/mhausenblas/cnat-kubebuilder/cmd/manager      [no test files]
go build -o bin/manager github.com/mhausenblas/cnat-kubebuilder/cmd/manager
```

Let's see what has changed, focusing on the two directories that have received updates and additions:

```
$ tree config/ pkg/
config/
├── crds
│   └── cnat_v1alpha1_at.yaml
├── default
│   ├── kustomization.yaml
│   ├── manager_auth_proxy_patch.yaml
│   ├── manager_image_patch.yaml
│   └── manager_prometheus_metrics_patch.yaml
├── manager
│   └── manager.yaml
├── rbac
│   ├── auth_proxy_role.yaml
│   ├── auth_proxy_role_binding.yaml
│   ├── auth_proxy_service.yaml
│   ├── rbac_role.yaml
│   └── rbac_role_binding.yaml
└── samples
    └── cnat_v1alpha1_at.yaml
pkg/
```

```
├── apis
│   ├── addtoscheme_cnat_v1alpha1.go
│   ├── apis.go
│   └── cnat
│       ├── group.go
│       └── v1alpha1
│           ├── at_types.go
│           ├── at_types_test.go
│           ├── doc.go
│           ├── register.go
│           ├── v1alpha1_suite_test.go
│           └── zz_generated.deepcopy.go
├── controller
│   ├── add_at.go
│   ├── at
│   │   ├── at_controller.go
│   │   ├── at_controller_suite_test.go
│   │   └── at_controller_test.go
│   └── controller.go
└── webhook
    └── webhook.go

11 directories, 27 files
```

Note the addition of *cnat_v1alpha1_at.yaml* in *config/crds/*, which is the CRD, as well as *cnat_v1alpha1_at.yaml* (yes, the same name) in *config/samples/*, representing a custom resource example instance of the CRD. Further, in *pkg/* we see a number of new files, most importantly *apis/cnat/v1alpha1/at_types.go* and *controller/at/at_controller.go*, both of which we will modify next.

Next, we create a dedicated namespace, `cnat`, in Kubernetes and use it as the default, setting the context as follows (as a good practice, always use a dedicated namespace, not the `default` one):

```
$ kubectl create ns cnat && \
  kubectl config set-context $(kubectl config current-context) --namespace=cnat
```

We install the CRD with:

```
$ make install
go run vendor/sigs.k8s.io/controller-tools/cmd/controller-gen/main.go all
CRD manifests generated under 'config/crds'
RBAC manifests generated under 'config/rbac'
kubectl apply -f config/crds
customresourcedefinition.apiextensions.k8s.io/ats.cnat.programming-kubernetes.info created
```

And now we can launch the operator locally:

```
$ make run
go generate ./pkg/... ./cmd/...
go fmt ./pkg/... ./cmd/...
go vet ./pkg/... ./cmd/...
go run ./cmd/manager/main.go
{"level":"info","ts":1559152740.0550249,"logger":"entrypoint",
  "msg":"setting up client for manager"}
{"level":"info","ts":1559152740.057556,"logger":"entrypoint",
  "msg":"setting up manager"}
{"level":"info","ts":1559152740.1396701,"logger":"entrypoint",
```

```
   "msg":"Registering Components."}
{"level":"info","ts":1559152740.1397,"logger":"entrypoint",
   "msg":"setting up scheme"}
{"level":"info","ts":1559152740.139773,"logger":"entrypoint",
   "msg":"Setting up controller"}
{"level":"info","ts":1559152740.139831,"logger":"kubebuilder.controller",
   "msg":"Starting EventSource","controller":"at-controller",
   "source":"kind source: /, Kind="}
{"level":"info","ts":1559152740.139929,"logger":"kubebuilder.controller",
   "msg":"Starting EventSource","controller":"at-controller",
   "source":"kind source: /, Kind="}
{"level":"info","ts":1559152740.139971,"logger":"entrypoint",
   "msg":"setting up webhooks"}
{"level":"info","ts":1559152740.13998,"logger":"entrypoint",
   "msg":"Starting the Cmd."}
{"level":"info","ts":1559152740.244628,"logger":"kubebuilder.controller",
   "msg":"Starting Controller","controller":"at-controller"}
{"level":"info","ts":1559152740.344791,"logger":"kubebuilder.controller",
   "msg":"Starting workers","controller":"at-controller","worker count":1}
```

Leave the terminal session running and, in a new session, install the CRD, validate it, and create the sample custom resource like so:

```
$ kubectl apply -f config/crds/cnat_v1alpha1_at.yaml
customresourcedefinition.apiextensions.k8s.io/ats.cnat.programming-kubernetes.info
configured

$ kubectl get crds
NAME                                      CREATED AT
ats.cnat.programming-kubernetes.info      2019-05-29T17:54:51Z

$ kubectl apply -f config/samples/cnat_v1alpha1_at.yaml
at.cnat.programming-kubernetes.info/at-sample created
```

If you now look at the output of the session where make run runs, you should notice the following output:

```
...
{"level":"info","ts":1559153311.659829,"logger":"controller",
   "msg":"Creating Deployment","namespace":"cnat","name":"at-sample-deployment"}
{"level":"info","ts":1559153311.678407,"logger":"controller",
   "msg":"Updating Deployment","namespace":"cnat","name":"at-sample-deployment"}
{"level":"info","ts":1559153311.6839428,"logger":"controller",
   "msg":"Updating Deployment","namespace":"cnat","name":"at-sample-deployment"}
{"level":"info","ts":1559153311.693443,"logger":"controller",
   "msg":"Updating Deployment","namespace":"cnat","name":"at-sample-deployment"}
{"level":"info","ts":1559153311.7023401,"logger":"controller",
   "msg":"Updating Deployment","namespace":"cnat","name":"at-sample-deployment"}
{"level":"info","ts":1559153332.986961,"logger":"controller",#
   "msg":"Updating Deployment","namespace":"cnat","name":"at-sample-deployment"}
```

This tells us that the overall setup was successful! Now that we've completed the scaffolding and successfully launched the cnat operator, we can move on to the actual core task: implementing the cnat business logic with Kubebuilder.

Business Logic

For starters, we'll change *config/crds/cnat_v1alpha1_at.yaml* (*http://bit.ly/2N1jQNb*) and *config/samples/cnat_v1alpha1_at.yaml* (*http://bit.ly/2Xs1F7c*) to our own definitions of the cnat CRD and custom resource values, re-using the same structures as in "Following sample-controller" on page 106.

In terms of the business logic, we have two parts to implement in the operator:

- In *pkg/apis/cnat/v1alpha1/at_types.go* (*http://bit.ly/31KNLfO*) we modify the AtSpec struct to include the respective fields, such as schedule and command. Note that you must run make whenever you change something here in order to regenerate dependent files. Kubebuilder uses the Kubernetes generators (described in Chapter 5) and ships its own set of generators (e.g., to generate the CRD manifest).

- In *pkg/controller/at/at_controller.go* (*http://bit.ly/2Iwormg*) we modify the Recon cile(request reconcile.Request) method to create a pod at the time defined in Spec.Schedule.

In *at_types.go*:

```
const (
    PhasePending = "PENDING"
    PhaseRunning = "RUNNING"
    PhaseDone    = "DONE"
)

// AtSpec defines the desired state of At
type AtSpec struct {
    // Schedule is the desired time the command is supposed to be executed.
    // Note: the format used here is UTC time https://www.utctime.net
    Schedule string `json:"schedule,omitempty"`
    // Command is the desired command (executed in a Bash shell) to be executed.
    Command string `json:"command,omitempty"`
}

// AtStatus defines the observed state of At
type AtStatus struct {
    // Phase represents the state of the schedule: until the command is executed
    // it is PENDING, afterwards it is DONE.
    Phase string `json:"phase,omitempty"`
}
```

In *at_controller.go* we implement the state transition between the three phases, PEND ING to RUNNING to DONE:

```
func (r *ReconcileAt) Reconcile(req reconcile.Request) (reconcile.Result, error) {
    reqLogger := log.WithValues("namespace", req.Namespace, "at", req.Name)
    reqLogger.Info("=== Reconciling At")
    // Fetch the At instance
    instance := &cnatv1alpha1.At{}
    err := r.Get(context.TODO(), req.NamespacedName, instance)
```

```
if err != nil {
    if errors.IsNotFound(err) {
        // Request object not found, could have been deleted after
        // reconcile request—return and don't requeue:
        return reconcile.Result{}, nil
    }
        // Error reading the object—requeue the request:
    return reconcile.Result{}, err
}

// If no phase set, default to pending (the initial phase):
if instance.Status.Phase == "" {
    instance.Status.Phase = cnatv1alpha1.PhasePending
}

// Now let's make the main case distinction: implementing
// the state diagram PENDING -> RUNNING -> DONE
switch instance.Status.Phase {
case cnatv1alpha1.PhasePending:
    reqLogger.Info("Phase: PENDING")
    // As long as we haven't executed the command yet, we need to check if
    // it's already time to act:
    reqLogger.Info("Checking schedule", "Target", instance.Spec.Schedule)
    // Check if it's already time to execute the command with a tolerance
    // of 2 seconds:
    d, err := timeUntilSchedule(instance.Spec.Schedule)
    if err != nil {
        reqLogger.Error(err, "Schedule parsing failure")
        // Error reading the schedule. Wait until it is fixed.
        return reconcile.Result{}, err
    }
    reqLogger.Info("Schedule parsing done", "Result", "diff",
        fmt.Sprintf("%v", d))
    if d > 0 {
        // Not yet time to execute the command, wait until the scheduled time
        return reconcile.Result{RequeueAfter: d}, nil
    }
    reqLogger.Info("It's time!", "Ready to execute", instance.Spec.Command)
    instance.Status.Phase = cnatv1alpha1.PhaseRunning
case cnatv1alpha1.PhaseRunning:
    reqLogger.Info("Phase: RUNNING")
    pod := newPodForCR(instance)
    // Set At instance as the owner and controller
    err := controllerutil.SetControllerReference(instance, pod, r.scheme)
    if err != nil {
        // requeue with error
        return reconcile.Result{}, err
    }
    found := &corev1.Pod{}
    nsName := types.NamespacedName{Name: pod.Name, Namespace: pod.Namespace}
    err = r.Get(context.TODO(), nsName, found)
    // Try to see if the pod already exists and if not
    // (which we expect) then create a one-shot pod as per spec:
    if err != nil && errors.IsNotFound(err) {
        err = r.Create(context.TODO(), pod)
        if err != nil {
        // requeue with error
            return reconcile.Result{}, err
        }
```

```
            reqLogger.Info("Pod launched", "name", pod.Name)
        } else if err != nil {
            // requeue with error
            return reconcile.Result{}, err
        } else if found.Status.Phase == corev1.PodFailed ||
                found.Status.Phase == corev1.PodSucceeded {
            reqLogger.Info("Container terminated", "reason",
                found.Status.Reason, "message", found.Status.Message)
            instance.Status.Phase = cnatv1alpha1.PhaseDone
        } else {
            // Don't requeue because it will happen automatically when the
            // pod status changes.
            return reconcile.Result{}, nil
        }
    case cnatv1alpha1.PhaseDone:
        reqLogger.Info("Phase: DONE")
        return reconcile.Result{}, nil
    default:
        reqLogger.Info("NOP")
        return reconcile.Result{}, nil
    }

    // Update the At instance, setting the status to the respective phase:
    err = r.Status().Update(context.TODO(), instance)
    if err != nil {
        return reconcile.Result{}, err
    }

    // Don't requeue. We should be reconcile because either the pod
    // or the CR changes.
    return reconcile.Result{}, nil
}
```

Note here that the Update call at the end operates on the */status* subresource (see "Status subresource" on page 81) instead of the whole CR. Hence, here we follow the best practice of a spec-status split.

Now, once the CR example-at is created, we see the following output of the locally executed operator:

```
$ make run
...
{"level":"info","ts":1555063897.488535,"logger":"controller",
  "msg":"=== Reconciling At","namespace":"cnat","at":"example-at"}
{"level":"info","ts":1555063897.488621,"logger":"controller",
  "msg":"Phase: PENDING","namespace":"cnat","at":"example-at"}
{"level":"info","ts":1555063897.4886441,"logger":"controller",
  "msg":"Checking schedule","namespace":"cnat","at":"example-at",
  "Target":"2019-04-12T10:12:00Z"}
{"level":"info","ts":1555063897.488703,"logger":"controller",
  "msg":"Schedule parsing done","namespace":"cnat","at":"example-at",
  "Result":"2019-04-12 10:12:00 +0000 UTC with a diff of 22.511336s"}
{"level":"info","ts":1555063907.489264,"logger":"controller",
  "msg":"=== Reconciling At","namespace":"cnat","at":"example-at"}
{"level":"info","ts":1555063907.489402,"logger":"controller",
  "msg":"Phase: PENDING","namespace":"cnat","at":"example-at"}
{"level":"info","ts":1555063907.489428,"logger":"controller",
  "msg":"Checking schedule","namespace":"cnat","at":"example-at",
```

```
    "Target":"2019-04-12T10:12:00Z"}
{"level":"info","ts":1555063907.489486,"logger":"controller",
    "msg":"Schedule parsing done","namespace":"cnat","at":"example-at",
    "Result":"2019-04-12 10:12:00 +0000 UTC with a diff of 12.510551s"}
{"level":"info","ts":1555063917.490178,"logger":"controller",
    "msg":"=== Reconciling At","namespace":"cnat","at":"example-at"}
{"level":"info","ts":1555063917.4902349,"logger":"controller",
    "msg":"Phase: PENDING","namespace":"cnat","at":"example-at"}
{"level":"info","ts":1555063917.490247,"logger":"controller",
    "msg":"Checking schedule","namespace":"cnat","at":"example-at",
    "Target":"2019-04-12T10:12:00Z"}
{"level":"info","ts":1555063917.490278,"logger":"controller",
    "msg":"Schedule parsing done","namespace":"cnat","at":"example-at",
    "Result":"2019-04-12 10:12:00 +0000 UTC with a diff of 2.509743s"}
{"level":"info","ts":1555063927.492718,"logger":"controller",
    "msg":"=== Reconciling At","namespace":"cnat","at":"example-at"}
{"level":"info","ts":1555063927.49283,"logger":"controller",
    "msg":"Phase: PENDING","namespace":"cnat","at":"example-at"}
{"level":"info","ts":1555063927.492857,"logger":"controller",
    "msg":"Checking schedule","namespace":"cnat","at":"example-at",
    "Target":"2019-04-12T10:12:00Z"}
{"level":"info","ts":1555063927.492915,"logger":"controller",
    "msg":"Schedule parsing done","namespace":"cnat","at":"example-at",
    "Result":"2019-04-12 10:12:00 +0000 UTC with a diff of -7.492877s"}
{"level":"info","ts":1555063927.4929411,"logger":"controller",
    "msg":"It's time!","namespace":"cnat","at":
    "example-at","Ready to execute":"echo YAY"}
{"level":"info","ts":1555063927.626236,"logger":"controller",
    "msg":"=== Reconciling At","namespace":"cnat","at":"example-at"}
{"level":"info","ts":1555063927.626303,"logger":"controller",
    "msg":"Phase: RUNNING","namespace":"cnat","at":"example-at"}
{"level":"info","ts":1555063928.07445,"logger":"controller",
    "msg":"Pod launched","namespace":"cnat","at":"example-at",
    "name":"example-at-pod"}
{"level":"info","ts":1555063928.199562,"logger":"controller",
    "msg":"=== Reconciling At","namespace":"cnat","at":"example-at"}
{"level":"info","ts":1555063928.199645,"logger":"controller",
    "msg":"Phase: DONE","namespace":"cnat","at":"example-at"}
{"level":"info","ts":1555063937.631733,"logger":"controller",
    "msg":"=== Reconciling At","namespace":"cnat","at":"example-at"}
{"level":"info","ts":1555063937.631783,"logger":"controller",
    "msg":"Phase: DONE","namespace":"cnat","at":"example-at"}
...
```

To verify whether our custom controller has done its job, execute:

```
$ kubectl get at,pods
NAME                                                   AGE
at.cnat.programming-kubernetes.info/example-at         11m

NAME                 READY   STATUS       RESTARTS   AGE
pod/example-at-pod   0/1     Completed    0          38s
```

Great! The example-at-pod has been created, and now it's time to see the result of the operation:

```
$ kubectl logs example-at-pod
YAY
```

When you're done developing the custom controller, using local mode as shown here, you'll likely want to build a container image out of it. This custom controller container image can subsequently be used, for example, in a Kubernetes deployment. You can use the following command to generate the container image and push it into the repo *quay.io/pk/cnat*:

```
$ export IMG=quay.io/pk/cnat:v1

$ make docker-build

$ make docker-push
```

With this we move on to the Operator SDK, which shares some of Kubebuilder's code base and APIs.

The Operator SDK

To make it easier to build Kubernetes applications, CoreOS/Red Hat has put together the Operator Framework. Part of that is the Operator SDK (*http://bit.ly/2KtpK7D*), which enables developers to build operators without requiring deep knowledge of Kubernetes APIs.

The Operator SDK provides the tools to build, test, and package operators. While there is much more functionality available in the SDK, especially around testing, we focus here on implementing our cnat (*http://bit.ly/2RpHhON*) operator with the SDK (see the corresponding directory in our Git repository (*http://bit.ly/2FpCtE9*)).

First things first: make sure to install the Operator SDK (*http://bit.ly/2ZBQlCT*) and check if all dependencies are available:

```
$ dep version
dep:
 version     : v0.5.1
 build date  : 2019-03-11
 git hash    : faa6189
 go version  : go1.12
 go compiler : gc
 platform    : darwin/amd64
 features    : ImportDuringSolve=false

$ operator-sdk --version
operator-sdk version v0.6.0
```

Bootstrapping

Now it's time to bootstrap the cnat operator as follows:

```
$ operator-sdk new cnat-operator && cd cnat-operator
```

Next, and very similar to Kubebuilder, we add an API—or simply put: initialize the custom controller like so:

```
$ operator-sdk add api \
          --api-version=cnat.programming-kubernetes.info/v1alpha1 \
          --kind=At

$ operator-sdk add controller \
          --api-version=cnat.programming-kubernetes.info/v1alpha1 \
          --kind=At
```

These commands generate the necessary boilerplate code as well as a number of helper functions, such as the deep-copy functions `DeepCopy()`, `DeepCopyInto()`, and `DeepCopyObject()`.

Now we're in a position to apply the autogenerated CRD to the Kubernetes cluster:

```
$ kubectl apply -f deploy/crds/cnat_v1alpha1_at_crd.yaml

$ kubectl get crds
NAME                                      CREATED AT
ats.cnat.programming-kubernetes.info      2019-04-01T14:03:33Z
```

Let's launch our `cnat` custom controller locally. With this, it can start processing requests:

```
$ OPERATOR_NAME=cnatop operator-sdk up local --namespace "cnat"
INFO[0000] Running the operator locally.
INFO[0000] Using namespace cnat.
{"level":"info","ts":1555041531.871706,"logger":"cmd",
  "msg":"Go Version: go1.12.1"}
{"level":"info","ts":1555041531.871785,"logger":"cmd",
  "msg":"Go OS/Arch: darwin/amd64"}
{"level":"info","ts":1555041531.8718028,"logger":"cmd",
  "msg":"Version of operator-sdk: v0.6.0"}
{"level":"info","ts":1555041531.8739321,"logger":"leader",
  "msg":"Trying to become the leader."}
{"level":"info","ts":1555041531.8743382,"logger":"leader",
  "msg":"Skipping leader election; not running in a cluster."}
{"level":"info","ts":1555041536.1611362,"logger":"cmd",
  "msg":"Registering Components."}
{"level":"info","ts":1555041536.1622112,"logger":"kubebuilder.controller",
  "msg":"Starting EventSource","controller":"at-controller",
  "source":"kind source: /, Kind="}
{"level":"info","ts":1555041536.162519,"logger":"kubebuilder.controller",
  "msg":"Starting EventSource","controller":"at-controller",
  "source":"kind source: /, Kind="}
{"level":"info","ts":1555041539.978822,"logger":"metrics",
  "msg":"Skipping metrics Service creation; not running in a cluster."}
{"level":"info","ts":1555041539.978875,"logger":"cmd",
  "msg":"Starting the Cmd."}
{"level":"info","ts":1555041540.179469,"logger":"kubebuilder.controller",
  "msg":"Starting Controller","controller":"at-controller"}
{"level":"info","ts":1555041540.280784,"logger":"kubebuilder.controller",
  "msg":"Starting workers","controller":"at-controller","worker count":1}
```

Our custom controller will remain in this state until we create a CR, *ats.cnat.programming-kubernetes.info*. So let's do that:

```
$ cat deploy/crds/cnat_v1alpha1_at_cr.yaml
apiVersion: cnat.programming-kubernetes.info/v1alpha1
```

```
kind: At
metadata:
  name: example-at
spec:
  schedule: "2019-04-11T14:56:30Z"
  command: "echo YAY"

$ kubectl apply -f deploy/crds/cnat_v1alpha1_at_cr.yaml

$ kubectl get at
NAME                                              AGE
at.cnat.programming-kubernetes.info/example-at    54s
```

Business Logic

In terms of the business logic, we have two parts to implement in the operator:

- In *pkg/apis/cnat/v1alpha1/at_types.go* (*http://bit.ly/31Ip2sF*) we modify the AtSpec struct to include the respective fields, such as schedule and command, and use operator-sdk generate k8s to regenerate code, as well as using the operator-sdk generate openapi command for the OpenAPI bits.

- In *pkg/controller/at/at_controller.go* (*http://bit.ly/2Fpo5Mi*) we modify the Recon cile(request reconcile.Request) method to create a pod at the time defined in Spec.Schedule.

The changes applied to the bootstrapped code in greater detail are as follows (focusing on the relevant bits). In *at_types.go*:

```
// AtSpec defines the desired state of At
// +k8s:openapi-gen=true
type AtSpec struct {
    // Schedule is the desired time the command is supposed to be executed.
    // Note: the format used here is UTC time https://www.utctime.net
    Schedule string `json:"schedule,omitempty"`
    // Command is the desired command (executed in a Bash shell) to be executed.
    Command string `json:"command,omitempty"`
}

// AtStatus defines the observed state of At
// +k8s:openapi-gen=true
type AtStatus struct {
    // Phase represents the state of the schedule: until the command is executed
    // it is PENDING, afterwards it is DONE.
    Phase string `json:"phase,omitempty"`
}
```

In *at_controller.go* we implement the state diagram for the three phases, PENDING to RUNNING to DONE.

The `controller-runtime` (*http://bit.ly/2ZFtDKd*) is another SIG API Machinery–owned project, aimed at providing a common set of low-level functionality for building controllers in the form of Go packages. See Chapter 4 for more details.

As both Kubebuilder and the Operator SDK share the controller runtime, the `Recon cile()` function is in fact the same:

```go
func (r *ReconcileAt) Reconcile(request reconcile.Request) (reconcile.Result, error) {
    the-same-as-for-kubebuilder
}
```

Once the CR `example-at` is created, we see the following output of the locally executed operator:

```
$ OPERATOR_NAME=cnatop operator-sdk up local --namespace "cnat"
INFO[0000] Running the operator locally.
INFO[0000] Using namespace cnat.
...
{"level":"info","ts":1555044934.023597,"logger":"controller_at",
 "msg":"=== Reconciling At","namespace":"cnat","at":"example-at"}
{"level":"info","ts":1555044934.023713,"logger":"controller_at",
 "msg":"Phase: PENDING","namespace":"cnat","at":"example-at"}
{"level":"info","ts":1555044934.0237482,"logger":"controller_at",
 "msg":"Checking schedule","namespace":"cnat","at":
 "example-at","Target":"2019-04-12T04:56:00Z"}
{"level":"info","ts":1555044934.02382,"logger":"controller_at",
 "msg":"Schedule parsing done","namespace":"cnat","at":"example-at",
 "Result":"2019-04-12 04:56:00 +0000 UTC with a diff of 25.976236s"}
{"level":"info","ts":1555044934.148148,"logger":"controller_at",
 "msg":"=== Reconciling At","namespace":"cnat","at":"example-at"}
{"level":"info","ts":1555044934.148224,"logger":"controller_at",
 "msg":"Phase: PENDING","namespace":"cnat","at":"example-at"}
{"level":"info","ts":1555044934.148243,"logger":"controller_at",
 "msg":"Checking schedule","namespace":"cnat","at":"example-at",
 "Target":"2019-04-12T04:56:00Z"}
{"level":"info","ts":1555044934.1482902,"logger":"controller_at",
 "msg":"Schedule parsing done","namespace":"cnat","at":"example-at",
 "Result":"2019-04-12 04:56:00 +0000 UTC with a diff of 25.85174s"}
{"level":"info","ts":1555044944.1504588,"logger":"controller_at",
 "msg":"=== Reconciling At","namespace":"cnat","at":"example-at"}
{"level":"info","ts":1555044944.150568,"logger":"controller_at",
 "msg":"Phase: PENDING","namespace":"cnat","at":"example-at"}
{"level":"info","ts":1555044944.150599,"logger":"controller_at",
 "msg":"Checking schedule","namespace":"cnat","at":"example-at",
 "Target":"2019-04-12T04:56:00Z"}
{"level":"info","ts":1555044944.150663,"logger":"controller_at",
 "msg":"Schedule parsing done","namespace":"cnat","at":"example-at",
 "Result":"2019-04-12 04:56:00 +0000 UTC with a diff of 15.84938s"}
{"level":"info","ts":1555044954.385175,"logger":"controller_at",
 "msg":"=== Reconciling At","namespace":"cnat","at":"example-at"}
{"level":"info","ts":1555044954.3852649,"logger":"controller_at",
 "msg":"Phase: PENDING","namespace":"cnat","at":"example-at"}
{"level":"info","ts":1555044954.385288,"logger":"controller_at",
 "msg":"Checking schedule","namespace":"cnat","at":"example-at",
 "Target":"2019-04-12T04:56:00Z"}
```

```
{"level":"info","ts":1555044954.38534,"logger":"controller_at",
 "msg":"Schedule parsing done","namespace":"cnat","at":"example-at",
 "Result":"2019-04-12 04:56:00 +0000 UTC with a diff of 5.614691s"}
{"level":"info","ts":1555044964.518383,"logger":"controller_at",
 "msg":"=== Reconciling At","namespace":"cnat","at":"example-at"}
{"level":"info","ts":1555044964.5184839,"logger":"controller_at",
 "msg":"Phase: PENDING","namespace":"cnat","at":"example-at"}
{"level":"info","ts":1555044964.518566,"logger":"controller_at",
 "msg":"Checking schedule","namespace":"cnat","at":"example-at",
 "Target":"2019-04-12T04:56:00Z"}
{"level":"info","ts":1555044964.5186381,"logger":"controller_at",
 "msg":"Schedule parsing done","namespace":"cnat","at":"example-at",
 "Result":"2019-04-12 04:56:00 +0000 UTC with a diff of -4.518596s"}
{"level":"info","ts":1555044964.5186849,"logger":"controller_at",
 "msg":"It's time!","namespace":"cnat","at":"example-at",
 "Ready to execute":"echo YAY"}
{"level":"info","ts":1555044964.642559,"logger":"controller_at",
 "msg":"=== Reconciling At","namespace":"cnat","at":"example-at"}
{"level":"info","ts":1555044964.642622,"logger":"controller_at",
 "msg":"Phase: RUNNING","namespace":"cnat","at":"example-at"}
{"level":"info","ts":1555044964.911037,"logger":"controller_at",
 "msg":"=== Reconciling At","namespace":"cnat","at":"example-at"}
{"level":"info","ts":1555044964.9111192,"logger":"controller_at",
 "msg":"Phase: RUNNING","namespace":"cnat","at":"example-at"}
{"level":"info","ts":1555044966.038684,"logger":"controller_at",
 "msg":"=== Reconciling At","namespace":"cnat","at":"example-at"}
{"level":"info","ts":1555044966.038771,"logger":"controller_at",
 "msg":"Phase: DONE","namespace":"cnat","at":"example-at"}
{"level":"info","ts":1555044966.708663,"logger":"controller_at",
 "msg":"=== Reconciling At","namespace":"cnat","at":"example-at"}
{"level":"info","ts":1555044966.708749,"logger":"controller_at",
 "msg":"Phase: DONE","namespace":"cnat","at":"example-at"}
...
```

Here you can see the three phases of our operator: PENDING until timestamp 1555044964.518566, then RUNNING, then DONE.

To validate the function of our custom controller and check the result of the operation, enter:

```
$ kubectl get at,pods
NAME                                                    AGE
at.cnat.programming-kubernetes.info/example-at          23m

NAME                    READY    STATUS       RESTARTS    AGE
pod/example-at-pod      0/1      Completed    0           46s

$ kubectl logs example-at-pod
YAY
```

When you're done developing the custom controller, using local mode as shown here, you'll likely want to build a container image out of it. This custom controller container image can subsequently be used, for example, in a Kubernetes deployment. You can use the following command to generate the container image:

```
$ operator-sdk build $REGISTRY/PROJECT/IMAGE
```

Here are some further resources to learn more about the Operator SDK and examples around it:

- "A Complete Guide to Kubernetes Operator SDK" (*http://bit.ly/2RqkGSf*) by Toader Sebastian on BanzaiCloud
- Rob Szumski's blog post "Building a Kubernetes Operator for Prometheus and Thanos" (*http://bit.ly/2KvgHmu*)
- "Kubernetes Operator Development Guidelines for Improved Usability" (*http://bit.ly/31P7rPC*) from CloudARK on ITNEXT

To wrap up this chapter, let's look at some alternative ways to write custom controllers and operators.

Other Approaches

In addition to, or potentially in combination with, the approaches we've discussed, you might want to have a look at the following projects, libraries, and tools:

Metacontroller (https://metacontroller.app)
> The basic idea of Metacontroller is to provide you with a declarative specification of the state and changes, interfacing with JSON, based on a level-triggered reconciliation loop. That is, you receive JSON describing the observed state and return JSON describing your desired state. This is especially useful for rapid development of automation in dynamic scripting languages like Python or JavaScript. In addition to simple controllers, Metacontroller allows you to compose APIs into higher-level abstractions—for example, BlueGreenDeployment (*http://bit.ly/31KNTfi*).

KUDO (https://kudo.dev)
> Similar to Metacontroller, KUDO provides a declarative approach to building Kubernetes operators, covering the entire application lifecycle. In a nutshell, it's Mesosphere's experience from Apache Mesos frameworks, ported to Kubernetes. KUDO is highly opinionated but also easy to use and requires little to no coding; essentially, all you have to specify is a collection of Kubernetes manifests with a built-in logic to define what is executed when.

Rook operator kit (http://bit.ly/2J34faw)
> This is a common library for implementing operators. It originated from the Rook operator but has been spun out into a separate, independent project.

ericchiang/k8s (http://bit.ly/2ZHc5h0)
> This is a slimmed-down Go client by Eric Chiang generated using the Kubernetes protocol buffer support. It behaves similarly to the official Kubernetes client-go, but imports only two external dependencies. While it comes with certain lim-

itations—for example, in terms of cluster access configuration (*http://bit.ly/2ZBQIxh*)—it is a simple-to-use Go package.

kutil *(http://bit.ly/2Fq3ojh)*
AppsCode provides Kubernetes client-go add-ons via kutil.

CLI-client-based approaches
A client-side approach, mainly for experimentation and testing, is to leverage kubectl programmatically (e.g., the kubecuddler (*http://bit.ly/2L3CDoi*) library).

 While we focus on writing operators using the Go programming language in this book, you can write operators in other languages. Two notable examples are Flant's Shell-operator (*http://bit.ly/2ZxkZ0m*), which enables you to write operators in good old shell scripts, and Zalando's Kopf (Kubernetes operators framework) (*http://bit.ly/2WRXU6Q*), a Python framework and a library.

As mentioned at the beginning of this chapter, the operator field is rapidly evolving, and more and more practitioners are sharing their knowledge in the form of code and best practices, so keep an eye on new tooling here. Make sure to check out online resources and forums, such as the #kubernetes-operators, #kubebuilder, and #client-go-docs channels on the Kubernetes Slack, to learn about new approaches and/or discuss issues and receive help when you're stuck.

Uptake and Future Directions

The jury is still out on which of the approaches to write operators will be the most popular and widely used. In the context of the Kubernetes project, there are activities in several SIGs when it comes to CRs and controllers. The main stakeholder is the SIG API Machinery (*http://bit.ly/2RuTPEp*), which owns CRs and controllers and is responsible for the Kubebuilder (*http://bit.ly/2I8w9mz*) project. The Operator SDK has increased its efforts to align with the Kubebuilder API, so there's a lot of overlap.

Summary

In this chapter we had a look at different tools allowing you to write custom controllers and operators more efficiently. Traditionally, following the sample-controller was the only option out there, but with Kubebuilder and the Operator SDK you now have two options that allow you to focus on the business logic of your custom controller rather than dealing with boilerplate. And luckily these two tools share a lot of APIs and code, so moving from one to the other should not be too difficult.

Now, let's see how to deliver the results of our labor—that is, how to package and ship the controllers we've been writing.

## CHAPTER 7

Shipping Controllers and Operators

Now that you're familiar with the development of custom controllers, let's move on to the topic of how to make your custom controllers and operators production-ready. In this chapter we'll discuss the operational aspects of controllers and operators, showing you how to package them, walking you through best practices for running controllers in production, and making sure that your extension points don't break your Kubernetes cluster, security, or performance-wise.

Lifecycle Management and Packaging

In this section we consider the lifecycle management of operators. That is, we will discuss how to package and ship your controller or operator, as well as how to handle upgrades. When you're ready to ship your operator to users, you'll need a way for them to install it. For this, you need to package the respective artifacts, such as YAML manifests that define the controller binary (typically as a Kubernetes deployment), along with the CRDs and security-related resources, such as service accounts and the necessary RBAC permissions. Once your targeted users have a certain version of the operator running, you will also want to have a mechanism in place for upgrading the controller, considering versioning and potentially zero-downtime upgrades.

Let's start with the low-hanging fruit: packaging and delivering your controllers so that a user can install it in a straightforward manner.

Packaging: The Challenge

While Kubernetes defines resources with manifests, typically written in YAML, a low-level interface to declare the state of resources, these manifest files have shortcomings. Most importantly in the context of packaging containerized apps, the YAML manifests are static; that is, all values in a YAML manifest are fixed. This means that if you want to change the container image in a deployment manifest (*http://bit.ly/2WZ1uRD*), for example, you have to create a new manifest.

Let's look at a concrete example. Assume you have the following Kubernetes deployment encoded in a YAML manifest called *mycontroller.yaml*, representing the custom controller you'd like users to install:

```yaml
apiVersion: apps/v1beta1
kind: Deployment
metadata:
  name: mycustomcontroller
spec:
  replicas: 1
  template:
    metadata:
      labels:
        app: customcontroller
    spec:
      containers:
      - name: thecontroller
        image: example/controller:0.1.0
        ports:
        - containerPort: 9999
        env:
        - name: REGION
          value: eu-west-1
```

Imagine the environment variable `REGION` defines certain runtime properties of your controller, such as the availability of other services like a managed service mesh. In other words, while the default value of `eu-west-1` might be a sensible one, users can and likely will overwrite it, based on their own preferences or policies.

Now, given that the YAML manifest *mycontroller.yaml* itself is a static file with all values defined at the time of writing—and clients such as `kubectl` don't inherently support variable parts in the manifest—how do you enable users to supply variable values or overwrite existing values at runtime? That is, how in the preceding example can a user set `REGION` to, say, `us-east-2` when they're installing it, using (for example) `kubectl apply`?

To overcome these limitations of build-time, static YAML manifests in Kubernetes, there are a few options to templatize the manifests (Helm, for example) or otherwise enable variable input (Kustomize), depending on user-provided values or runtime properties.

Helm

Helm (*https://helm.sh*), which touts itself as *the* package manager for Kubernetes, was originally developed by Deis and is now a Cloud Native Computing Foundation (CNCF (*https://www.cncf.io*)) project with major contributors from Microsoft, Google, and Bitnami (now part of VMware).

Helm helps you to install and upgrade Kubernetes applications by defining and applying so-called charts, effectively parameterized YAML manifests. Here is an excerpt of an example chart template (*http://bit.ly/2XmLk3R*):

```
apiVersion: apps/v1
kind: Deployment
metadata:
  name: {{ include "flagger.fullname" . }}
...
spec:
  replicas: 1
  strategy:
    type: Recreate
  selector:
    matchLabels:
      app.kubernetes.io/name: {{ template "flagger.name" . }}
      app.kubernetes.io/instance: {{ .Release.Name }}
  template:
    metadata:
      labels:
        app.kubernetes.io/name: {{ template "flagger.name" . }}
        app.kubernetes.io/instance: {{ .Release.Name }}
    spec:
      serviceAccountName: {{ template "flagger.serviceAccountName" . }}
      containers:
        - name: flagger
          securityContext:
            readOnlyRootFilesystem: true
            runAsUser: 10001
          image: "{{ .Values.image.repository }}:{{ .Values.image.tag }}"
```

As you can see, variables are encoded in {{ ._Some.value.here_ }} format, which happens to be Go templates (*http://bit.ly/2N2Q3DW*).

To install a chart, you can run the `helm install` command. While Helm has several ways to find and install charts, the easiest is to use one of the official stable charts:

```
# get the latest list of charts:
$ helm repo update

# install MySQL:
$ helm install stable/mysql
Released smiling-penguin

# list running apps:
$ helm ls
NAME             VERSION   UPDATED                   STATUS     CHART
smiling-penguin  1         Wed Sep 28 12:59:46 2016  DEPLOYED   mysql-0.1.0

# remove it:
$ helm delete smiling-penguin
Removed smiling-penguin
```

In order to package your controller, you will need to create a Helm chart for it and publish it somewhere, by default to a public repository indexed and accessible through the Helm Hub (*https://hub.helm.sh*), as depicted in Figure 7-1.

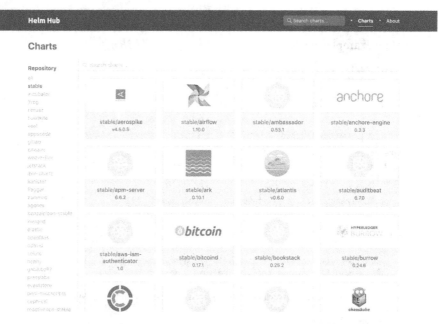

Figure 7-1. Helm Hub screenshot showing publicly available Helm charts

For further guidance on how to create Helm charts, peruse the following resources at your leisure:

- Bitnami's excellent article "How to Create Your First Helm Chart" (*http://bit.ly/2ZIlODJ*).

- "Using S3 as a Helm Repository" (*http://bit.ly/2KzwLDY*), if you want to keep the charts in your own organization.

- The official Helm docs: "The Chart Best Practices Guide" (*http://bit.ly/31GbayW*).

Helm is popular, partly because of its ease of use for end users. However, some argue that the current Helm architecture introduces security risks (*http://bit.ly/2WXM5vZ*). The good news is that the community is actively working on addressing those.

Kustomize

Kustomize (*https://kustomize.io*) provides a declarative approach to configuration customization of Kubernetes manifest files, adhering to the familiar Kubernetes API. It was introduced in mid-2018 (*http://bit.ly/2L5Ec5f*) and is now a Kubernetes SIG CLI project.

You can install (*http://bit.ly/2Y3JeCV*) Kustomize on your machine, as a standalone, or, if you have a more recent kubectl version (newer than 1.14), it is shipped (*http://bit.ly/2IEYqRG*) with kubectl and activated with the -k command-line flag.

So, Kustomize lets you customize the raw YAML manifest files, without touching the original manifest. But how does this work in practice? Let's assume you want to package our cnat custom controller; you'd define a file called *kustomize.yaml* that looks something like:

```
imageTags:
  - name: quay.io/programming-kubernetes/cnat-operator
    newTag: 0.1.0
resources:
- cnat-controller.yaml
```

Now you can apply this to the *cnat-controller.yaml* file, say, with the following content:

```
apiVersion: apps/v1beta1
kind: Deployment
metadata:
  name: cnat-controller
spec:
  replicas: 1
  template:
    metadata:
      labels:
        app: cnat
    spec:
      containers:
      - name: custom-controller
        image: quay.io/programming-kubernetes/cnat-operator
```

Use kustomize build and—leaving the *cnat-controller.yaml* file unchanged!—the output is then:

```
apiVersion: apps/v1beta1
kind: Deployment
metadata:
  name: cnat-controller
spec:
  replicas: 1
  template:
    metadata:
      labels:
        app: cnat
    spec:
      containers:
      - name: custom-controller
        image: quay.io/programming-kubernetes/cnat-operator:0.1.0
```

The output of kustomize build can then, for example, be used in a kubectl apply command, with all the customizations (*http://bit.ly/2LbCDTr*) applied for you, automatically.

For a more detailed walk-through of Kustomize and how to use it, check out the following resources:

- Sébastien Goasguen's blog post "Configuring Kubernetes Applications with kustomize" (*http://bit.ly/2JbgJOR*).
- Kevin Davin's post "Kustomize—The right way to do templating in Kubernetes" (*http://bit.ly/2JpJgPm*).
- The video "TGI Kubernetes 072: Kustomize and friends" (*http://bit.ly/2XoHm6C*), where you can watch Joe Beda apply it.

Given the native support of Kustomize in kubectl, it's likely that an increasing number of users will adopt it. Note that while it solves some problems (customization), there are other areas of the lifecycle management, such as validations and upgrades, that may require you to use Kustomize together with languages such as Google's CUE (*http://bit.ly/32heAZI*).

To wrap up this packaging topic, let's review some other solutions practitioners use.

Other Packaging Options

Some notable alternatives to the aforementioned packaging options—and the many others in the wild (*http://bit.ly/2X553FE*)—are:

UNIX tooling
> In order to customize values of raw Kubernetes manifests, you can use a range of CLI tools such as sed, awk, or jq in shell scripts. This is a popular solution and, at least until the arrival of Helm, likely the most widely used option—not least because it minimizes dependencies and is rather portable across *nix environments.

Traditional configuration management systems
> You can use any of the traditional configuration management systems, such as Ansible, Puppet, Chef, or Salt, to package and deliver your operator.

Cloud-native languages
> A new generation of so-called cloud-native programming languages (*http://bit.ly/2Rwh5lu*), such as Pulumi and Ballerina, allows for, among other things, packaging and lifecycle management of Kubernetes-native apps.

ytt (https://get-ytt.io)
> With ytt you have another option for a YAML templating tool using a language that is itself a modified version of Google's configuration language Starlark (*http://bit.ly/2NaqoJh*). It operates semantically on the YAML structures and focuses on reusability.

Ksonnet (https://ksonnet.io)

A configuration management tool for Kubernetes manifests, originally developed by Heptio (now VMware), Ksonnet has been deprecated and is not actively worked on anymore, so use it at your own risk.

Read more about the options discussed here in Jesse Suen's post "The State of Kubernetes Configuration Management: An Unsolved Problem" (*http://bit.ly/2N9BkXM*).

Now that we've discussed the packaging options in general, let's look at best practices for packaging and shipping controllers and operators.

Packaging Best Practices

When packaging and publishing your operator, make sure you are aware of the following best practices. These apply regardless of which mechanism you choose (Helm, Kustomize, shell scripts, etc.):

- Provide a proper access control setup: this means defining a dedicated service account for the controller along with the RBAC permissions on a least-privileges basis; see "Getting the Permissions Right" on page 139 for further details.

- Consider the scope of your custom controller: will it look after CRs in one namespace or more than one namespace? Check out Alex Ellis's Twitter conversation (*http://bit.ly/2ZHd5S7*) about the pros and cons of the different approaches.

- Test and profile your controller so that you have an idea of its footprint and scalability. For example, Red Hat has put together a detailed set of requirements with instructions in the OperatorHub contribution (*http://bit.ly/2IEplx4*) guide.

- Make sure the CRDs and controller are well documented, ideally with the inline docs available on godoc.org (*https://godoc.org*) and a set of usage examples; see Banzai Cloud's bank-vaults (*http://bit.ly/2XtfPVB*) operator for inspiration.

Lifecycle Management

A broader and more holistic approach, compared to package/ship, is that of lifecycle management. The basic idea is to consider the entire supply chain, from development to shipping to upgrades, and automate as much as possible. In this area, CoreOS (and later Red Hat) was again a trailblazer: applying the same logic that led to operators to their lifecycle management. In other words: in order to install and later upgrade the custom controller of an operator, you'd have a dedicated operator that knows how to, well, handle operators. And indeed, part of the Operator Framework—which also provides the Operator SDK, as discussed in "The Operator SDK" on page 123—is the so-called Operator Lifecycle Manager (*http://bit.ly/2HIfDcR*) (OLM).

Jimmy Zelinskie, one of the main people behind OLM, phrased (*http://bit.ly/ 2KEfoSu*) it as follows:

> OLM does a lot for Operator authors, but it also solves an important problem that not many people have thought about yet: how do you effectively manage first-class extensions to Kubernetes over time?

In a nutshell, OLM provides a declarative way to install and upgrade operators and their dependencies, complementary packaging solutions such as Helm. It's up to you if you want to buy into the full-blown OLM solution or create an ad hoc solution for the versioning and upgrading challenge; however, you should have some strategy in place here. For certain areas—for example, the certification process (*http://bit.ly/ 2KBlymy*) for the Operator Hub by Red Hat—it's not only recommended but mandatory for any nontrivial deployment scenario, even if you don't aim at the Hub.

Production-Ready Deployments

In this section we review and discuss how to make your custom controllers and operators production-ready. The following is a high-level checklist:

- Use Kubernetes deployments (*http://bit.ly/2q7vR7Y*) or DaemonSets to supervise your custom controller so that they are restarted automatically when they fail— and fail they will.

- Implement health checks through dedicated endpoints for liveness and readiness probes. This, together with the previous step, makes your operations more resilient.

- Consider a leader-follower/standby model to make sure that even when your controller pod crashes, someone else can take over. Note, however, that synchronizing state is a nontrivial task.

- Provide access control resources, such as service account and roles, applying the least-privileges principle; see "Getting the Permissions Right" on page 139 for details.

- Consider automated builds, including testing. Some more tips are available in "Automated Builds and Testing" on page 142.

- Proactively tackle monitoring and logging; see "Custom Controllers and Observability" on page 142 for the what and how.

We also suggest that you peruse the aforementioned article "Kubernetes Operator Development Guidelines for Improved Usability" (*http://bit.ly/31P7rPC*) to learn more.

Getting the Permissions Right

Your custom controller is part of the Kubernetes control plane. It needs to read the state of resources, create resources inside as well as (potentially) outside Kubernetes, and communicate the state of its own resources. For all of this, the custom controller needs the right set of permissions, expressed through a set of role-based access control (RBAC)–related settings. Getting this right is the topic of this section.

First things first: *always* create a dedicated service account (*http://bit.ly/2RwoSQp*) to run your controller. In other words: *never* use the `default` service account in a namespace.[1]

To make your life easier, you can define a `ClusterRole` with the necessary RBAC rules along with a `RoleBinding` to bind it to a specific namespace, effectively reusing the role across namespaces, as explained in the Using RBAC Authorization (*http://bit.ly/2LdVFsj*) entry.

Following the least-privileges principle, assign only the permissions necessary for the controller to carry out its work. For example, if a controller only manages pods, there is no need to provide it with the permissions to list or create deployments or services. Also, make sure that the controller does not install the CRDs and/or the admission webhooks. In other words, the controller *should not* have permissions to manage CRDs and webhooks.

Common tooling for creating custom controllers, as discussed in Chapter 6, typically provides functionality for generating RBAC rules out-of-the-box. For example, Kubebuilder generates the following (*http://bit.ly/2RRCyFO*) RBAC assets, along with an operator:

```
$ ls -al rbac/
total 40
drwx------  7 mhausenblas  staff   224 12 Apr 09:52 .
drwx------  7 mhausenblas  staff   224 12 Apr 09:55 ..
-rw-------  1 mhausenblas  staff   280 12 Apr 09:49 auth_proxy_role.yaml
-rw-------  1 mhausenblas  staff   257 12 Apr 09:49 auth_proxy_role_binding.yaml
-rw-------  1 mhausenblas  staff   449 12 Apr 09:49 auth_proxy_service.yaml
-rw-r--r--  1 mhausenblas  staff  1044 12 Apr 10:50 rbac_role.yaml
-rw-r--r--  1 mhausenblas  staff   287 12 Apr 10:50 rbac_role_binding.yaml
```

Looking at the autogenerated RBAC roles and bindings reveals a fine-grained setup. In *rbac_role.yaml* you can find:

```
apiVersion: rbac.authorization.k8s.io/v1
kind: ClusterRole
metadata:
  creationTimestamp: null
```

---

1 See also Luc Juggery's post "Kubernetes Tips: Using a ServiceAccount" (*http://bit.ly/2X0fjKK*) for a detailed discussion of service account usage.

```
      name: manager-role
    rules:
    - apiGroups:
      - apps
      resources:
      - deployments
      verbs: ["get", "list", "watch", "create", "update", "patch", "delete"]
    - apiGroups:
      - apps
      resources:
      - deployments/status
      verbs: ["get", "update", "patch"]
    - apiGroups:
      - cnat.programming-kubernetes.info
      resources:
      - ats
      verbs: ["get", "list", "watch", "create", "update", "patch", "delete"]
    - apiGroups:
      - cnat.programming-kubernetes.info
      resources:
      - ats/status
      verbs: ["get", "update", "patch"]
    - apiGroups:
      - admissionregistration.k8s.io
      resources:
      - mutatingwebhookconfigurations
      - validatingwebhookconfigurations
      verbs: ["get", "list", "watch", "create", "update", "patch", "delete"]
    - apiGroups:
      - ""
      resources:
      - secrets
      verbs: ["get", "list", "watch", "create", "update", "patch", "delete"]
    - apiGroups:
      - ""
      resources:
      - services
      verbs: ["get", "list", "watch", "create", "update", "patch", "delete"]
```

Looking at these permissions that Kubebuilder generates in v1, you'll likely be a little taken aback.[2] We certainly were: best practice tells us that a controller, if it does not have very good reasons for doing so, should not be able to:

- Write resources that are only read in the code, generally. For example, if you only watch services and deployments, do remove the create, update, patch, and delete verbs in the role.

- Access all secrets; that is, always restrict this to the most minimal set of secrets necessary.

- Write MutatingWebhookConfigurations or ValidatingWebhookConfigurations. This is equivalent to getting access to any resource in the cluster.

---

2 We did, however, raise Issue 748 (*http://bit.ly/2J7Qys4*) against the Kubebuilder project.

- Write `CustomResourceDefinitions`. Note that this is not allowed in the cluster role just shown, but it's important to mention here, nevertheless: CRD creation should be done by a separate process, not by the controller itself.
- Write the */status* subresource (see "Subresources" on page 81) of foreign resources that it is not managing. For example, deployments here are not managed by the `cnat` controller and should not be in scope.

Kubebuilder, of course, is not really able to understand what your controller code is actually doing. So it's not surprising that the generated RBAC rules are far too relaxed. We recommend double-checking the permissions and reducing them to the absolute minimum, following the preceding checklist.

Having read access to all secrets in the system gives a controller access to all service account tokens. This is equivalent to having access to all passwords in the cluster. Having write access to `Muta tingWebhookConfigurations` or `ValidatingWebhookConfigura tions` allows you to intercept and manipulate every API request in the system. This opens the door to rootkits in a Kubernetes cluster. Both are obviously highly dangerous and considered antipatterns, so it's best to avoid them.

To avoid having too much power—that is, to restrict access rights to those that are absolutely necessary—consider using audit2rbac (*http://bit.ly/2IDW1qm*). This tool uses audit logs to generate an appropriate set of permissions, leading to more secure setups and fewer headaches down the road.

From *rbac_role_binding.yaml* you can learn:

```
apiVersion: rbac.authorization.k8s.io/v1
kind: ClusterRoleBinding
metadata:
  creationTimestamp: null
  name: manager-rolebinding
roleRef:
  apiGroup: rbac.authorization.k8s.io
  kind: ClusterRole
  name: manager-role
subjects:
- kind: ServiceAccount
  name: default
  namespace: system
```

For more best practices on RBAC and tooling around it, check out *RBAC.dev* (*https://rbac.dev*), a website dedicated to RBAC in Kubernetes. Let's move on now to testing and performance considerations for custom controllers.

Automated Builds and Testing

As a best practice in cloud-native land, consider an automated build of your custom controller. This is usually called *continuous build* or *continuous integration* (CI) and comprises unit tests, integration tests, building the container image, and potentially even sanity or smoke (*http://bit.ly/1Z9jXp5*) tests. The Cloud Native Computing Foundation (CNCF) maintains an interactive listing (*http://bit.ly/2J2vy4L*) of the many open source CI tools available.

When building your controller, keep in mind that it should consume as few compute resources as possible, while at the same time serving as many clients as possible. Each CR, based on the CRD(s) you define, is a proxy for a client. But how do you know how much it consumes, if and where it leaks memory, and how well it scales?

You can and indeed should carry out a number of tests, once the development of your custom controller stabilizes. These can include the following, but may not be limited to them:

- Performance-related tests, as found in Kubernetes itself (*http://bit.ly/2X556g8*) as well as the kboom (*http://bit.ly/2Fuy4zU*) tool, can provide you with data around scaling and resource footprints.
- Soak tests—for example, the ones used in Kubernetes (*http://bit.ly/2KBZmZc*)— aim at long-term usage, from several hours to days, with the goal of unveiling any leaking of resources, like files or main memory.

As a best practice, these tests should be part of your CI pipeline. In other words, automate the building of the custom controller, testing, and packaging from day one. For a concrete example setup we encourage you to check out Marko Mudrinić's excellent post "Spawning Kubernetes Clusters in CI for Integration and E2E tests" (*http://bit.ly/2FwN1RU*).

Next, we'll look at best practices that provide the basis for effective troubleshooting: built-in support for observability.

Custom Controllers and Observability

In this section we look at *observability* aspects of your custom controllers, specifically logging and monitoring.

Logging

Make sure you provide enough logging information to aid troubleshooting (*http://bit.ly/2WXD85D*) (in production). As usual in a containerized setup, log information is sent to `stdout`, where it can be consumed either on a per-pod basis with the `kubectl logs` command or in an aggregated form. Aggregates can be provided using cloud-provider-specific solutions, such as Stackdriver in Google Cloud or Cloud-Watch in AWS, or bespoke solutions like the Elasticsearch-Logstash-Kibana/Elasticsearch-Fluentd-Kibana stack. See also *Kubernetes Cookbook* (*http://bit.ly/2FTgJzk*) by Sébastien Goasguen and Michael Hausenblas (O'Reilly) for recipes on this topic.

Let's look at an example excerpt of our cnat custom controller log:

```
{ "level":"info",
  "ts":1555063927.492718,
  "logger":"controller",
  "msg":"=== Reconciling At" }
{ "level":"info",
  "ts":1555063927.49283,
  "logger":"controller",
  "msg":"Phase: PENDING" }
{ "level":"info",
  "ts":1555063927.492857,
  "logger":"controller",
  "msg":"Checking schedule" }
{ "level":"info",
  "ts":1555063927.492915,
  "logger":"controller",
  "msg":"Schedule parsing done" }
```

The *how* of logging: in general, we prefer structured logging (*http://bit.ly/31TPRu3*) and adjustable log levels, at least debug and info. There are two methods widely used across the Kubernetes code base, and unless you have good reasons not to, you should consider using those:

- The logger interface—for example, as found in *httplog.go* (*http://bit.ly/2WWV54w*), along with a concrete type (respLogger)—captures things like the status and errors.

- klog (*http://bit.ly/31OJxUu*), a fork of Google's glog, is a structured logger used throughout Kubernetes, and while it has its idiosyncrasies, it's worth knowing.

The *what* of logging: make sure to have detailed log information for the normal case of your business logic operation. For example, from our Operator SDK implementation of the cnat controller, in *at_controller.go* (*http://bit.ly/2Fpo5Mi*), set up the logger like so:

```
reqLogger := log.WithValues("namespace", request.Namespace, "at", request.Name)
```

And then in the business logic, in the Reconcile(request reconcile.Request) function:

```
case cnatv1alpha1.PhasePending:
  reqLogger.Info("Phase: PENDING")
  // As long as we haven't executed the command yet, we need to check if it's
  // already time to act:
  reqLogger.Info("Checking schedule", "Target", instance.Spec.Schedule)
  // Check if it's already time to execute the command with a tolerance of
```

```
// 2 seconds:
d, err := timeUntilSchedule(instance.Spec.Schedule)
if err != nil {
  reqLogger.Error(err, "Schedule parsing failure")
  // Error reading the schedule. Wait until it is fixed.
  return reconcile.Result{}, err
}
reqLogger.Info("Schedule parsing done", "Result", "diff", fmt.Sprintf("%v", d))
if d > 0 {
  // Not yet time to execute the command, wait until the scheduled time
  return reconcile.Result{RequeueAfter: d}, nil
}
reqLogger.Info("It's time!", "Ready to execute", instance.Spec.Command)
instance.Status.Phase = cnatv1alpha1.PhaseRunning
```

This Go snippet gives you a good idea of what to log, and especially when to use `reqLogger.Info` and `reqLogger.Error`.

With Logging 101 out of the way, let's move on to a related topic: metrics!

Monitoring, instrumentation, and auditing

A great open source, container-ready monitoring solution you can use across environments (on-premises and in the cloud) is Prometheus (*https://prometheus.io*). Alerting on each event is not practical, so you might want to think about who needs to be informed about what kind of event. For example, you could have a policy that node-related or namespace-related events are handled by infrastructure admins, and namespace admins or developers are paged for pod-level events. In this context, in order to visualize the metrics you've gathered, the most popular solution is certainly Grafana (*https://grafana.com*); see Figure 7-2 for an example of Prometheus metrics visualized in Grafana, taken from the Prometheus documentation (*http://bit.ly/2Oi4YcA*).

If you are using a service mesh—for example, based on the Envoy proxy (*https://envoy.com*) (like Istio or App Mesh), or Linkerd—then instrumentation typically comes for free or is achievable with minimal (configuration) effort. Otherwise, you will have to use the respective libraries, such as those provided by Prometheus (*http://bit.ly/2xb2qmv*), to expose the relevant metrics in your code yourself. In this context, you might also want to check out the fledgling Service Mesh Interface (SMI (*https://smi-spec.io*)) project, introduced in early 2019, which aims to provide a standardized interface for service meshes, based on CRs and controllers.

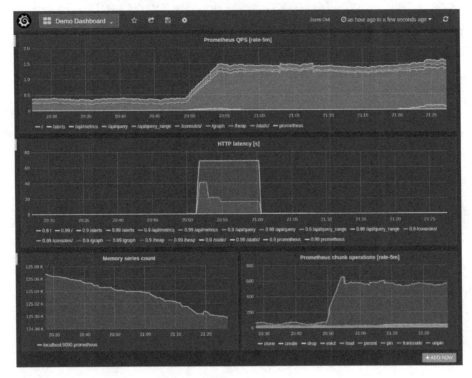

Figure 7-2. Prometheus metrics visualized in Grafana

Another useful feature Kubernetes offers via the API server is auditing (*http://bit.ly/ 2O4WBkL*), which allows you to record a sequence of activities affecting the cluster. Different strategies are available in the auditing policy, from no logging to logging event metadata, request bodies, and response bodies. You can choose between a simple log backend and using a webhook for integrating with third-party systems.

Summary

This chapter focused on how to make your operators production-ready by discussing operational aspects of controllers and operators, including packaging, security, and performance.

With this we've covered the basics of writing and using custom Kubernetes controllers and operators, so now we move on to another way to extend Kubernetes: developing a custom API server.

## CHAPTER 8

Custom API Servers

As an alternative to CustomResourceDefinitions, you can use a custom API server. Custom API servers can serve API groups with resources the same way the main Kubernetes API server does. In contrast to CRDs, there are hardly any limits to what you can do with a custom API server.

This chapter begins by listing a number of reasons why CRDs might not be the right solution for your use case. It describes the aggregation pattern that makes it possible to extend the Kubernetes API surface with a custom API server. Finally, you'll learn to actually implement a custom API server using Golang.

Use Cases for Custom API Servers

A custom API server can be used in place of CRDs. It can do everything that CRDs can do and offers nearly infinite flexibility. Of course, this comes at a cost: complexity of both development and operation.

Let's look at some limits of CRDs as of the time of this writing (when Kubernetes 1.14 was the stable release). CRDs:

- Use etcd as their storage medium (or whatever the Kubernetes API server uses).
- Do not support protobuf, only JSON.
- Support only two kinds of subresources: /status and /scale (see "Subresources" on page 81).

- Do not support graceful deletion.[1] Finalizers can simulate this but do not allow a custom graceful deletion time.

- Add significantly to the Kubernetes API server's CPU load, because all algorithms are implemented in a generic way (for example, validation).

- Implement only standard CRUD semantics for the API endpoints.

- Do not support cohabitation of resources (i.e., resources in different API groups or resources of different names that share storage).[2]

A custom API server, in contrast, does not have these restrictions. A custom API server:

- Can use any storage medium. There are custom API servers, such as:

  — The metrics API server (*http://bit.ly/2FvgfAV*), which stores data in memory for maximum performance

  — API servers mirroring a Docker registry in OpenShift (*http://redhat.com/open shift*)

  — API servers writing to a time series database

  — API servers mirroring cloud APIs

  — API servers mirroring other API objects, like projects in OpenShift (*http:// redhat.com/openshift*) that mirror Kubernetes namespaces

- Can provide protobuf support like all native Kubernetes resources do. For this you must create a *.proto* file by using go-to-protobuf (*http://bit.ly/31OLSie*) and then using the protobuf compiler `protoc` to generate serializers, which are then compiled into the binary.

- Can provide any custom subresource; for example, the Kubernetes API server provides */exec*, */logs*, */port-forward*, and more, most of which use very custom protocols like WebSockets or HTTP/2 streaming.

- Can implement graceful deletion as Kubernetes does for pods. `kubectl` waits for the deletion, and the user can even provide a custom graceful termination period.

- Can implement all operations like validation, admission, and conversion in the most efficient way using Golang, without a roundtrip through webhooks, which add further latency. This can matter for high performance use cases or if there is

---

1 Graceful deletion means that the client can pass a graceful deletion period as part of the deletion call. The actual deletion is done by a controller asynchronously (the `kubelet` does that for pods) by doing a forced deletion. This way pods have time to cleanly shut down.

2 Kubernetes uses cohabitation to migrate resources (e.g., deployments from the `extensions/v1beta1` API group) to subject-specific API groups (e.g., `apps/v1`). CRDs have no concept of shared storage.

---

a large number of objects. Think about pod objects in a huge cluster with thousands of nodes, and two magnitudes more pods.

- Can implement custom semantics, like the atomic reservation of a service IP in the core v1 `Service` kind. At the moment the service is created, a unique service IP is assigned and directly returned. To a limited degree, special semantics like this can of course be implemented with admission webhooks (see "Admission Webhooks" on page 226), though those webhooks can never reliably know whether the passed object was actually created or updated: they are called optimistically, but a later step in the request pipeline might cancel the request. In other words: side effects in webhooks are tricky because there is no undo trigger if a request fails.

- Can serve resources that have a common storage mechanism (i.e., a common etcd key path prefix) but live in different API groups or are named differently. For example, Kubernetes stores deployments and other resources in the API group `extensions/v1` and then moves them to more specific API groups like `apps/v1`.

In other words, custom API servers are a solution for situations where CRDs are still limited. In transitional scenarios where it is important to not break resource compatibility when moving to new semantics, custom API servers are often much more flexible.

Example: A Pizza Restaurant

To learn how custom API servers are implemented, in this section we will look at an example project: a custom API server implementing a pizza restaurant API. Let's take a look at the requirements.

We want to create two kinds in the `restaurant.programming-kubernetes.info` API group:

`Topping`
 Pizza toppings (e.g., salami, mozzarella, or tomato)

`Pizza`
 The type of pizza offered in the restaurant

The toppings are cluster-wide resources and hold only a floating-point value for the cost of one unit of the topping. An instance is as simple as:

```
apiVersion: restaurant.programming-kubernetes.info/v1alpha1
kind: Topping
metadata:
  name: mozzarella
spec:
  cost: 1.0
```

Each pizza can have an arbitrary number of toppings; for example:

```
apiVersion: restaurant.programming-kubernetes.info/v1alpha1
kind: Pizza
metadata:
  name: margherita
spec:
  toppings:
  - mozzarella
  - tomato
```

The list of toppings is ordered (like any list in YAML or JSON), but the order does not really matter for the semantics of the type. The customer will get the same pizza in any case. We want to allow duplicates in the list in order to allow, say, a pizza with extra cheese.

All this can be implemented easily with CRDs. Now let's add some requirements that go beyond the basic CRD capabilities:[3]

- We want to allow only toppings in a pizza specification that have a corresponding Topping object.

- We also want to assume that we first introduced this API as a v1alpha1 version but eventually learned that we want another representation of the toppings in the v1beta1 version of the same API.

In other words, we want to have two versions and convert seamlessly between them.

The full implementation of this API as a custom API server can be found at the book's GitHub repository (*http://bit.ly/2x9C3gR*). In the rest of this chapter, we will go through all the major parts of that project and learn how it works. In the process, you'll see a lot of the concepts presented in the previous chapter in a different light: namely, the Golang implementation that is also behind the Kubernetes API server. A number of design decisions highlighted in CRDs also will become clearer.

Hence, we highly recommend you read through this chapter even if you don't plan to go the route of a custom API server. Maybe the concepts presented here will be made available for CRDs as well in the future, in which case having knowledge of custom API servers will be useful to you.

The Architecture: Aggregation

Before going into the technical implementation details, we want to take a higher-level view of the custom API server architecture in the context of a Kubernetes cluster.

---

3 We'll see in Chapter 9 that CRD conversion and admission webhooks available in the latest Kubernetes versions also allow us to add these features to CRDs.

Custom API servers are processes serving API groups, usually built using the generic API server library *k8s.io/apiserver* (*http://bit.ly/2X3joNX*). These processes can run inside or outside of the cluster. In the former case, they run inside pods, with a service in front.

The main Kubernetes API server, called kube-apiserver, is always the first point of contact for kubectl and other API clients. API groups served by a custom API server are proxied by the kube-apiserver process to the custom API server process. In other words, the kube-apiserver process knows about all of the custom API servers and the API groups they serve, in order to be able to proxy the right requests to them.

The component doing this proxying is inside the kube-apiserver process and is called kube-aggregator (*http://bit.ly/2X10C9W*). The process of proxying API requests to the custom API server is called *API aggregation*.

Let's look a bit more into the path of requests targeted at a custom API server, but coming in at the Kubernetes API server TCP socket (see Figure 8-1):

1. Requests are received by the Kubernetes API server.

2. They pass the handler chain consisting of authentication, audit logging, impersonation, max-in-flight throttling, authorization, and more (the figure is just a sketch and is not complete).

3. As the Kubernetes API server knows the aggregated APIs, it can intercept requests to the HTTP path */apis/aggregated-API-group-name*.

4. The Kubernetes API server forwards the request to the custom API server.

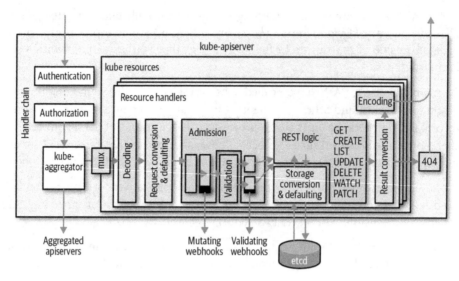

Figure 8-1. Kubernetes main API server kube-apiserver with an integrated kube-aggregator

The kube-aggregator proxies requests under the HTTP path for an API group version (i.e., everything under */apis/group-name/version*). It does not have to know the actual served resources in the API group version.

In contrast, the kube-aggregator serves the discovery endpoints */apis* and */apis/group-name* of all aggregated custom API servers itself (it uses the defined order explained in the following section) and returns the results without talking to the aggregated custom API servers. Instead it uses the information from the APIService resource. Let's look at this process in detail.

API Services

For the Kubernetes API server to know about the API groups a custom API server serves, one APIService object must be created in the apiregistration.k8s.io/v1 API group. These objects list only the API groups and versions, not resources or any further details:

```
apiVersion: apiregistration.k8s.io/v1beta1
kind: APIService
metadata:
  name: name
spec:
  group: API-group-name
  version: API-group-version
  service:
    namespace: custom-API-server-service-namespace
    name: -API-server-service
```

```
caBundle: base64-caBundle
insecureSkipTLSVerify: bool
groupPriorityMinimum: 2000
versionPriority: 20
```

The name is arbitrary, but for clarity we suggest you use a name that identifies the API group name and version—e.g., *group-name-version*.

The service can be a normal `ClusterIP` service (*http://bit.ly/2X0zEEu*) in the cluster, or it can be an `ExternalName` service with a given DNS name for out-of-cluster custom API servers. In both cases, the port must be 443. No other service port is supported (at the time of this writing). Service target port mapping allows any chosen, preferably nonrestricted, higher port to be used for the custom API server pods, so this is not a major restriction.

The certificate authority (CA) bundle is used for the Kubernetes API server to trust the contacted service. Note that API requests can contain confidential data. To avoid man-in-the-middle attacks, it is highly recommended that you set the `caBundle` field and not use the `insecureSkipTLSVerify` alternative. This is especially important for any production cluster, including a mechanism for certificate rotation.

Finally, there are two priorities in the `APIService` object. These have some tricky semantics, described in the Golang code documentation for the `APIService` type:

```
// GroupPriorityMininum is the priority this group should have at least. Higher
// priority means that the group is preferred by clients over lower priority ones.
// Note that other versions of this group might specify even higher
// GroupPriorityMinimum values such that the whole group gets a higher priority.
//
// The primary sort is based on GroupPriorityMinimum, ordered highest number to
// lowest (20 before 10). The secondary sort is based on the alphabetical
// comparison of the name of the object (v1.bar before v1.foo). We'd recommend
// something like: *.k8s.io (except extensions) at 18000 and PaaSes
// (OpenShift, Deis) are recommended to be in the 2000s
GroupPriorityMinimum int32 `json:"groupPriorityMinimum"`

// VersionPriority controls the ordering of this API version inside of its
// group. Must be greater than zero. The primary sort is based on
// VersionPriority, ordered highest to lowest (20 before 10). Since it's inside
// of a group, the number can be small, probably in the 10s. In case of equal
// version priorities, the version string will be used to compute the order
// inside a group. If the version string is "kube-like", it will sort above non
// "kube-like" version strings, which are ordered lexicographically. "Kube-like"
// versions start with a "v", then are followed by a number (the major version),
// then optionally the string "alpha" or "beta" and another number (the minor
// version). These are sorted first by GA > beta > alpha (where GA is a version
// with no suffix such as beta or alpha), and then by comparing major version,
// then minor version. An example sorted list of versions:
// v10, v2, v1, v11beta2, v10beta3, v3beta1, v12alpha1, v11alpha2, foo1, foo10.
VersionPriority int32 `json:"versionPriority"`
```

In other words, the `GroupPriorityMinimum` value determines where the group is prioritized. If multiple `APIService` objects for different versions differ, the highest value rules.

The second priority just orders the versions among each other to define the preferred version to be used by dynamic clients.

Here is a list of the `GroupPriorityMinimum` values for the native Kubernetes API groups:

```
var apiVersionPriorities = map[schema.GroupVersion]priority{
    {Group: "", Version: "v1"}: {group: 18000, version: 1},
    {Group: "extensions", Version: "v1beta1"}: {group: 17900, version: 1},
    {Group: "apps", Version: "v1beta1"}:                       {group: 17800, version: 1},
    {Group: "apps", Version: "v1beta2"}:                       {group: 17800, version: 9},
    {Group: "apps", Version: "v1"}:                            {group: 17800, version: 15},
    {Group: "events.k8s.io", Version: "v1beta1"}:             {group: 17750, version: 5},
    {Group: "authentication.k8s.io", Version: "v1"}:          {group: 17700, version: 15},
    {Group: "authentication.k8s.io", Version: "v1beta1"}:     {group: 17700, version: 9},
    {Group: "authorization.k8s.io", Version: "v1"}:           {group: 17600, version: 15},
    {Group: "authorization.k8s.io", Version: "v1beta1"}:      {group: 17600, version: 9},
    {Group: "autoscaling", Version: "v1"}:                     {group: 17500, version: 15},
    {Group: "autoscaling", Version: "v2beta1"}:                {group: 17500, version: 9},
    {Group: "autoscaling", Version: "v2beta2"}:                {group: 17500, version: 1},
    {Group: "batch", Version: "v1"}:                           {group: 17400, version: 15},
    {Group: "batch", Version: "v1beta1"}:                      {group: 17400, version: 9},
    {Group: "batch", Version: "v2alpha1"}:                     {group: 17400, version: 9},
    {Group: "certificates.k8s.io", Version: "v1beta1"}:       {group: 17300, version: 9},
    {Group: "networking.k8s.io", Version: "v1"}:              {group: 17200, version: 15},
    {Group: "networking.k8s.io", Version: "v1beta1"}:         {group: 17200, version: 9},
    {Group: "policy", Version: "v1beta1"}:                     {group: 17100, version: 9},
    {Group: "rbac.authorization.k8s.io", Version: "v1"}:      {group: 17000, version: 15},
    {Group: "rbac.authorization.k8s.io", Version: "v1beta1"}: {group: 17000, version: 12},
    {Group: "rbac.authorization.k8s.io", Version: "v1alpha1"}: {group: 17000, version: 9},
    {Group: "settings.k8s.io", Version: "v1alpha1"}:          {group: 16900, version: 9},
    {Group: "storage.k8s.io", Version: "v1"}:                 {group: 16800, version: 15},
    {Group: "storage.k8s.io", Version: "v1beta1"}:            {group: 16800, version: 9},
    {Group: "storage.k8s.io", Version: "v1alpha1"}:           {group: 16800, version: 1},
    {Group: "apiextensions.k8s.io", Version: "v1beta1"}:      {group: 16700, version: 9},
    {Group: "admissionregistration.k8s.io", Version: "v1"}:   {group: 16700, version: 15},
    {Group: "admissionregistration.k8s.io", Version: "v1beta1"}: {group: 16700, version: 12},
    {Group: "scheduling.k8s.io", Version: "v1"}:              {group: 16600, version: 15},
    {Group: "scheduling.k8s.io", Version: "v1beta1"}:         {group: 16600, version: 12},
    {Group: "scheduling.k8s.io", Version: "v1alpha1"}:        {group: 16600, version: 9},
    {Group: "coordination.k8s.io", Version: "v1"}:            {group: 16500, version: 15},
    {Group: "coordination.k8s.io", Version: "v1beta1"}:       {group: 16500, version: 9},
    {Group: "auditregistration.k8s.io", Version: "v1alpha1"}: {group: 16400, version: 1},
    {Group: "node.k8s.io", Version: "v1alpha1"}:              {group: 16300, version: 1},
    {Group: "node.k8s.io", Version: "v1beta1"}:               {group: 16300, version: 9},
}
```

So using 2000 for PaaS-like APIs means that they are placed at the end of this list.[4]

The order of the API groups plays a role during the REST mapping process in kubectl (see "REST Mapping" on page 63). This means it has actual influence on the user experience. If there are conflicting resource names or short names, the one with the highest `GroupPriorityMinimum` value wins.

---

4 PaaS stands for Platform as a Service.

Also, in the special case of replacing of an API group version using a custom API server, this priority ordering might be of use. For example, you could replace a native Kubernetes API group with a modified one (for whatever reason) by placing the custom API service at a position with a lower `GroupPriorityMinimum` value than the one in the upper table.

Note again that the Kubernetes API server does not need to know the list of resources for either of the discovery endpoints /apis, and /apis/group-name, or for proxying. The list of resources is returned only via the third discovery endpoint, /apis/group-name/version. But as we have seen in the previous section, this endpoint is served by the aggregated custom API server, not by `kube-aggregator`.

Inner Structure of a Custom API Server

A custom API server resembles most of the parts that make up the Kubernetes API server, though of course with different API group implementations, and without an embedded `kube-aggregator` or an embedded `apiextension-apiserver` (which serves CRDs). This leads to nearly the same architectural picture (shown in Figure 8-2) as the one in Figure 8-1:

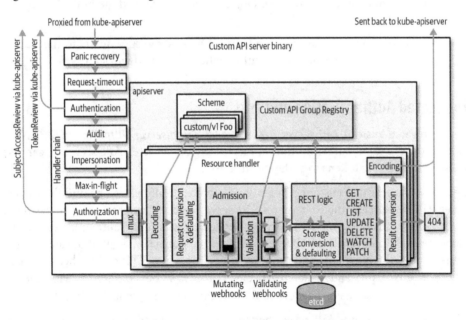

Figure 8-2. An aggregated custom API server based on k8s.io/apiserver

We observe a number of things. An aggregated API server:

- Has the same basic internal structure as the Kubernetes API server.

- Has its own handler chain, including authentication, audit, impersonation, max-in-flight throttling, and authorization (we will explain throughout this chapter why this is necessary; see, for example, "Delegated Authorization" on page 157).

- Has its own resource handler pipeline, including decoding, conversion, admission, REST mapping, and encoding.

- Calls admission webhooks.

- Might write to etcd (it can use a different storage backend, though). The etcd cluster does not have to be the same as the one used by the Kubernetes API server.

- Has its own scheme and registry implementation for custom API groups. The registry implementation might differ and be customized to any degree.

- Does authentication again. It usually does client certificate authentication and token-based authentication, calling back to the Kubernetes API server with a TokenAccessReview request. We will discuss the authentication and trust architecture in more detail shortly.

- Does its own auditing. This means the Kubernetes API server audits certain fields, but only on the meta level. Object-level auditing is done in the aggregated custom API server.

- Does its own authentication using SubjectAccessReview requests to the Kubernetes API server. We will discuss authorization in more detail shortly.

Delegated Authentication and Trust

An aggregated custom API server (based on *k8s.io/apiserver* (*http://bit.ly/2X3joNX*)) is built on the same authentication library as the Kubernetes API server. It can use client certificates or tokens to authenticate a user.

Because an aggregated custom API server is architecturally placed behind the Kubernetes API server (i.e., the Kubernetes API server receives requests and proxies them to the aggregated custom API server), requests are already authenticated by the Kubernetes API server. The Kubernetes API server stores the result of the authentication—that is, the username and group membership—in HTTP request headers, usually X-Remote-User and X-Remote-Group (these can be configured with the --requestheader-username-headers and --requestheader-group-headers flags).

The aggregated custom API server has to know when to trust these headers; otherwise, any other caller could claim to have done authentication and could set these headers. This is handled by a special request header client CA. It is stored in the config map *kube-system/extension-apiserver-authentication* (filename *requestheader-client-ca-file*). Here is an example:

```
apiVersion: v1
kind: ConfigMap
metadata:
  name: extension-apiserver-authentication
  namespace: kube-system
data:
  client-ca-file: |
    -----BEGIN CERTIFICATE-----
    ...
    -----END CERTIFICATE-----
  requestheader-allowed-names: '["aggregator"]'
  requestheader-client-ca-file: |
    -----BEGIN CERTIFICATE-----
    ...
    -----END CERTIFICATE-----
  requestheader-extra-headers-prefix: '["X-Remote-Extra-"]'
  requestheader-group-headers: '["X-Remote-Group"]'
  requestheader-username-headers: '["X-Remote-User"]'
```

With this information, an aggregated custom API server with default settings will authenticate:

- Clients using client certificates matching the given *client-ca-file*
- Clients preauthenticated by the Kubernetes API server whose requests are forwarded using the given *requestheader-client-ca-file* and whose username and group memberships are stored in the given HTTP headers X-Remote-Group and X-Remote-User

Last but not least, there is a mechanism called TokenAccessReview that forwards bearer tokens (received via the HTTP header Authorization: bearer *token*) back to the Kubernetes API server in order to verify whether they are valid. The token access review mechanism is disabled by default but can optionally be enabled; see "Options and Config Pattern and Startup Plumbing" on page 160.

We will see in the following sections how delegated authentication is actually set up. While we've gone into detail about this mechanism here, inside an aggregated custom API server this is mostly done automatically by the *k8s.io/apiserver* library. But knowing what is going on behind the curtain is certainly valuable, especially where security is involved.

Delegated Authorization

After authentication has been done, each request must be authorized. Authorization is based on the username and group list. The default authorization mechanism in Kubernetes is role-based access control (RBAC).

RBAC maps identities to roles, and roles to authorization rules, which finally accept or reject requests. We won't go into all the details here about RBAC authorization objects like roles and cluster roles, or role bindings and cluster role bindings (see

"Getting the Permissions Right" on page 139 for more). From an architectural point of view it is enough to know that an aggregated custom API server authorizes requests using delegated authorization via `SubjectAccessReviews`. It does not evaluate RBAC rules itself but instead delegates evaluation to the Kubernetes API server.

Why Aggregated API Servers Always Have to Do Another Authorization Step

Each request received by the Kubernetes API server and forwarded to an aggregated custom API server passes authentication and authorization (see Figure 8-1). This means an aggregated custom API server could skip the delegated authorization part for such requests.

But this preauthorization is not guaranteed and might go away at any time (there are plans to split `kube-aggregator` from `kube-apiserver` for better security and more scalability in the future). In addition, requests going directly to the aggregated custom API server (e.g., authenticated via client certificates or token access review) do not pass the Kubernetes API server and therefore are not preauthorized.

In other words, skipping delegated authorization opens up a security hole and is therefore highly discouraged.

Let's look at delegated authorization in more detail now.

A subject access review is sent from the aggregated custom API server to the Kubernetes API server on a request (if it does not find an answer in its authorization cache). Here is an example of such a review object:

```
apiVersion: authorization.k8s.io/v1
kind: SubjectAccessReview
spec:
  resourceAttributes:
    group: apps
    resource: deployments
    verb: create
    namespace: default
    version: v1
    name: example
  user: michael
  groups:
  - system:authenticated
  - admins
  - authors
```

The Kubernetes API server receives this from the aggregated custom API server, evaluates the RBAC rules in the cluster, and makes a decision, returning a `SubjectAccessReview` object with a status field set; for example:

```
apiVersion: authorization.k8s.io/v1
kind: SubjectAccessReview
```

```
status:
  allowed: true
  denied: false
  reason: "rule foo allowed this request"
```

Note here that it is possible that both `allowed` and `denied` are `false`. This means that the Kubernetes API server could not make a decision, in which case another authorizer inside an aggregated custom API server can make a decision (API servers implement an authorization chain that is queried one by one, with delegated authorization being one of the authorizers in that chain). This can be used to model nonstandard authorization logic—that is, if in certain cases there are no RBAC rules but an external authorization system is used instead.

Note that for performance reasons, the delegated authorization mechanism maintains a local cache in each aggregated custom API server. By default, it caches 1,024 authorization entries with:

- 5 minutes expiry for allowed authorization requests
- 30 seconds expiry for denied authorization requests

These values can be customized via `--authorization-webhook-cache-authorized-ttl` and `--authorization-webhook-cache-unauthorized-ttl`.

We'll see in the following sections how delegated authorization is set up in code. Again, as with authentication, inside an aggregated custom API server delegated authorization is mostly done automatically by the *k8s.io/apiserver* library.

Writing Custom API Servers

In the previous sections we looked at the architecture of aggregated API servers. In this section we want to look at the implementation of an aggregated custom API server in Golang.

The main Kubernetes API server is implemented via the *k8s.io/apiserver* library. A custom API server will use the very same code. The main difference is that our custom API server will run in-cluster. This means that it can assume that a kube-apiserver is available in the cluster and use it to do delegated authorization and to retrieve other kube-native resources.

We also assume that an `etcd` cluster is available and ready to be used by the aggregated custom API server. It is not important whether this `etcd` is dedicated or shared with the Kubernetes API server. Our custom API server will use a different `etcd` key space to avoid conflicts.

The code examples in this chapter refer to the example code on GitHub (*http://bit.ly/2x9C3gR*), so look there for the complete source code. We will show only the most interesting excerpt here, but you can always go to the complete example project, experiment with it, and—very important for learning—run it in a real cluster.

This pizza-apiserver project implements the example API shown in "Example: A Pizza Restaurant" on page 149.

Options and Config Pattern and Startup Plumbing

1. The *k8s.io/apiserver* library uses an *options and config pattern* to create a running API server.

We'll start with a couple of option structs that are bound to flags. Take them from *k8s.io/apiserver* and add our custom options. Option structs from *k8s.io/apiserver* can be tweaked in-code for special use cases, and the provided flags can be applied to a flag set in order to be accessible to the user.

In the example (*http://bit.ly/2x9C3gR*) we start very simply by basing everything on the RecommendedOptions. These recommended options set up everything as needed for a "normal" aggregated custom API server for simple APIs, like this:

```
import (
    ...
    informers "github.com/programming-kubernetes/pizza-apiserver/pkg/
    generated/informers/externalversions"
)

const defaultEtcdPathPrefix = "/registry/restaurant.programming-kubernetes.info"

type CustomServerOptions struct {
    RecommendedOptions *genericoptions.RecommendedOptions
    SharedInformerFactory informers.SharedInformerFactory
}

func NewCustomServerOptions(out, errOut io.Writer) *CustomServerOptions {
    o := &CustomServerOptions{
        RecommendedOptions: genericoptions.NewRecommendedOptions(
            defaultEtcdPathPrefix,
            apiserver.Codecs.LegacyCodec(v1alpha1.SchemeGroupVersion),
            genericoptions.NewProcessInfo("pizza-apiserver", "pizza-apiserver"),
        ),
    }

    return o
}
```

The CustomServerOptions embed RecommendedOptions and add one field on top. NewCustomServerOptions is the constructor that fills the CustomServerOptions struct with default values.

Let's look into some of the more interesting details:

- `defaultEtcdPathPrefix` is the `etcd` prefix for all of our keys. As a key space, we use */registry/pizza-apiserver.programming-kubernetes.info*, clearly distinct from Kubernetes keys.

- `SharedInformerFactory` is the process-wide shared informer factory for our own CRs to avoid unnecessary informers for the same resources (see Figure 3-5). Note that it is imported from the generated informer code in our project and not from `client-go`.

- `NewRecommendedOptions` sets everything up for an aggregated custom API server with default values.

Let's take a quick look at `NewRecommendedOptions`:

```
return &RecommendedOptions{
    Etcd:            NewEtcdOptions(storagebackend.NewDefaultConfig(prefix, codec)),
    SecureServing:   sso.WithLoopback(),
    Authentication: NewDelegatingAuthenticationOptions(),
    Authorization:  NewDelegatingAuthorizationOptions(),
    Audit:           NewAuditOptions(),
    Features:        NewFeatureOptions(),
    CoreAPI:         NewCoreAPIOptions(),
    ExtraAdmissionInitializers:
      func(c *server.RecommendedConfig) ([]admission.PluginInitializer, error) {
          return nil, nil
      },
    Admission:       NewAdmissionOptions(),
    ProcessInfo:     processInfo,
    Webhook:         NewWebhookOptions(),
}
```

All of these can be tweaked if necessary. For example, if a custom default serving port is desired, `RecommendedOptions.SecureServing.SecureServingOptions.BindPort` can be set.

Let's briefly go through the existing option structs:

- `Etcd` configures the storage stack that reads and write to `etcd`.

- `SecureServing` configures everything around HTTPS (i.e., ports, certificates, etc.)

- `Authentication` sets up delegated authentication as described in "Delegated Authentication and Trust" on page 156.

- `Authorization` sets up delegated authorization as described in "Delegated Authorization" on page 157.

- `Audit` sets up the auditing output stack. This is disabled by default, but can be set to output an audit log file or to send audit events to an external backend.

- `Features` configures feature gates of alpha and beta features.

- CoreAPI holds a path to a kubeconfig file to access the main API server. This defaults to using the in-cluster configuration.

- Admission is a stack of mutating and validating admission plug-ins that execute for every incoming API request. This can be extended with custom in-code admission plug-ins, or the default admission chain can be tweaked for the custom API server.

- ExtraAdmissionInitializers allows us to add more initializers for admission. Initializers implement the plumbing of, for example, informers or clients through the custom API server. See "Admission" on page 189 for more about custom admission.

- ProcessInfo holds information for event object creation (i.e., a process name and a namespace). We have set it to pizza-apiserver for both values.

- Webhook configures how webhooks operate (e.g., general setting for authentication and admission webhook). It is set up with good defaults for a custom API server that runs inside of a cluster. For API servers outside of the cluster, this would be the place to configure how it can reach the webhook.

Options are coupled with flags; that is, they are conventionally on the same abstraction level as flags. As a rule of thumb, options do not hold "running" data structures. They are used during startup and then converted to configuration or server objects, which are then run.

Options can be validated via the Validate() error method. This method will also check that the user-provided flag values make logical sense.

Options can be completed in order to set default values, which should not show up in the flags' help text but which are necessary to get a complete set of options.

Options are converted to a server configuration ("config") by the Config() (*api server.Config, error) method. This is done by starting with a recommended default configuration and then applying the options to it:

```
func (o *CustomServerOptions) Config() (*apiserver.Config, error) {
    err := o.RecommendedOptions.SecureServing.MaybeDefaultWithSelfSignedCerts(
        "localhost", nil, []net.IP{net.ParseIP("127.0.0.1")},
    )
    if err != nil {
        return nil, fmt.Errorf("error creating self-signed cert: %v", err)
    }

    [... omitted o.RecommendedOptions.ExtraAdmissionInitializers ...]

    serverConfig := genericapiserver.NewRecommendedConfig(apiserver.Codecs)
    err = o.RecommendedOptions.ApplyTo(serverConfig, apiserver.Scheme);
    if err != nil {
        return nil, err
    }
```

```
    config := &apiserver.Config{
        GenericConfig: serverConfig,
        ExtraConfig:   apiserver.ExtraConfig{},
    }
    return config, nil
}
```

The config created here contains runnable data structures; in other words, configs are runtime objects, in contrast to the options, which correspond to flags. The line o.Rec ommendedOptions.SecureServing.MaybeDefaultWithSelfSignedCerts creates self-signed certificates in case the user has not passed flags for pregenerated certificates.

As we've described, genericapiserver.NewRecommendedConfig returns a default recommended configuration, and RecommendedOptions.ApplyTo changes it according to flags (and other customized options).

The config struct of the pizza-apiserver project itself is just a wrapper around the RecommendedConfig for our example custom API server:

```
type ExtraConfig struct {
    // Place your custom config here.
}

type Config struct {
    GenericConfig *genericapiserver.RecommendedConfig
    ExtraConfig   ExtraConfig
}

// CustomServer contains state for a Kubernetes custom api server.
type CustomServer struct {
    GenericAPIServer *genericapiserver.GenericAPIServer
}

type completedConfig struct {
    GenericConfig genericapiserver.CompletedConfig
    ExtraConfig   *ExtraConfig
}

type CompletedConfig struct {
    // Embed a private pointer that cannot be instantiated outside of
    // this package.
    *completedConfig
}
```

If more state for a running custom API server is necessary, ExtraConfig is the place to put it.

Similarly to option structs, the config has a Complete() CompletedConfig method that sets default values. Because it is necessary to actually call Complete() for the underlying configuration, it is common to enforce that via the type system by introducing the unexported completedConfig data type. The idea here is that only a call to Complete() can turn a Config into a completeConfig. The compiler will complain if this call is not done:

```
func (cfg *Config) Complete() completedConfig {
    c := completedConfig{
        cfg.GenericConfig.Complete(),
        &cfg.ExtraConfig,
    }

    c.GenericConfig.Version = &version.Info{
        Major: "1",
        Minor: "0",
    }

    return completedConfig{&c}
}
```

Finally, the completed config can be turned into a `CustomServer` runtime struct via the `New()` constructor:

```
// New returns a new instance of CustomServer from the given config.
func (c completedConfig) New() (*CustomServer, error) {
    genericServer, err := c.GenericConfig.New(
        "pizza-apiserver",
        genericapiserver.NewEmptyDelegate(),
    )
    if err != nil {
        return nil, err
    }

    s := &CustomServer{
        GenericAPIServer: genericServer,
    }

    [ ... omitted API installation ...]

    return s, nil
}
```

Note that we have intentionally omitted the API installation part here. We'll come back to this in "API Installation" on page 186 (i.e., how you wire the *registries* into the custom API server during startup). A registry implements the API and storage semantics of an API group. We will see this for the restaurant API group in "Registry and Strategy" on page 181.

The `CustomServer` object can finally be started with the `Run(stopCh <-chan struct{})` error method. This is called by the `Run` method of the options in our example. That is, `CustomServerOptions.Run`:

- Creates the config
- Completes the config
- Creates the `CustomServer`
- Calls `CustomServer.Run`

This is the code:

```
func (o CustomServerOptions) Run(stopCh <-chan struct{}) error {
    config, err := o.Config()
    if err != nil {
        return err
    }

    server, err := config.Complete().New()
    if err != nil {
        return err
    }

    server.GenericAPIServer.AddPostStartHook("start-pizza-apiserver-informers",
        func(context genericapiserver.PostStartHookContext) error {
            config.GenericConfig.SharedInformerFactory.Start(context.StopCh)
            o.SharedInformerFactory.Start(context.StopCh)
            return nil
        },
    )

    return server.GenericAPIServer.PrepareRun().Run(stopCh)
}
```

The `PrepareRun()` call wires up the OpenAPI specification and might do other post-API-installation operations. After calling it, the `Run` method starts the actual server. It blocks until `stopCh` is closed.

This example also wires a *post-start hook* named `start-pizza-apiserver-informers`. As the name suggests, a post-start hook is called after the HTTPS server is up and listening. Here, it starts the shared informer factories.

Note that even local in-process informers of resources provided by the custom API server itself speak via HTTPS to the localhost interface. So it makes sense to start them after the server is up and the HTTPS port is listening.

Also note that the */healthz* endpoint returns success only after all post-start hooks have finished successfully.

With all the little plumbing pieces in place, the `pizza-apiserver` project wraps everything up into a `cobra` command:

```
// NewCommandStartCustomServer provides a CLI handler for 'start master' command
// with a default CustomServerOptions.
func NewCommandStartCustomServer(
    defaults *CustomServerOptions,
    stopCh <-chan struct{},
) *cobra.Command {
    o := *defaults
    cmd := &cobra.Command{
        Short: "Launch a custom API server",
        Long:  "Launch a custom API server",
        RunE: func(c *cobra.Command, args []string) error {
            if err := o.Complete(); err != nil {
                return err
            }
            if err := o.Validate(); err != nil {
                return err
```

```
        }
        if err := o.Run(stopCh); err != nil {
            return err
        }
        return nil
    },
}

flags := cmd.Flags()
o.RecommendedOptions.AddFlags(flags)

return cmd
}
```

With `NewCommandStartCustomServer` the `main()` method of the process is pretty simple:

```
func main() {
    logs.InitLogs()
    defer logs.FlushLogs()

    stopCh := genericapiserver.SetupSignalHandler()
    options := server.NewCustomServerOptions(os.Stdout, os.Stderr)
    cmd := server.NewCommandStartCustomServer(options, stopCh)
    cmd.Flags().AddGoFlagSet(flag.CommandLine)
    if err := cmd.Execute(); err != nil {
        klog.Fatal(err)
    }
}
```

Note especially the call to `SetupSignalHandler`: it wires Unix signal handling. On `SIGINT` (triggered when you press Ctrl-C in a terminal) and `SIGKILL`, the stop channel is closed. The stop channel is passed to the running custom API server, and it shuts down when the stop channel is closed. Hence, the main loop will initiate a shutdown when one of the signals is received. This shutdown is graceful in the sense that running requests are finished (for up to 60 seconds by default) before termination. It also makes sure that all requests are sent to the audit backend and no audit data is dropped. After all that, `cmd.Execute()` will return and the process will terminate.

The First Start

Now we have everything in place to start the custom API server for the first time. Assuming you have a cluster configured in *~/.kube/config*, you can use it for delegated authentication and authorization:

```
$ cd $GOPATH/src/github.com/programming-kubernetes/pizza-apiserver
$ etcd &
$ go run . --etcd-servers localhost:2379 \
    --authentication-kubeconfig ~/.kube/config \
    --authorization-kubeconfig ~/.kube/config \
    --kubeconfig ~/.kube/config
I0331 11:33:25.702320   64244 plugins.go:158]
  Loaded 3 mutating admission controller(s) successfully in the following order:
    NamespaceLifecycle,MutatingAdmissionWebhook,PizzaToppings.
I0331 11:33:25.702344   64244 plugins.go:161]
```

```
Loaded 1 validating admission controller(s) successfully in the following order:
    ValidatingAdmissionWebhook.
I0331 11:33:25.714148    64244 secure_serving.go:116] Serving securely on [::]:443
```

It will start up and start serving the generic API endpoints:

```
$ curl -k https://localhost:443/healthz
ok
```

We can also list the discovery endpoint, but the result is not very satisfying yet—we have not created an API, so the discovery is empty:

```
$ curl -k https://localhost:443/apis
{
  "kind": "APIGroupList",
  "groups": []
}
```

Let's take a look from a higher level:

- We have started a custom API server with the recommended options and config.
- We have a standard handler chain that includes delegated authentication, delegated authorization, and auditing.
- We have an HTTPS server running and serving requests for the generic endpoints: */logs*, */metrics*, */version*, */healthz*, and */apis*.

Figure 8-3 shows this from 10,000 feet.

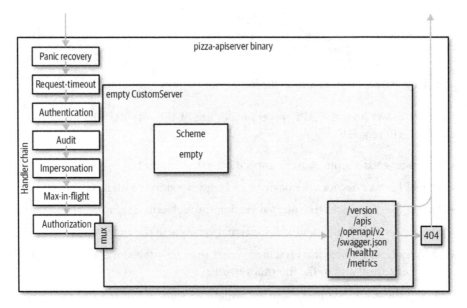

Figure 8-3. The custom API server without APIs

Internal Types and Conversion

Now that we've set up a running custom API server, it's time to actually implement APIs. Before doing so, we have to understand API versions and how they are handled inside of an API server.

Every API server serves a number of resources and versions (see Figure 2-3). Some resources have multiple versions. To make multiple versions of a resource possible, the API server converts between versions.

To avoid quadratic growth of necessary conversions between versions, API servers use an *internal version* when implementing the actual API logic. The internal version is also often called *hub version* because it is a kind of hub that every other version is converted to and from (see Figure 8-4). The internal API logic is implemented just once for that hub version.

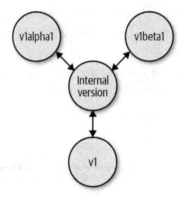

Figure 8-4. Conversion from and to the hub version

Figure 8-5 shows how the API servers make use of the internal version in the life-cycle of an API request:

- The user sends a request using a specific version (e.g., v1).
- The API server decodes the payload and converts it to the internal version.
- The API server passes the internal version through admission and validation.
- The API logic is implemented for internal versions in the registry.
- etcd reads and writes the versioned object (e.g., v2—the storage version); that is, it converts from and to the internal version.
- Finally, the result is converted to the request version, in this case, v1.

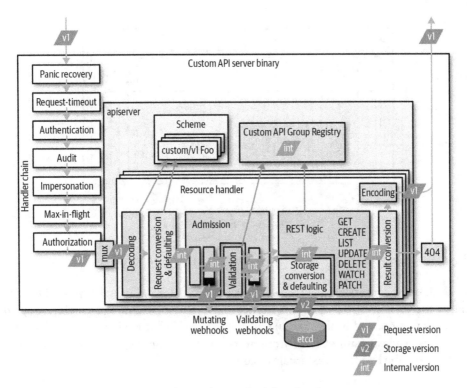

Figure 8-5. Conversion of API objects during the lifecycle of a request

On each edge between the internal hub version and the external version, a conversion takes place. In Figure 8-6, you can count the number of conversions per request handler. In a writing operation (like creation and update), at least four conversions are done, and even more if admission webhooks are deployed in the cluster. As you can see, conversion is a crucial operation in every API implementation.

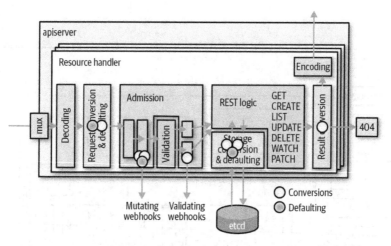

Figure 8-6. Conversions and defaulting during the lifecycle of a request

In addition to conversion, Figure 8-6 also shows when *defaulting* takes place. Default-ing is the process of filling in unspecified field values. Defaulting is highly coupled with conversion, and is always done on the external version when it comes in from the user's request, from `etcd` or from an admission webhook, but never when con-verted from the hub to the external version.

Conversion is crucial for the API server mechanics. It is also crucial that all conversions (back and forth) must be correct in the sense of being *roundtrippable*. Roundtrippable means that we can convert back and forth in the version graph (Figure 8-4) starting with ran-dom values, and we never lose any information; that is, conversions are bijective, or one-to-one. For example, we must be able to go from a random (but valid) `v1` object to the internal hub type, then to `v1alpha1`, back to the internal hub type, and then back to `v1`. The resulting object must be equivalent to the original.

Making types roundtrippable often requires a lot of thought; it nearly always drives the API design of new versions and also influ-ences the extension of old types in order to store the information that new versions carry.

In short: getting roundtripping right is hard—very hard at times. See "Roundtrip Testing" on page 177 to learn how roundtripping can be tested effectively.

Defaulting logic can changed during the lifecycle of an API server. Imagine you add a new field to a type. The user might have old objects stored on disk, or the `etcd` may have old objects. If that new field has a default, this field value is set when the old, stored objects are sent to the API server, or when the user retrieves one of the old objects from etcd. It looks like the new field has existed forever, while in reality the defaulting process in the API server sets the field values during the processing of the request.

Writing the API Types

As we have seen, to add an API to the custom API server, we have to write the internal hub version types and the external version types and convert between them. This is what we'll look at now for the pizza example project (*http://bit.ly/2x9C3gR*).

API types are traditionally placed into the *pkg/apis/group-name* package of the project with *pkg/apis/group-name/types.go* for internal types and *pkg/apis/group-name/version/types.go* for the external versions). So, for our example, *pkg/apis/restaurant, pkg/apis/restaurant/v1alpha1/types.go*, and *pkg/apis/restaurant/v1beta1/types.go*.

Conversions will be created at *pkg/apis/group-name/version/zz_generated.conversion.go* (for conversion-gen output) and *pkg/apis/group-name/version/conversion.go* for custom conversions written by the developer.

In a similar way, defaulting code will be created for defaulter-gen output at *pkg/apis/group-name/version/zz_generated.defaults.go* and at *pkg/apis/group-name/version/defaults.go* for custom defaulting code written by the developer. We have both *pkg/apis/restaurant/v1alpha1/defaults.go* and *pkg/apis/restaurant/v1beta1/defaults.go* in our example.

We go into more detail about conversion and defaulting in "Conversions" on page 172 and "Defaulting" on page 176.

With the exception of conversion and defaulting, we've seen most of this process already for CustomResourceDefinitions in "Anatomy of a type" on page 88. Native types for the external versions in our custom API server are defined exactly the same way.

In addition, we have *pkg/apis/group-name/types.go* for the internal types, the hub types. The main difference is that in the latter the SchemeGroupVersion in the *register.go* file references runtime.APIVersionInternal (which is a shortcut for "__internal").

```
// SchemeGroupVersion is group version used to register these objects
var SchemeGroupVersion = schema.GroupVersion{Group: GroupName, Version:
runtime.APIVersionInternal}
```

Another difference between pkg/apis/*group-name*/types.go and the external type files is the lack of JSON and protobuf tags.

JSON tags are used by some generators to detect whether a *types.go* file is for an external version or the internal version. So always drop those tags when copying and pasting external types in order to create or update the internal types.

Last but not least, there is a helper to install all versions of an API group into a scheme. This helper is traditionally placed in *pkg/apis/group-name/install/install.go*. For our custom API server *pkg/apis/restaurant/install/install.go*, it looks as simple as this:

```
// Install registers the API group and adds types to a scheme
func Install(scheme *runtime.Scheme) {
    utilruntime.Must(restaurant.AddToScheme(scheme))
    utilruntime.Must(v1beta1.AddToScheme(scheme))
    utilruntime.Must(v1alpha1.AddToScheme(scheme))
    utilruntime.Must(scheme.SetVersionPriority(
        v1beta1.SchemeGroupVersion,
        v1alpha1.SchemeGroupVersion,
    ))
}
```

Because we have multiple versions, the priority has to be defined. This order will be used to determine the default storage version of the resource. It used to also play a role in version selection in internal clients (clients that return internal version objects; refer back to the note "Versioned Clients and Internal Clients in the Past" on page 52). But internal clients are deprecated and are going away. Even code inside an API server will use an external version client in the future.

Conversions

Conversion takes an object in one version and converts it into an object in another version. Conversion is implemented through conversion functions, some of them manually written (placed into *pkg/apis/group-name/version/conversion.go* by convention), and others autogenerated by conversion-gen (*http://bit.ly/31RewiP*) (placed by convention into *pkg/apis/group-name/version/zz_generated.conversion.go*).

Conversion is initiated via a scheme (see "Scheme" on page 65) using the Convert() method, passing the source object in and the target object out:

```
func (s *Scheme) Convert(in, out interface{}, context interface{}) error
```

The context is described as follows:

```
// ...an optional field that callers may use to pass info to conversion functions.
```

It is used only in very special cases and is usually nil. Later in the chapter we will look at the conversion function scope, which allows us to access this context from within conversion functions.

To do the actual conversion, the scheme knows about all the Golang API types, their GroupVersionKinds, and the conversion functions between GroupVersionKinds. For this, conversion-gen registers generated conversion functions via the local scheme builder. In our example custom API server, the *zz_generated.conversion.go* file starts like this:

```
func init() {
    localSchemeBuilder.Register(RegisterConversions)
}

// RegisterConversions adds conversion functions to the given scheme.
// Public to allow building arbitrary schemes.
func RegisterConversions(s *runtime.Scheme) error {
    if err := s.AddGeneratedConversionFunc(
        (*Topping)(nil),
        (*restaurant.Topping)(nil),
        func(a, b interface{}, scope conversion.Scope) error {
            return Convert_v1alpha1_Topping_To_restaurant_Topping(
                a.(*Topping),
                b.(*restaurant.Topping),
                scope,
            )
        },
    ); err != nil {
        return err
    }
    ...
    return nil
}

...
```

The function Convert_v1alpha1_Topping_To_restaurant_Topping() is generated. It takes a v1alpha1 object and converts it to the internal type.

> The preceding complicated type conversion turns the typed conversion function into a uniformly typed func(a, b interface{}, scope conversion.Scope) error. The scheme uses the latter types because it can call them without the use of reflection. Reflection is slow due to the many necessary allocations.

The manually written conversions in *conversion.go* take precedence during generation in the sense that conversion-gen skips generation for types if it finds a manually written function in the packages with the *Convert_source-package-basename_KindTo_target-package-basename_Kind* conversion function naming pattern. For example:

```
func Convert_v1alpha1_PizzaSpec_To_restaurant_PizzaSpec(
    in *PizzaSpec,
    out *restaurant.PizzaSpec,
    s conversion.Scope,
) error {
```

```
    ...
    return nil
}
```

In the simplest case, conversion functions just copy over values from the source to the target object. But for the previous example, which converts a `v1alpha1` pizza specification to the internal type, simple copying is not enough. We have to adapt the different structure, which actually looks like the following:

```
func Convert_v1alpha1_PizzaSpec_To_restaurant_PizzaSpec(
    in *PizzaSpec,
    out *restaurant.PizzaSpec,
    s conversion.Scope,
) error {
    idx := map[string]int{}
    for _, top := range in.Toppings {
        if i, duplicate := idx[top]; duplicate {
            out.Toppings[i].Quantity++
            continue
        }
        idx[top] = len(out.Toppings)
        out.Toppings = append(out.Toppings, restaurant.PizzaTopping{
            Name: top,
            Quantity: 1,
        })
    }

    return nil
}
```

Clearly, no code generation can be so clever as to foresee what the user intended when defining these different types.

Note that during conversion the source object must never be mutated. But it is completely normal and, often for performance reasons, highly recommended to reuse data structures of the source in the target object if the types match.

This is so important that we reiterate it in a warning, because it has implications not only for the implementation of conversion but also for callers of conversions and consumers of conversion output.

Conversion functions must not mutate the source object, but the output is allowed to share data structures with the source. This means that consumers of conversion output have to make sure not to mutate an object if the original object must not be mutated.

For example, assume you have a pod *core.Pod in the internal version, and you convert it to v1 as podv1 *corev1.Pod, and mutate the resulting podv1. This might also mutate the original pod. If the pod came from an informer, this is highly dangerous because informers have a shared cache and mutating pod makes the cache inconsistent.

So, be aware of this property of conversion and do deep copies if necessary to avoid undesired and potentially dangerous mutations.

While this sharing of data structures leads to some risk, it also can avoid unnecessary allocations in many situations. Generated code goes so far that the generator compares source and target structs and uses Golang's unsafe packages to convert pointers to structs of the same memory layout via a simple type conversion. Because the internal type and the v1beta1 types for a pizza in our example have the same memory layout, we get this:

```
func autoConvert_restaurant_PizzaSpec_To_v1beta1_PizzaSpec(
    in *restaurant.PizzaSpec,
    out *PizzaSpec,
    s conversion.Scope,
) error {
    out.Toppings = *(*[]PizzaTopping)(unsafe.Pointer(&in.Toppings))
    return nil
}
```

On the machine language level, this is a NOOP and therefore as fast as it can get. It avoids allocating a slice in this case and copying item by item from in to out.

Last but not least, some words about the third argument of conversion functions: the conversion scope conversion.Scope.

The conversion scope provides access to a number of conversion metalevel values. For example, it allows us to access the context value that is passed to the scheme's Convert(in, out interface{}, context interface{}) error method via:

```
s.Meta().Context
```

It also allows us to call the scheme conversion for subtypes via s.Convert, or without considering the registered conversion functions at all via s.DefaultConvert.

In most conversion cases, though, there is no need to use the scope at all. You can just ignore its existence for the sake of simplicity until you hit a tricky situation where more context than the source and target object is necessary.

Defaulting

Defaulting is the step in an API request's lifecycle that sets default values for omitted fields in incoming objects (from the client or from etcd). For example, a pod has a restartPolicy field. If the user does not specify it, a value will default to Always.

Imagine we are using a very old Kubernetes version around the year 2014. The field restartPolicy was just introduced to the system in the latest release at that time. After an upgrade of your cluster, there is a pod in etcd without the restartPolicy field. A kubectl get pod would read the old pod from etcd and the defaulting code would add the default value Always. From the user's point of view, magically the old pod suddenly has the new restartPolicy field.

Refer back to Figure 8-6 to see where defaulting takes place today in the Kubernetes request pipeline. Note that defaulting is done only for external types, not internal types.

Now let's look at the code that does defaulting. Defaulting is initiated by the *k8s.io/apiserver* code via the scheme, similarly to conversion. Hence, we have to register defaulting functions into the scheme for our custom types.

Again, similarly to conversions, most defaulting code is just generated with the defaulter-gen (*http://bit.ly/2J108vK*) binary. It traverses API types and creates defaulting functions in *pkg/apis/group-name/version/zz_generated.defaults.go*. The code doesn't do anything by default other than calling defaulting functions for the substructures.

You can define your own defaulting logic by following the defaulting function naming pattern SetDefaults*Kind*:

```
func SetDefaultsKind(obj *Type) {
    ...
}
```

In addition, and unlike with conversions, we have to call the registration of the generated function on the local scheme builder manually. This is unfortunately not done automatically:

```
func init() {
    localSchemeBuilder.Register(RegisterDefaults)
}
```

Here, RegisterDefaults is generated inside package *pkg/apis/group-name/version/zz_generated.defaults.go*.

For defaulting code, it is crucial to know when a field was set by the user and when it wasn't. This is not that clear in many cases.

Golang has zero values for every type and sets them if a field is not found in the passed JSON or protobuf. Imagine a default of `true` for a boolean field `foo`. The zero value is `false`. Unfortunately, it is not clear whether `false` was set due to the user's input or because `false` is just the zero value of booleans.

To avoid this situation, often a pointer type must be used in the Golang API types (e.g., `*bool` in the preceding case). A user-provided `false` would lead to a non-nil boolean pointer to a `false` value, and a user-provided `true` would lead to the non-nil boolean pointer and a `true` value. A not-provided field leads to `nil`. This can be detected in the defaulting code:

```
func SetDefaultsKind(obj *Type) {
    if obj.Foo == nil {
        x := true
        obj.Foo = &x
    }
}
```

This gives the desired semantics: "foo defaults to true."

This trick of using a pointer works for primitive types like strings. For maps and arrays, it is often hard to reach roundtrippability without identifying `nil` maps/arrays and empty maps/arrays. Most defaulters for maps and arrays in Kubernetes therefore apply the default in both cases, working around encoding and decoding bugs.

Roundtrip Testing

Getting conversions right is hard. Roundtrip tests are an essential tool to check automatically in a randomized test that conversions behave as planned and do not lose data when converting from and to all known group versions.

Roundtrip tests are usually placed with the *install.go* file (for example, into *pkg/apis/restaurant/install/roundtrip_test.go*) and just call the roundtrip test functions from API Machinery:

```
import (
    ...
    "k8s.io/apimachinery/pkg/api/apitesting/roundtrip"
    restaurantfuzzer "github.com/programming-kubernetes/pizza-apiserver/pkg/apis/
    restaurant/fuzzer"
)

func TestRoundTripTypes(t *testing.T) {
    roundtrip.RoundTripTestForAPIGroup(t, Install, restaurantfuzzer.Funcs)
}
```

Internally, the `RoundTripTestForAPIGroup` call installs the API group into a temporary scheme using the `Install` functions. Then it creates random objects in the internal version using the given fuzzer, and then converts them to some external version and back to internal. The resulting objects must be equivalent to the original. This test is done hundreds or thousand of times with all external versions.

A *fuzzer* is a function that return a slice of randomizer functions for the internal types and their subtypes. In our example, the fuzzer is placed into the package *pkg/apis/restaurant/fuzzer/fuzzer.go* and contains a randomizer for the spec struct:

```
// Funcs returns the fuzzer functions for the restaurant api group.
var Funcs = func(codecs runtimeserializer.CodecFactory) []interface{} {
    return []interface{}{
        func(s *restaurant.PizzaSpec, c fuzz.Continue) {
            c.FuzzNoCustom(s) // fuzz first without calling this function again

            // avoid empty Toppings because that is defaulted
            if len(s.Toppings) == 0 {
                s.Toppings = []restaurant.PizzaTopping{
                    {"salami", 1},
                    {"mozzarella", 1},
                    {"tomato", 1},
                }
            }

            seen := map[string]bool{}
            for i := range s.Toppings {
                // make quantity strictly positive and of reasonable size
                s.Toppings[i].Quantity = 1 + c.Intn(10)

                // remove duplicates
                for {
                    if !seen[s.Toppings[i].Name] {
                        break
                    }
                    s.Toppings[i].Name = c.RandString()
                }
                seen[s.Toppings[i].Name] = true
            }
        },
    }
}
```

If no randomizer function is given, the underlying library *github.com/google/gofuzz* (*http://bit.ly/2KJrb27*) will generically try to fuzz the object by setting random values for base types and diving recursively into pointers, structs, maps, and slices, eventually calling custom randomizer functions if they are given by the developer.

When writing a randomizer function for one of the types, it is convenient to call c.FuzzNoCustom(s) first. It randomizes the given object s and also calls custom functions for substructures, but not for s itself. Then the developer can restrict and fix the random values to make the object valid.

It is important to make fuzzers as general as possible in order to cover as many valid objects as possible. If the fuzzer is too restrictive, the test coverage will be bad. In many cases during the development of Kubernetes, regressions were not caught because the fuzzers in place were not good.

On the other hand, a fuzzer only has to consider objects that validate and are the projection of actual objects definable in the external versions. Often you have to restrict the random values set by c.FuzzNoCustom(s) in a way that the randomized object becomes valid. For example, a string holding a URL does not have to round-trip for arbitrary values if validation will reject arbitrary strings anyway.

Our preceding PizzaSpec example first calls c.FuzzNoCustom(s) and then fixes up the object by:

- Defaulting the nil case for toppings
- Setting a reasonable quantity for each topping (without that, the conversion to v1alpha1 will explode in complexity, introducing high quantities into a string list)
- Normalizing the topping names, as we know that duplicated toppings in a pizza spec will never roundtrip (for the internal types, note that v1alpha1 types have duplication)

Validation

Incoming objects are validated shortly after they have been deserialized, defaulted, and converted to the internal version. Figure 8-5 showed earlier how validation is done between mutating admission plug-ins and validating admission plug-ins, long before the actual creation or update logic is executed.

This means validation has to be implemented only once for the internal version, not for all external versions. This has the advantage that it obviously saves implementation work and also ensures consistency between versions. On the other hand, it means that validation errors do not refer to the external version. This can actually be observed with Kubernetes resources, but in practice it is no big deal.

In this section, we'll look at the implementation of validation functions. The wiring into the custom API server—namely, calling validation from the strategy that configures the generic registry—will be covered in the next section. In other words, Figure 8-5 is slightly misleading in favor of visual simplicity.

For now it should be enough to look at the entry point into the validation inside the strategy:

```
func (pizzaStrategy) Validate(
    ctx context.Context, obj runtime.Object,
) field.ErrorList {
    pizza := obj.(*restaurant.Pizza)
    return validation.ValidatePizza(pizza)
}
```

This calls out to the Validate*Kind*(obj *Kind*) field.ErrorList validation function in the validation package of the API group pkg/apis/*group*/*validation*.

The validation functions return an error list. They are usually written in the same style, appending return values to an error list while recursively diving into the type, one validation function per struct:

```
// ValidatePizza validates a Pizza.
func ValidatePizza(f *restaurant.Pizza) field.ErrorList {
    allErrs := field.ErrorList{}

    errs := ValidatePizzaSpec(&f.Spec, field.NewPath("spec"))
    allErrs = append(allErrs, errs...)

    return allErrs
}

// ValidatePizzaSpec validates a PizzaSpec.
func ValidatePizzaSpec(
    s *restaurant.PizzaSpec,
    fldPath *field.Path,
) field.ErrorList {
    allErrs := field.ErrorList{}

    prevNames := map[string]bool{}
    for i := range s.Toppings {
        if s.Toppings[i].Quantity <= 0 {
            allErrs = append(allErrs, field.Invalid(
                fldPath.Child("toppings").Index(i).Child("quantity"),
                s.Toppings[i].Quantity,
                "cannot be negative or zero",
            ))
        }
        if len(s.Toppings[i].Name) == 0 {
            allErrs = append(allErrs, field.Invalid(
                fldPath.Child("toppings").Index(i).Child("name"),
                s.Toppings[i].Name,
                "cannot be empty",
            ))
        } else {
            if prevNames[s.Toppings[i].Name] {
                allErrs = append(allErrs, field.Invalid(
                    fldPath.Child("toppings").Index(i).Child("name"),
                    s.Toppings[i].Name,
                    "must be unique",
                ))
            }
            prevNames[s.Toppings[i].Name] = true
```

```
        }
    }
    return allErrs
}
```

Note how the field path is maintained using `Child` and `Index` calls. The field path is the JSON path, which is printed in case of errors.

Often there is an additional set of validation functions that differs slightly for updates (while the preceding set is used for creation). In our example API server, this could look like the following:

```
func (pizzaStrategy) ValidateUpdate(
    ctx context.Context,
    obj, old runtime.Object,
) field.ErrorList {
    objPizza := obj.(*restaurant.Pizza)
    oldPizza := old.(*restaurant.Pizza)
    return validation.ValidatePizzaUpdate(objPizza, oldPizza)
}
```

This can be used to verify that no read-only fields are changed. Often an update validation calls the normal validation functions as well and only adds checks relevant for the update.

Validation is the right place to restrict object names on creation—for example, to be single-word only, or to not include any non-alpha-numeric characters.

Actually, any `ObjectMeta` field can technically be restricted in a custom way, though that's not desirable for many fields because it might break core API machinery behavior. A number of resources restrict the names because, for example, the name will show up in other systems or in other contexts that require a specially formatted name.

But even if there are special `ObjectMeta` validations in place in a custom API server, the generic registry will validate against generic rules in any case, after the custom validation has passed. This allows us to return more specific error messages from the custom code first.

Registry and Strategy

So far, we have seen how API types are defined and validate. The next step is the implementation of the REST logic for those API types. Figure 8-7 shows the registry as a central part of the implementation of an API group. The generic REST request handler code in *k8s.io/apiserver* calls out to the registry.

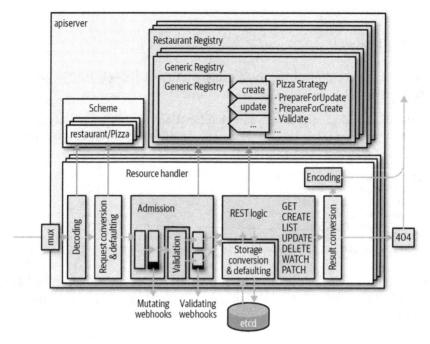

Figure 8-7. Resource storage and generic registry

Generic registry

The REST logic is usually implemented by what is called the *generic registry*. It is—as the name suggests—a generic implementation of the registry interfaces in the package *k8s.io/apiserver/pkg/registry/rest*.

The generic registry implements the default REST behavior for "normal" resources. Nearly all Kubernetes resources use this implementation. Only a few, specifically those that do not persist objects (e.g., `SubjectAccessReview`; see "Delegated Authorization" on page 157), have custom implementations.

In *k8s.io/apiserver/pkg/registry/rest/rest.go* you will find many interfaces, loosely corresponding to HTTP verbs and certain API functionalities. If an interface is implemented by a registry, the API endpoint code will offer certain REST features. Because the generic registry implements most of the *k8s.io/apiserver/pkg/registry/rest* interfaces, resources that use it will support all the default Kubernetes HTTP verbs (see "The HTTP Interface of the API Server" on page 20). Here is a list of those interfaces that are implemented, with the GoDoc description from the Kubernetes source code:

`CollectionDeleter`
An object that can delete a collection of RESTful resources

Creater
> An object that can create an instance of a RESTful object

CreaterUpdater
> A storage object that must support both create and update operations

Exporter
> An object that knows how to strip a RESTful resource for export

Getter
> An object that can retrieve a named RESTful resource

GracefulDeleter
> An object that knows how to pass deletion options to allow delayed deletion of a RESTful object

Lister
> An object that can retrieve resources that match the provided field and label criteria

Patcher
> A storage object that supports both get and update

Scoper
> An object that must be specified and indicates what scope the resource

Updater
> An object that can update an instance of a RESTful object

Watcher
> An object that should be implemented by all storage objects that want to offer the ability to watch for changes through the Watch API

Let's look at one of the interfaces, Creater:

```
// Creater is an object that can create an instance of a RESTful object.
type Creater interface {
    // New returns an empty object that can be used with Create after request
    // data has been put into it.
    // This object must be a pointer type for use with Codec.DecodeInto([]byte,
    // runtime.Object)
    New() runtime.Object

    // Create creates a new version of a resource.
    Create(
        ctx context.Context,
        obj runtime.Object,
        createValidation ValidateObjectFunc,
        options *metav1.CreateOptions,
    ) (runtime.Object, error)
}
```

A registry implementing this interface will be able to create objects. In contrast to `NamedCreater`, the name of the new object either comes from `ObjectMeta.Name` or is generated via `ObjectMeta.GenerateName`. If a registry implements `NamedCreater`, the name can also be passed through the HTTP path.

It is important to understand that the implemented interfaces determine which verbs will be supported by the API endpoint that is created while installing the API into the custom API server. See "API Installation" on page 186 for how this is done in the code.

Strategy

The generic registry can be customized to a certain degree using an object called a *strategy*. The strategy provides callbacks to functionality like validation, as we saw in "Validation" on page 179.

The strategy implements the REST strategy interfaces listed here with their GoDoc description (see *k8s.io/apiserver/pkg/registry/rest* for their definitions):

RESTCreateStrategy
:   Defines the minimum validation, accepted input, and name generation behavior to create an object that follows Kubernetes API conventions.

RESTDeleteStrategy
:   Defines deletion behavior on an object that follows Kubernetes API conventions.

RESTGracefulDeleteStrategy
:   Must be implemented by the registry that supports graceful deletion.

GarbageCollectionDeleteStrategy
:   Must be implemented by the registry that wants to orphan dependents by default.

RESTExportStrategy
:   Defines how to export a Kubernetes object.

RESTUpdateStrategy
:   Defines the minimum validation, accepted input, and name generation behavior to update an object that follows Kubernetes API conventions.

Let's look again at the strategy for the creation case:

```
type RESTCreateStrategy interface {
    runtime.ObjectTyper
    // The name generator is used when the standard GenerateName field is set.
    // The NameGenerator will be invoked prior to validation.
    names.NameGenerator

    // NamespaceScoped returns true if the object must be within a namespace.
    NamespaceScoped() bool
    // PrepareForCreate is invoked on create before validation to normalize
```

```
// the object. For example: remove fields that are not to be persisted,
// sort order-insensitive list fields, etc. This should not remove fields
// whose presence would be considered a validation error.
//
// Often implemented as a type check and an initailization or clearing of
// status. Clear the status because status changes are internal. External
// callers of an api (users) should not be setting an initial status on
// newly created objects.
PrepareForCreate(ctx context.Context, obj runtime.Object)
// Validate returns an ErrorList with validation errors or nil. Validate
// is invoked after default fields in the object have been filled in
// before the object is persisted. This method should not mutate the
// object.
Validate(ctx context.Context, obj runtime.Object) field.ErrorList
// Canonicalize allows an object to be mutated into a canonical form. This
// ensures that code that operates on these objects can rely on the common
// form for things like comparison. Canonicalize is invoked after
// validation has succeeded but before the object has been persisted.
// This method may mutate the object. Often implemented as a type check or
// empty method.
Canonicalize(obj runtime.Object)
}
```

The embedded ObjectTyper recognizes objects; that is, it checks whether an object in a request is supported by the registry. This is important to create the right kind of objects (e.g., via a "foo" resource, only "Foo" resources should be created).

The NameGenerator obviously generates names from the ObjectMeta.GenerateName field.

Via NamespaceScoped the strategy can support cluster-wide or namespaced resources by returning either false or true.

The PrepareForCreate method is called with the incoming object before validation.

The Validate method we've seen before in "Validation" on page 179: it's the entry point to the validation functions.

Finally, the Canonicalize method does normalization (e.g., sorting of slices).

Wiring a strategy into the generic registry

The strategy object is plugged into a generic registry instance. Here is the REST storage constructor for our custom API server on GitHub (*http://bit.ly/2Y0Mtyn*):

```
// NewREST returns a RESTStorage object that will work against API services.
func NewREST(
    scheme *runtime.Scheme,
    optsGetter generic.RESTOptionsGetter,
) (*registry.REST, error) {
    strategy := NewStrategy(scheme)

    store := &genericregistry.Store{
        NewFunc:       func() runtime.Object { return &restaurant.Pizza{} },
        NewListFunc:   func() runtime.Object { return &restaurant.PizzaList{} },
        PredicateFunc: MatchPizza,
```

```
            DefaultQualifiedResource: restaurant.Resource("pizzas"),

            CreateStrategy: strategy,
            UpdateStrategy: strategy,
            DeleteStrategy: strategy,
        }
    options := &generic.StoreOptions{
        RESTOptions: optsGetter,
        AttrFunc: GetAttrs,
    }
    if err := store.CompleteWithOptions(options); err != nil {
        return nil, err
    }
    return &registry.REST{store}, nil
}
```

It instantiates the generic registry object `genericregistry.Store` and sets a few fields. Many of these fields are optional and `store.CompleteWithOptions` will default them if they are not set by the developer.

You can see how the custom strategy is first instantiated via the `NewStrategy` constructor and then plugged into the registry for `create`, `update`, and `delete` operators.

In addition, the `NewFunc` is set to create a new object instance, and the `NewListFunc` field is set to create a new object list. The `PredicateFunc` translates a selector (which could be passed to a list request) into a predicate function, filtering runtime objects.

The returned object is a REST registry, just a simple wrapper in our example project (*http://bit.ly/2Rxcv6G*) around the generic registry object to make the type our own:

```
type REST struct {
    *genericregistry.Store
}
```

With this we have everything to instantiate our API and wire it into the custom API server. In the following section we'll see how to create an HTTP handler out of it.

API Installation

To activate an API in an API server, two steps are necessary:

1. The API version must be installed into the API type's (and conversion and defaulting functions') server scheme.

2. The API version must be installed into the server HTTP multiplexer (mux).

The first step is usually done using `init` functions somewhere centrally in the API server bootstrapping. This is done in *pkg/apiserver/apiserver.go* in our example custom API server, where the `serverConfig` and `CustomServer` objects are defined (see "Options and Config Pattern and Startup Plumbing" on page 160):

```
import (
    ...
    "k8s.io/apimachinery/pkg/runtime"
    "k8s.io/apimachinery/pkg/runtime/serializer"

    "github.com/programming-kubernetes/pizza-apiserver/pkg/apis/restaurant/install"
)

var (
    Scheme = runtime.NewScheme()
    Codecs = serializer.NewCodecFactory(Scheme)
)
```

Then for each API group that should be served, we call the `Install()` function:

```
func init() {
    install.Install(Scheme)
}
```

For technical reasons, we also have to add some discovery-related types to the scheme
(this will probably go away in future versions of *k8s.io/apiserver*):

```
func init() {
    // we need to add the options to empty v1
    // TODO: fix the server code to avoid this
    metav1.AddToGroupVersion(Scheme, schema.GroupVersion{Version: "v1"})
    // TODO: keep the generic API server from wanting this
    unversioned := schema.GroupVersion{Group: "", Version: "v1"}
    Scheme.AddUnversionedTypes(unversioned,
        &metav1.Status{},
        &metav1.APIVersions{},
        &metav1.APIGroupList{},
        &metav1.APIGroup{},
        &metav1.APIResourceList{},
    )
}
```

With this we have registered our API types in the global scheme, including conversion and defaulting functions. In other words, the empty scheme of Figure 8-3 now
knows everything about our types.

The second step is to add the API group to the HTTP mux. The generic API server
code embedded into our `CustomServer` struct provides the `InstallAPIGroup(api
GroupInfo *APIGroupInfo) error` method, which sets up the whole request pipeline
for an API group.

The only thing we have to do is to provide a properly filled `APIGroupInfo` struct. We
do this in the constructor `New() (*CustomServer, error)` of the `completedConfig`
type:

```
// New returns a new instance of CustomServer from the given config.
func (c completedConfig) New() (*CustomServer, error) {
    genericServer, err := c.GenericConfig.New("pizza-apiserver",
        genericapiserver.NewEmptyDelegate())
    if err != nil {
        return nil, err
    }
```

```
    s := &CustomServer{
        GenericAPIServer: genericServer,
    }

    apiGroupInfo := genericapiserver.NewDefaultAPIGroupInfo(restaurant.GroupName,
        Scheme, metav1.ParameterCodec, Codecs)

    v1alpha1storage := map[string]rest.Storage{}

    pizzaRest := pizzastorage.NewREST(Scheme, c.GenericConfig.RESTOptionsGetter)
    v1alpha1storage["pizzas"] = customregistry.RESTInPeace(pizzaRest)

    toppingRest := toppingstorage.NewREST(
        Scheme, c.GenericConfig.RESTOptionsGetter,
    )
    v1alpha1storage["toppings"] = customregistry.RESTInPeace(toppingRest)

    apiGroupInfo.VersionedResourcesStorageMap["v1alpha1"] = v1alpha1storage

    v1beta1storage := map[string]rest.Storage{}

    pizzaRest = pizzastorage.NewREST(Scheme, c.GenericConfig.RESTOptionsGetter)
    v1beta1storage["pizzas"] = customregistry.RESTInPeace(pizzaRest)

    apiGroupInfo.VersionedResourcesStorageMap["v1beta1"] = v1beta1storage

    if err := s.GenericAPIServer.InstallAPIGroup(&apiGroupInfo); err != nil {
        return nil, err
    }

    return s, nil
}
```

The `APIGroupInfo` has references to the generic registry that we customized in "Registry and Strategy" on page 181 via a strategy. For each group version and resource, we create an instance of the registry using the implemented constructors.

The `customregistry.RESTInPeace` wrapper is just a helper that panics when the registry constructors return an error:

```
func RESTInPeace(storage rest.StandardStorage, err error) rest.StandardStorage {
    if err != nil {
        err = fmt.Errorf("unable to create REST storage: %v", err)
        panic(err)
    }
    return storage
}
```

The registry itself is version-independent, as it operates on internal objects; refer back to Figure 8-5. Hence, we call the same registry constructor for each version.

The call to `InstallAPIGroup` finally leads us to a complete custom API server ready to serve our custom API group, as shown earlier in Figure 8-7.

After all this heavy plumbing, it is time to see our new API groups in action. For this we start up the server as shown in "The First Start" on page 166. But this time the discovery info is not empty but instead shows our newly registered resource:

```
$ curl -k https://localhost:443/apis
{
  "kind": "APIGroupList",
  "groups": [
    {
      "name": "restaurant.programming-kubernetes.info",
      "versions": [
        {
          "groupVersion": "restaurant.programming-kubernetes.info/v1beta1",
          "version": "v1beta1"
        },
        {
          "groupVersion": "restaurant.programming-kubernetes.info/v1alpha1",
          "version": "v1alpha1"
        }
      ],
      "preferredVersion": {
        "groupVersion": "restaurant.programming-kubernetes.info/v1beta1",
        "version": "v1beta1"
      },
      "serverAddressByClientCIDRs": [
        {
          "clientCIDR": "0.0.0.0/0",
          "serverAddress": ":443"
        }
      ]
    }
  ]
}
```

With this, we have nearly reached our goal to serve the restaurant API. We have wired the API group versions, conversions are in place, and validation is working.

What's missing is a check that a topping mentioned in a pizza actually exists in the cluster. We could add this in the validation functions. But traditionally these are just format validation functions, which are static and do not need other resources to run.

In contrast, more complex checks are implemented in admission—the topic of the next section.

Admission

Every request passes the chain of admission plug-ins after being unmarshaled, defaulted, and converted to internal types; refer back to Figure 8-2. More precisely, requests pass admission twice:

- The mutating plug-ins
- The validating plug-ins

Admission plug-ins can be both mutating and validating and therefore can potentially get called twice by the admission mechanism:

- Once in the mutation phase, called for all mutating plug-ins sequentially
- Once in the validation phase, called (potentially parallelized) for all validating plug-ins

More precisely, a plug-in can implement both the mutating and the validating admission interface, with two different methods for both cases.

Before the separation into mutating and validating, there was just one call to each plug-in. It was nearly impossible to keep an eye on which mutation each plug-in did and which admission plug-in order therefore made sense to lead to consistent behavior for the user.

This two-step architecture at least ensures that a validation is done at the end for all plug-ins, which guarantees consistency.

In addition, the chain (i.e., the order of plug-ins for both admission phases) is the same. Plug-ins are always enabled or disabled for both phases at the same time.

Admission plug-ins, at least those implemented in Golang as described in this chapter, work with internal types. In contrast, webhook admission plug-ins (see "Admission Webhooks" on page 226) are based on external types and involve conversion on the way to the webhook and back (in case of mutating webhooks).

But after all this theory, let's get into the code.

Implementation

An admission plug-in is a type implementing:

- The admission plug-in interface `Interface`
- Optionally the `MutatingInterface`
- Optionally the `ValidatingInterface`

All three can be found in the package *k8s.io/apiserver/pkg/admission*:

```
// Operation is the type of resource operation being checked for
// admission control
type Operation string.

// Operation constants
const (
    Create  Operation = "CREATE"
    Update  Operation = "UPDATE"
    Delete  Operation = "DELETE"
```

```
    Connect Operation = "CONNECT"
)

// Interface is an abstract, pluggable interface for Admission Control
// decisions.
type Interface interface {
    // Handles returns true if this admission controller can handle the given
    // operation where operation can be one of CREATE, UPDATE, DELETE, or
    // CONNECT.
    Handles(operation Operation) bool.
}

type MutationInterface interface {
    Interface

    // Admit makes an admission decision based on the request attributes.
    Admit(a Attributes, o ObjectInterfaces) (err error)
}

// ValidationInterface is an abstract, pluggable interface for Admission Control
// decisions.
type ValidationInterface interface {
    Interface

    // Validate makes an admission decision based on the request attributes.
    // It is NOT allowed to mutate.
    Validate(a Attributes, o ObjectInterfaces) (err error)
}
```

You see that the Interface method Handles is responsible for filtering on the operation. The mutating plug-ins are called via Admit and the validating plug-ins are called via Validate.

The ObjectInterfaces gives access to helpers usually implemented by a scheme:

```
type ObjectInterfaces interface {
    // GetObjectCreater is the ObjectCreater for the requested object.
    GetObjectCreater() runtime.ObjectCreater
    // GetObjectTyper is the ObjectTyper for the requested object.
    GetObjectTyper() runtime.ObjectTyper
    // GetObjectDefaulter is the ObjectDefaulter for the requested object.
    GetObjectDefaulter() runtime.ObjectDefaulter
    // GetObjectConvertor is the ObjectConvertor for the requested object.
    GetObjectConvertor() runtime.ObjectConvertor
}
```

The attributes passed to the plug-in (via Admit or Validate or both) basically contain all the information extractable from a request that is important to implementing advanced checks:

```
// Attributes is an interface used by AdmissionController to get information
// about a request that is used to make an admission decision.
type Attributes interface {
    // GetName returns the name of the object as presented in the request.
    // On a CREATE operation, the client may omit name and rely on the
    // server to generate the name. If that is the case, this method will
    // return the empty string.
    GetName() string
```

```
// GetNamespace is the namespace associated with the request (if any).
GetNamespace() string
// GetResource is the name of the resource being requested. This is not the
// kind. For example: pods.
GetResource() schema.GroupVersionResource
// GetSubresource is the name of the subresource being requested. This is a
// different resource, scoped to the parent resource, but it may have a
// different kind.
// For instance, /pods has the resource "pods" and the kind "Pod", while
// /pods/foo/status has the resource "pods", the sub resource "status", and
// the kind "Pod" (because status operates on pods). The binding resource for
// a pod, though, may be /pods/foo/binding, which has resource "pods",
// subresource "binding", and kind "Binding".
GetSubresource() string
// GetOperation is the operation being performed.
GetOperation() Operation
// IsDryRun indicates that modifications will definitely not be persisted for
// this request. This is to prevent admission controllers with side effects
// and a method of reconciliation from being overwhelmed.
// However, a value of false for this does not mean that the modification will
// be persisted, because it could still be rejected by a subsequent
// validation step.
IsDryRun() bool
// GetObject is the object from the incoming request prior to default values
// being applied.
GetObject() runtime.Object
// GetOldObject is the existing object. Only populated for UPDATE requests.
GetOldObject() runtime.Object
// GetKind is the type of object being manipulated. For example: Pod.
GetKind() schema.GroupVersionKind
// GetUserInfo is information about the requesting user.
GetUserInfo() user.Info

// AddAnnotation sets annotation according to key-value pair. The key
// should be qualified, e.g., podsecuritypolicy.admission.k8s.io/admit-policy,
//  where "podsecuritypolicy" is the name of the plugin, "admission.k8s.io"
// is the name of the organization, and "admit-policy" is the key
// name. An error is returned if the format of key is invalid. When
// trying to overwrite annotation with a new value, an error is
// returned. Both ValidationInterface and MutationInterface are
// allowed to add Annotations.
AddAnnotation(key, value string) error
}
```

In the mutating case—that is, in the implementation of the `Admit(a Attributes)` error method—the attributes can be mutated, or more precisely, the object returned from `GetObject() runtime.Object` can.

In the validating case, mutation is not allowed.

Both cases permit the call to `AddAnnotation(key, value string) error`, which allows us to add annotations that end up in the audit output of the API server. This can be helpful in order to understand why an admission plug-in mutated or rejected a request.

Rejection is signaled by returning a non-`nil` error from `Admit` or `Validate`.

It is good practice for mutating admission plug-ins to also validate the changes in the validating admission phase. The reason is that other plug-ins, including webhook admission plug-ins, might add further changes. If an admission plug-in guarantees that certain invariants are fulfilled, only the validation step can make sure this is really the case.

Admission plug-ins have to implement the `Handles(operation Operation) bool` method from the `admission.Interface` interfaces. There is a helper in the same package called `Handler`. It can be instantiated using `NewHandler(ops ...Operation) *Handler` and implements the `Handles` method by embedding `Handler` into the custom admission plug-in:

```
type CustomAdmissionPlugin struct {
    *admission.Handler
    ...
}
```

Admission plug-ins should always check the GroupVersionKind of the passed object first:

```
func (d *PizzaToppingsPlugin) Admit(
    a admission.Attributes,
    o ObjectInterfaces,
) error {
    // we are only interested in pizzas
    if a.GetKind().GroupKind() != restaurant.Kind("Pizza") {
        return nil
    }

    ...
}
```

and similarly for the validating case:

```
func (d *PizzaToppingsPlugin) Validate(
    a admission.Attributes,
    o ObjectInterfaces,
) error {
    // we are only interested in pizzas
    if a.GetKind().GroupKind() != restaurant.Kind("Pizza") {
        return nil
    }

    ...
}
```

The full example admission implementation looks like this:

```
// Admit ensures that the object in-flight is of kind Pizza.
// In addition checks that the toppings are known.
func (d *PizzaToppingsPlugin) Validate(
    a admission.Attributes,
    _ admission.ObjectInterfaces,
) error {
    // we are only interested in pizzas
    if a.GetKind().GroupKind() != restaurant.Kind("Pizza") {
        return nil
    }

    if !d.WaitForReady() {
        return admission.NewForbidden(a, fmt.Errorf("not yet ready"))
    }

    obj := a.GetObject()
    pizza := obj.(*restaurant.Pizza)
    for _, top := range pizza.Spec.Toppings {
        err := _, err := d.toppingLister.Get(top.Name)
        if err != nil && errors.IsNotFound(err) {
            return admission.NewForbidden(
                a,
                fmt.Errorf("unknown topping: %s", top.Name),
            )
        }
    }

    return nil
}
```

It takes the following steps:

1. Checks that the passed object is of the right kind

2. Forbids access before the informers are ready

3. Verifies via the toppings informer lister that each topping mentioned in the pizza specification actually exists as a Topping object in the cluster

Note here that the lister is just an interface to the informer in-memory store. So these Get calls will be fast.

Registering

Admission plug-ins must be registered. This is done through a `Register` function:

```
func Register(plugins *admission.Plugins) {
    plugins.Register(
        "PizzaTopping",
        func(config io.Reader) (admission.Interface, error) {
            return New()
        },
    )
}
```

This function is added to the plug-in list in the `RecommendedOptions` (see "Options and Config Pattern and Startup Plumbing" on page 160):

```
func (o *CustomServerOptions) Complete() error {
    // register admission plugins
    pizzatoppings.Register(o.RecommendedOptions.Admission.Plugins)

    // add admisison plugins to the RecommendedPluginOrder
    oldOrder := o.RecommendedOptions.Admission.RecommendedPluginOrder
    o.RecommendedOptions.Admission.RecommendedPluginOrder =
        append(oldOrder, "PizzaToppings")

    return nil
}
```

Here, the `RecommendedPluginOrder` list is prepopulated with the generic admission plug-ins, which every API server should keep enabled to be a good API convention citizen in the cluster.

It is best practice not to touch the order. One reason is that getting the order right is far from trivial. Of course, adding a custom plug-in at a location other than the end of the list is fine, if it is strictly necessary for the plug-in behavior.

The user of the custom API server will be able to disable a custom admission plug-in with the usual admission chain configuration flags (`--disable-admission-plugins`, for example). By default our own plug-in is enabled, because we don't explicitly disable it.

Admission plug-ins can be configured using a configuration file. To do so, we parse the output of the `io.Reader` in the `Register` function shown previously. The `--admission-control-config-file` allows us to pass a configuration file to the plug-in, like so:

```
kind: AdmissionConfiguration
apiVersion: apiserver.k8s.io/v1alpha1
plugins:
- name: CustomAdmissionPlugin
  path: custom-admission-plugin.yaml
```

Alternatively, we can do inline configuration to have all our admission configuration in one place:

```
kind: AdmissionConfiguration
apiVersion: apiserver.k8s.io/v1alpha1
plugins:
- name: CustomAdmissionPlugin
  configuration:
    your-custom-yaml-inline-config
```

We briefly mentioned that our admission plug-in uses the toppings informer to check for the existence of toppings mentioned in the pizza. We have not talked about how to wire that into the admission plug-in. Let's do this now.

Plumbing resources

Admission plug-ins often need clients and informers or other resources to implement their behavior. We can do this resource plumbing using plug-in initializers.

There are a number of standard plug-in initializers. If your plug-in wants to be called by them, it has to implement certain interfaces with callback methods (for more on this, see *k8s.io/apiserver/pkg/admission/initializer*):

```
// WantsExternalKubeClientSet defines a function that sets external ClientSet
// for admission plugins that need it.
type WantsExternalKubeClientSet interface {
    SetExternalKubeClientSet(kubernetes.Interface)
    admission.InitializationValidator
}

// WantsExternalKubeInformerFactory defines a function that sets InformerFactory
// for admission plugins that need it.
type WantsExternalKubeInformerFactory interface {
    SetExternalKubeInformerFactory(informers.SharedInformerFactory)
    admission.InitializationValidator
}

// WantsAuthorizer defines a function that sets Authorizer for admission
// plugins that need it.
type WantsAuthorizer interface {
    SetAuthorizer(authorizer.Authorizer)
    admission.InitializationValidator
}

// WantsScheme defines a function that accepts runtime.Scheme for admission
// plugins that need it.
type WantsScheme interface {
    SetScheme(*runtime.Scheme)
    admission.InitializationValidator
}
```

Implement some of these and the plug-in gets called during launch, in order to get access to, say, Kubernetes resources or the API server global scheme.

In addition, the `admission.InitializationValidator` interface is supposed to be implemented to do a final check that the plug-in is properly set up:

```
// InitializationValidator holds ValidateInitialization functions, which are
// responsible for validation of initialized shared resources and should be
```

```
// implemented on admission plugins.
type InitializationValidator interface {
    ValidateInitialization() error
}
```

Standard initializers are great, but we need access to the toppings informer. So, let's look at how to add our own initializers. An initializer consists of:

- A Wants* interface (e.g., WantsRestaurantInformerFactory), which should be implemented by an admission plug-in:

  ```
  // WantsRestaurantInformerFactory defines a function that sets
  // InformerFactory for admission plugins that need it.
  type WantsRestaurantInformerFactory interface {
      SetRestaurantInformerFactory(informers.SharedInformerFactory)
      admission.InitializationValidator
  }
  ```

- The initializer struct, implementing admission.PluginInitializer:

  ```
  func (i restaurantInformerPluginInitializer) Initialize(
      plugin admission.Interface,
  ) {
      if wants, ok := plugin.(WantsRestaurantInformerFactory); ok {
          wants.SetRestaurantInformerFactory(i.informers)
      }
  }
  ```

  In other words, the Initialize() method checks that the passed plug-in implements the corresponding custom initializer Wants* interface. If that is the case, the initializer will call the method on the plug-in.

- Plumbing of the initializer constructor into RecommendedOptions.Extra \AdmissionInitializers (see "Options and Config Pattern and Startup Plumbing" on page 160):

  ```
  func (o *CustomServerOptions) Config() (*apiserver.Config, error) {
      ...
      o.RecommendedOptions.ExtraAdmissionInitializers =
          func(c *genericapiserver.RecommendedConfig) (
              []admission.PluginInitializer, error,
          ) {
              client, err := clientset.NewForConfig(c.LoopbackClientConfig)
              if err != nil {
                  return nil, err
              }
              informerFactory := informers.NewSharedInformerFactory(
                  client, c.LoopbackClientConfig.Timeout,
              )
              o.SharedInformerFactory = informerFactory
              return []admission.PluginInitializer{
                  custominitializer.New(informerFactory),
              }, nil
          }

      ...
  }
  ```

This code creates a loopback client for the restaurant API group, creates a corresponding informer factory, stores it in the options o, and returns a plug-in initializer for it.

Syncing Informers

If informers are used in admission plug-ins, always check first that the informers are synced before using them in the actual Admit() or Validate() functions. Reject requests with a Forbidden error before that is the case.

Using the Handler helper struct described in "Implementation" on page 190, we can do this using the Handler.WaitForReady() function easily:

```
if !d.WaitForReady() {
    return admission.NewForbidden(
        a, fmt.Errorf("not yet ready to handle request"),
    )
}
```

To include a custom informer HasSynced() method in this WaitForReady() method, add it to the ready functions from the initializer implementation, like so:

```
func (d *PizzaToppingsPlugin) SetRestaurantInformerFactory(
f informers.SharedInformerFactory) {
    d.toppingLister = f.Restaurant().V1Alpha1().Toppings().Lister()
    d.SetReadyFunc(f.Restaurant().V1Alpha1().Toppings().Informer().HasSynced)
}
```

As promised, admission is the last step in the implementation to complete our custom API server for the restaurant API group. Now we want to see it in action, but not artificially on the local machine, but rather in a real Kubernetes cluster. This means we have to take a look at the deployment of an aggregated custom API server.

Deploying Custom API Servers

In "API Services" on page 152, we saw the APIService object, which is used to register the custom API server API group versions with the aggregator inside the Kubernetes API server:

```
apiVersion: apiregistration.k8s.io/v1beta1
kind: APIService
metadata:
  name: name
spec:
  group: API-group-name
  version: API-group-version
  service:
    namespace: custom-API-server-service-namespace
    name: custom-API-server-service
```

```
caBundle: base64-caBundle
insecureSkipTLSVerify: bool
groupPriorityMinimum: 2000
versionPriority: 20
```

The `APIService` object points to a service. Usually, this service will be a normal cluster IP service: that is, the custom API server is deployed into the cluster using pods. The service forwards the requests to the pods.

Let's look at the Kubernetes manifest to implement this.

Deployment Manifests

We have the following manifests (found in the example code on GitHub (*http://bit.ly/2J6CVIz*)) that will be part of an in-cluster deployment of a custom API service:

- An `APIService` for both versions `v1alpha1`:

```
apiVersion: apiregistration.k8s.io/v1beta1
kind: APIService
metadata:
  name: v1alpha1.restaurant.programming-kubernetes.info
spec:
  insecureSkipTLSVerify: true
  group: restaurant.programming-kubernetes.info
  groupPriorityMinimum: 1000
  versionPriority: 15
  service:
    name: api
    namespace: pizza-apiserver
  version: v1alpha1
```

...and `v1beta1`:

```
apiVersion: apiregistration.k8s.io/v1beta1
kind: APIService
metadata:
  name: v1alpha1.restaurant.programming-kubernetes.info
spec:
  insecureSkipTLSVerify: true
  group: restaurant.programming-kubernetes.info
  groupPriorityMinimum: 1000
  versionPriority: 15
  service:
    name: api
    namespace: pizza-apiserver
  version: v1alpha1
```

Note here that we set `insecureSkipTLSVerify`. This is OK for development but inadequate for any production deployment. We'll see how to fix this in "Certificates and Trust" on page 205.

- A `Service` in front of the custom API server instances running in the cluster:

```
apiVersion: v1
kind: Service
metadata:
```

```
    name: api
    namespace: pizza-apiserver
spec:
  ports:
  - port: 443
    protocol: TCP
    targetPort: 8443
  selector:
    apiserver: "true"
```

- A `Deployment` (as shown here) or `DaemonSet` for the custom API server pods:

```
apiVersion: apps/v1
kind: Deployment
metadata:
  name: pizza-apiserver
  namespace: pizza-apiserver
  labels:
    apiserver: "true"
spec:
  replicas: 1
  selector:
    matchLabels:
      apiserver: "true"
  template:
    metadata:
      labels:
        apiserver: "true"
    spec:
      serviceAccountName: apiserver
      containers:
      - name: apiserver
        image: quay.io/programming-kubernetes/pizza-apiserver:latest
        imagePullPolicy: Always
        command: ["/pizza-apiserver"]
        args:
        - --etcd-servers=http://localhost:2379
        - --cert-dir=/tmp/certs
        - --secure-port=8443
        - --v=4
      - name: etcd
        image: quay.io/coreos/etcd:v3.2.24
        workingDir: /tmp
```

- A namespace for the service and the deployment to live in:

```
apiVersion: v1
kind: Namespace
metadata:
  name: pizza-apiserver
spec: {}
```

Often, the aggregated API server is deployed to some nodes reserved for control plane pods, usually called *masters*. In that case, a `DaemonSet` is a good choice to run one custom API server instance per master node. This leads to a high availability setup. Note, that API servers are stateless, which means they can easily be deployed multiple times and no leader election is necessary.

With these manifests, we are nearly done. As is so often the case, though, a secure deployment needs some more thought. You might have noticed that the pods (defined via the preceding deployment) use a custom service account, `apiserver`. This can be created via another manifest:

```
kind: ServiceAccount
apiVersion: v1
metadata:
  name: apiserver
  namespace: pizza-apiserver
```

This service account needs a number of permissions, which we can add via RBAC objects.

Setting Up RBAC

The service account of an API service first needs some generic permissions to participate in:

namespace lifecycle

Objects can be created only in an existing namespace, and are deleted when the namespace is deleted. For this the API server has to get, list, and watch namespaces.

admission webhooks

Admission webhooks configured via `MutatingWebhookConfigurations` and `ValidatedWebhookConfigurations` are called from each API server independently. For this the admission mechanism in our custom API server has to get, list, and watch these resources.

We configure both by creating an RBAC cluster role:

```
kind: ClusterRole
apiVersion: rbac.authorization.k8s.io/v1
metadata:
  name: aggregated-apiserver-clusterrole
rules:
- apiGroups: [""]
  resources: ["namespaces"]
  verbs: ["get", "watch", "list"]
- apiGroups: ["admissionregistration.k8s.io"]
  resources: ["mutatingwebhookconfigurations", "validatingwebhookconfigurations"]
  verbs: ["get", "watch", "list"]
```

and binding it to our service account `apiserver` via a `ClusterRoleBinding`:

```
apiVersion: rbac.authorization.k8s.io/v1
kind: ClusterRoleBinding
metadata:
  name: pizza-apiserver-clusterrolebinding
roleRef:
  apiGroup: rbac.authorization.k8s.io
  kind: ClusterRole
```

```
  name: aggregated-apiserver-clusterrole
subjects:
- kind: ServiceAccount
  name: apiserver
  namespace: pizza-apiserver
```

For delegated authentication and authorization, the service account has to be bound
to the preexisting RBAC role extension-apiserver-authentication-reader:

```
apiVersion: rbac.authorization.k8s.io/v1
kind: RoleBinding
metadata:
  name: pizza-apiserver-auth-reader
  namespace: kube-system
roleRef:
  apiGroup: rbac.authorization.k8s.io
  kind: Role
  name: extension-apiserver-authentication-reader
subjects:
- kind: ServiceAccount
  name: apiserver
  namespace: pizza-apiserver
```

and the preexisting RBAC cluster role system:auth-delegator:

```
apiVersion: rbac.authorization.k8s.io/v1
kind: ClusterRoleBinding
metadata:
  name: pizza-apiserver:system:auth-delegator
roleRef:
  apiGroup: rbac.authorization.k8s.io
  kind: ClusterRole
  name: system:auth-delegator
subjects:
- kind: ServiceAccount
  name: apiserver
  namespace: pizza-apiserver
```

Running the Custom API Server Insecurely

Now with all manifests in place and RBAC set up, let's deploy the API server to a real
cluster.

From a checkout of the GitHub repository (*http://bit.ly/2x9C3gR*), and with configured kubectl with cluster-admin privileges (this is needed because RBAC rules can
never escalate access):

```
$ cd $GOPATH/src/github.com/programming-kubernetes/pizza-apiserver
$ cd artifacts/deployment
$ kubectl apply -f ns.yaml # create the namespace first
$ kubectl apply -f .        # creating all manifests described above
```

Now the custom API server is launching:

```
$ kubectl get pods -A
NAMESPACE      NAME                              READY STATUS           AGE
pizza-apiserver pizza-apiserver-7779f8d486-8fpgj 0/2  ContainerCreating 1s
$ # some moments later
```

```
$ kubectl get pods -A
pizza-apiserver pizza-apiserver-7779f8d486-8fpgj 2/2  Running          75s
```

When it is running, we double-check that the Kubernetes API server does aggregation (i.e., proxying of requests). First check via `APIServices` whether the Kubernetes API server thinks that our custom API server is available:

```
$ kubectl get apiservices v1alpha1.restaurant.programming-kubernetes.info
NAME                                             SERVICE            AVAILABLE
v1alpha1.restaurant.programming-kubernetes.info pizza-apiserver/api True
```

This looks good. Let's try to list pizzas, with logging enabled to see whether something goes wrong:

```
$ kubectl get pizzas --v=7
...
... GET https://localhost:58727/apis?timeout=32s
...
... GET https://localhost:58727/apis/restaurant.programming-kubernetes.info/
                          v1alpha1?timeout=32s
...
... GET https://localhost:58727/apis/restaurant.programming-kubernetes.info/
                          v1beta1/namespaces/default/pizzas?limit=500
... Request Headers:
...   Accept: application/json;as=Table;v=v1beta1;g=meta.k8s.io, application/json
...   User-Agent: kubectl/v1.15.0 (darwin/amd64) kubernetes/f873d2a
... Response Status: 200 OK in 6 milliseconds
No resources found.
```

This looks very good. We see that `kubectl` queries the discovery information to find out what a pizza is. It queries the *restaurant.programming-kubernetes.info/v1beta1* API to list the pizzas. Unsurprisingly, there aren't any yet. But we can of course change that:

```
$ cd ../examples
$ # install toppings first
$ ls topping* | xargs -n 1 kubectl create -f
$ kubectl create -f pizza-margherita.yaml
pizza.restaurant.programming-kubernetes.info/margherita created
$ kubectl get pizza -o yaml margherita
apiVersion: restaurant.programming-kubernetes.info/v1beta1
kind: Pizza
metadata:
  creationTimestamp: "2019-05-05T13:39:52Z"
  name: margherita
  namespace: default
  resourceVersion: "6"
  pizzas/margherita
  uid: 42ab6e88-6f3b-11e9-8270-0e37170891d3
spec:
  toppings:
  - name: mozzarella
    quantity: 1
  - name: tomato
    quantity: 1
status: {}
```

This looks awesome. But the margherita pizza was easy. Let's try defaulting in action by creating an empty pizza that does not list any toppings:

```
apiVersion: restaurant.programming-kubernetes.info/v1alpha1
kind: Pizza
metadata:
  name: salami
spec:
```

Our defaulting should turn this into a salami pizza with a salami topping. Let's try:

```
$ kubectl create -f empty-pizza.yaml
pizza.restaurant.programming-kubernetes.info/salami created
$ kubectl get pizza -o yaml salami
apiVersion: restaurant.programming-kubernetes.info/v1beta1
kind: Pizza
metadata:
  creationTimestamp: "2019-05-05T13:42:42Z"
  name: salami
  namespace: default
  resourceVersion: "8"
  pizzas/salami
  uid: a7cb7af2-6f3b-11e9-8270-0e37170891d3
spec:
  toppings:
  - name: salami
    quantity: 1
  - name: mozzarella
    quantity: 1
  - name: tomato
    quantity: 1
status: {}
```

This looks like a delicious salami pizza.

Now let's check whether our custom admission plug-in is working. We first delete all pizzas and toppings, and then try to re-create the pizzas:

```
$ kubectl delete pizzas --all
pizza.restaurant.programming-kubernetes.info "margherita" deleted
pizza.restaurant.programming-kubernetes.info "salami" deleted
$ kubectl delete toppings --all
topping.restaurant.programming-kubernetes.info "mozzarella" deleted
topping.restaurant.programming-kubernetes.info "salami" deleted
topping.restaurant.programming-kubernetes.info "tomato" deleted
$ kubectl create -f pizza-margherita.yaml
Error from server (Forbidden): error when creating "pizza-margherita.yaml":
 pizzas.restaurant.programming-kubernetes.info "margherita" is forbidden:
    unknown topping: mozzarella
```

No margherita without mozzarella, like in any good Italian restaurant.

Looks like we are done implementing what we described in "Example: A Pizza Restaurant" on page 149. But not quite. Security. Again. We have not taken care of the proper certificates. A malicious pizza seller could try to get between our users and the custom API server because the Kubernetes API server just accepts any serving certificates without checking them. Let's fix this.

Certificates and Trust

The `APIService` object contains the `caBundle` field. This configures how the aggregator (inside the Kubernetes API server) trusts the custom API server. This CA bundle contains the certificate (and intermediate certificates) used to verify that the aggregated API server has the identity it claims to have. For any serious deployment, put the corresponding CA bundle into this field.

 While `insecureSkipTLSVerify` is allowed in an `APIService` in order to disable certification verification, it is a bad idea to use this in a production setup. The Kubernetes API server sends requests to a trusted aggregated API server. Setting `insecureSkipTLSVerify` to true means that any other actor can claim to be the aggregated API server. This is obviously insecure and should not be used in production environments.

The reverse trust from the custom API server to the Kubernetes API server, and its preauthentication of requests, is described in "Delegated Authentication and Trust" on page 156. We don't have to do anything extra.

Back to the pizza example: to make it secure, we need a serving certificate and a key for the custom API server in the deployment. We put both into a `serving-cert` secret and mount it into the pod at */var/run/apiserver/serving-cert/tls.{crt,key}*. Then we use the *tls.crt* file as CA in the `APIService`. This can all be found in the example code on GitHub (*http://bit.ly/2XxtJWP*).

The certificate-generation logic is scripted in a Makefile (*http://bit.ly/2KGn0nw*).

Note that in a real-world scenario we'd probably have some kind of cluster or company CA we can plug into the `APIService`.

To see it in action, either start with a new cluster or just reuse the previous one and apply the new, secure manifests:

```
$ cd ../deployment-secure
$ make
openssl req -new -x509 -subj "/CN=api.pizza-apiserver.svc"
   -nodes -newkey rsa:4096
   -keyout tls.key -out tls.crt -days 365
Generating a 4096 bit RSA private key
.....................++
......................................................................++
writing new private key to 'tls.key'
...
$ ls *.yaml | xargs -n 1 kubectl apply -f
clusterrolebinding.rbac.authorization.k8s.io/pizza-apiserver:system:auth-delegator unchanged
rolebinding.rbac.authorization.k8s.io/pizza-apiserver-auth-reader unchanged
deployment.apps/pizza-apiserver configured
namespace/pizza-apiserver unchanged
clusterrolebinding.rbac.authorization.k8s.io/pizza-apiserver-clusterrolebinding unchanged
```

```
clusterrole.rbac.authorization.k8s.io/aggregated-apiserver-clusterrole unchanged
serviceaccount/apiserver unchanged
service/api unchanged
secret/serving-cert created
apiservice.apiregistration.k8s.io/v1alpha1.restaurant.programming-kubernetes.info configured
apiservice.apiregistration.k8s.io/v1beta1.restaurant.programming-kubernetes.info configured
```

Note here the correct common name CN=api.pizza-apiserver.svc in the certificate. The Kubernetes API server proxies the request to the *api/pizza-apiserver* service and hence its DNS name must be put into the certificate.

We double-check that we really have disabled the insecureSkipTLSVerify flag in the APIService:

```
$ kubectl get apiservices v1alpha1.restaurant.programming-kubernetes.info -o yaml
apiVersion: apiregistration.k8s.io/v1
kind: APIService
metadata:
  name: v1alpha1.restaurant.programming-kubernetes.info
  ...
spec:
  caBundle: LS0tLS1C...
  group: restaurant.programming-kubernetes.info
  groupPriorityMinimum: 1000
  service:
    name: api
    namespace: pizza-apiserver
  version: v1alpha1
  versionPriority: 15
status:
  conditions:
  - lastTransitionTime: "2019-05-05T14:07:07Z"
    message: all checks passed
    reason: Passed
    status: "True"
    type: Available
artifacts/deploymen
```

This looks as expected: insecureSkipTLSVerify is gone and the caBundle field is filled with a base64 value of our certificate And: the service is still available.

Now let's see whether kubectl can still query the API:

```
$ kubectl get pizzas
No resources found.
$ cd ../examples
$ ls topping* | xargs -n 1 kubectl create -f
topping.restaurant.programming-kubernetes.info/mozzarella created
topping.restaurant.programming-kubernetes.info/salami created
topping.restaurant.programming-kubernetes.info/tomato created
$ kubectl create -f pizza-margherita.yaml
pizza.restaurant.programming-kubernetes.info/margherita created
```

The margherita pizza is back. This time it is perfectly secured. No chance for a malicious pizza seller to start a man-in-the-middle attack. Buon appetito!

Sharing etcd

Aggregated API servers using the `RecommendOptions` (see "Options and Config Pattern and Startup Plumbing" on page 160) use `etcd` for storage. This means that any deployment of a custom API server requires an `etcd` cluster to be available.

This cluster can be in-cluster—for example, deployed using the `etcd` operator (*http:// bit.ly/2JTz8SK*). This operator allows us to launch and administrate an `etcd` cluster in a declarative way. The operator will do updates, up and down scaling, and backup. This reduces the operational overhead a lot.

Alternatively, the `etcd` of the cluster control plane (i.e., that of `kube-apiserver`) can be used. Depending on the environment—self-deployed, on-premise, or hosted services like Google Container Engine (GKE)—this might be viable, or it might be impossible because the user has no access to the cluster at all (as is the case with GKE). In the viable cases, the custom API server has to use a key path that is distinct from the one used by the Kubernetes API server or other `etcd` consumers. In our example custom API server, it looks like this:

```
const defaultEtcdPathPrefix =
    "/registry/pizza-apiserver.programming-kubernetes.github.com"

func NewCustomServerOptions() *CustomServerOptions {
    o := &CustomServerOptions{
        RecommendedOptions: genericoptions.NewRecommendedOptions(
            defaultEtcdPathPrefix,
            ...
        ),
    }

    return o
}
```

This `etcd` path prefix is different from Kubernetes API server paths, which use different group API names.

Last but not least, `etcd` can be proxied. The project etcdproxy-controller (*http://bit.ly/ 2Na2VrN*) implements this mechanism using the operator pattern; that is, etcd proxies can be deployed automatically to the cluster and configured using `EtcdProxy` objects.

The `etcd` proxies will automatically do key mapping, so it is guaranteed that `etcd` key prefixes will not conflict. This allows us to share `etcd` clusters for multiple aggregated API servers without worrying that one aggregated API server reads or changes the data of another one. This will improve security in an environment where shared `etcd` clusters are required, for example, due to resource constraints or to avoid operational overhead.

Depending on the context, one of these options must be chosen. Finally, aggregated API servers can of course also use other storage backends, at least in theory, as it requires a lot of custom code to implement the *k8s.io/apiserver* storage interfaces.

Summary

This was a pretty large chapter, and you made it to the end. You've gotten a lot of background about APIs in Kubernetes and how they are implemented.

We saw how aggregation of custom API servers fits into the architecture of a Kubernetes cluster. We saw how a custom API server receives requests that are proxies from the Kubernetes API server. We have seen how the Kubernetes API server preauthenticates these requests, and how API groups are implemented, with external versions and internal versions. We learned how objects are decoded into the Golang structs, how they are defaulted, how they are converted to internal types, and how they go through admission and validation and finally reach the registry. We saw how a strategy is plugged into a generic registry to implement "normal" Kubernetes-like REST resources, how we can add custom admissions, and how to configure a custom admission plug-in with a custom initializer. We now know how to do all the plumbing to start up a custom API server with a multiversion API group, and how to deploy the API group in a cluster with `APIServices`. We saw how to configure RBAC rules to allow the custom API server to do its job. We discussed how `kubectl` queries API groups. Finally, we learned how to secure the connection to our custom API server with certificates.

This was a lot. Now you have a much better understanding of what APIs are in Kubernetes and how they are implemented, and hopefully you are motivated to do one or more of the following:

- Implement your own custom API server
- Learn about the inner workings of Kubernetes
- Contribute to Kubernetes in the future

We hope that you have found this a good starting point.

## CHAPTER 9

Advanced Custom Resources

In this chapter we walk you through advanced topics about CRs: versioning, conversion, and admission controllers.

With multiple versions, CRDs become much more serious and are much less distinguishable from Golang-based API resources. Of course, at the same time the complexity considerably grows, both in development and maintenance but also operationally. We call these features "advanced" because they move CRDs from being a manifest (i.e., purely declarative) into the Golang world (i.e., into a real software development project).

Even if you do not plan to build a custom API server and instead intend to directly switch to CRDs, we highly recommend not skipping Chapter 8. Many of the concepts around advanced CRDs have direct counterparts in the world of custom API servers and are motivated by them. Reading Chapter 8 will make it much easier to understand this chapter as well.

The code for all the examples shown and discussed here is available via the GitHub repository (*http://bit.ly/2RBSjAl*).

Custom Resource Versioning

In Chapter 8 we saw how resources are available through different API versions. In the example of the custom API server, the pizza resources exist in version `v1alpha1` and `v1beta1` at the same time (see "Example: A Pizza Restaurant" on page 149). Inside of the custom API server, each object in a request is first converted from the API endpoint version to an internal version (see "Internal Types and Conversion" on page 168 and Figure 8-5) and then converted back to an external version for storage and to return a response. The conversion mechanism is implemented by conversion functions, some of them manually written, and some generated (see "Conversions" on page 172).

Versioning APIs is a powerful mechanism to adapt and improve APIs while keeping compatibility for older clients. Versioning plays a central role everywhere in Kubernetes to promote alpha APIs to beta and eventually to general availability (GA). During this process APIs often change structure or are extended.

For a long time, versioning was a feature available only through aggregated API servers as presented in Chapter 8. Any serious API needs versioning eventually, as it is not acceptable to break compatibility with consumers of the API.

Luckily, versioning for CRDs has been added very recently to Kubernetes—as alpha in Kubernetes 1.14 and promoted to beta in 1.15. Note that conversion requires OpenAPI v3 validation schemas that are *structural* (see "Validating Custom Resources" on page 76). Structural schema are basically what tools like Kubebuilder produce anyway. We will discuss the technical details in "Structural Schemas" on page 238.

We'll show you how versioning works here as it will play a central role in many serious applications of CRs in the near future.

Revising the Pizza Restaurant

To learn how CR conversion works, we'll reimplement the pizza restaurant example from Chapter 8, this time purely with CRDs—that is, without the aggregated API server involved.

For conversion, we will concentrate on the `Pizza` resource:

```
apiVersion: restaurant.programming-kubernetes.info/v1alpha1
kind: Pizza
metadata:
  name: margherita
spec:
  toppings:
  - mozzarella
  - tomato
```

This object should have a different representation of the toppings slice in the `v1beta1` version:

```
apiVersion: restaurant.programming-kubernetes.info/v1beta1
kind: Pizza
metadata:
  name: margherita
spec:
  toppings:
  - name: mozzarella
    quantity: 1
  - name: tomato
    quantity: 1
```

While in v1alpha1, repetition of toppings is used to represent an extra cheese pizza, we do this in v1beta1 by using a quantity field for each topping. The order of toppings does not matter.

We want to implement this translation—converting from v1alpha1 to v1beta1 and back. Before we do so, though, let's define the API as a CRD. Note here that we cannot have an aggregated API server and CRDs of the same GroupVersion in the same cluster. So make sure that the APIServices from Chapter 8 are removed before continuing with the CRDs here.

```
apiVersion: apiextensions.k8s.io/v1beta1
kind: CustomResourceDefinition
metadata:
  name: pizzas.restaurant.programming-kubernetes.info
spec:
  group: restaurant.programming-kubernetes.info
  names:
    kind: Pizza
    listKind: PizzaList
    plural: pizzas
    singular: pizza
  scope: Namespaced
  version: v1alpha1
  versions:
  - name: v1alpha1
    served: true
    storage: true
    schema: ...
  - name: v1beta1
    served: true
    storage: false
    schema: ...
```

The CRD defines two versions: v1alpha1 and v1beta1. We set the former as the storage version (see Figure 9-1), meaning every object to be stored in etcd is first converted to v1alpha1.

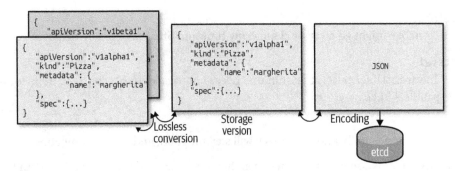

Figure 9-1. Conversion and storage version

As the CRD is defined currently, we can create an object as v1alpha1 and retrieve it as v1beta1, but both API endpoints return the same object. This is obviously not what we want. But we'll improve this very soon.

But before we do that, we'll set up the CRD in a cluster and create a margherita pizza:

```
apiVersion: restaurant.programming-kubernetes.info/v1alpha1
kind: Pizza
metadata:
  name: margherita
spec:
  toppings:
  - mozzarella
  - tomato
```

We register the preceding CRD and then create the margherita object:

```
$ kubectl create -f pizza-crd.yaml
$ kubectl create -f margherita-pizza.yaml
```

As expected, we get back the same object for both versions:

```
$ kubectl get pizza margherita -o yaml
apiVersion: restaurant.programming-kubernetes.info/v1beta1
kind: Pizza
metadata:
  creationTimestamp: "2019-04-14T11:39:20Z"
  generation: 1
  name: margherita
  namespace: pizza-apiserver
  resourceVersion: "47959"
  selfLink: /apis/restaurant.programming-kubernetes.info/v1beta1/namespaces/pizza-apiserver/
  pizzas/margherita
  uid: f18427f0-5ea9-11e9-8219-124e4d2dc074
spec:
  toppings:
  - mozzarella
  - tomato
```

Kubernetes uses the canonical version order; that is:

v1alpha1

Unstable: might go away or change any time and often disabled by default.

v1beta1

Towards stable: exists at least in one release in parallel to v1; contract: no incompatible API changes.

v1

Stable or generally available (GA): will stay for good, and will be compatible.

The GA versions come first in that order, then the betas, and then the alphas, with the major version ordered from high to low and the same for the minor version. Every CRD version not fitting into this pattern comes last, ordered alphabetically.

In our case, the preceding `kubectl get pizza` therefore returns `v1beta1`, although the created object was in version `v1alpha1`.

Conversion Webhook Architecture

Now let's add the conversion from `v1alpha1` to `v1beta1` and back. CRD conversions are implemented via webhooks in Kubernetes. Figure 9-2 shows the flow:

1. The client (e.g., our `kubectl get pizza margherita`) requests a version.

2. `etcd` has stored the object in some version.

3. If the versions do not match, the storage object is sent to the webhook server for conversion. The webhook returns a response with the converted object.

4. The converted object is sent back to the client.

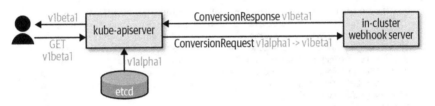

Figure 9-2. Conversion webhook

We have to implement this webhook server. Before doing so, let's look at the webhook API. The Kubernetes API server sends a `ConversionReview` object in the API group `apiextensions.k8s.io/v1beta1`:

```
type ConversionReview struct {
    metav1.TypeMeta `json:",inline"`
    Request *ConversionRequest
    Response *ConversionResponse
}
```

The request field is set in the payload sent to the webhook. The response field is set in the response.

The request looks like this:

```
type ConversionRequest struct {
    ...

    // `desiredAPIVersion` is the version to convert given objects to.
    // For example, "myapi.example.com/v1."
    DesiredAPIVersion string

    // `objects` is the list of CR objects to be converted.
    Objects []runtime.RawExtension
}
```

The `DesiredAPIVersion` string has the usual `apiVersion` format we know from TypeMeta: *group/version*.

The objects field has a number of objects. It is a slice because for one list request for pizzas, the webhook will receive one conversion request, with this slice being all objects for the list request.

The webhook converts and sets the response:

```
type ConversionResponse struct {
    ...

    // `convertedObjects` is the list of converted versions of `request.objects`
    // if the `result` is successful otherwise empty. The webhook is expected to
    // set apiVersion of these objects to the ConversionRequest.desiredAPIVersion.
    // The list must also have the same size as input list with the same objects
    // in the same order (i.e. equal UIDs and object meta).
    ConvertedObjects []runtime.RawExtension

    // `result` contains the result of conversion with extra details if the
    // conversion failed. `result.status` determines if the conversion failed
    // or succeeded. The `result.status` field is required and represents the
    // success or failure of the conversion. A successful conversion must set
    // `result.status` to `Success`. A failed conversion must set `result.status`
    // to `Failure` and provide more details in `result.message` and return http
    // status 200. The `result.message` will be used to construct an error
    // message for the end user.
    Result metav1.Status
}
```

The result status tells the Kubernetes API server whether the conversion was successful.

But when in the request pipeline is our conversion webhook actually called? What kind of input object can we expect? To understand this better, take a look at the general request pipeline in Figure 9-3: all those solid and striped circles are where conversion takes place in the *k8s.io/apiserver* code.

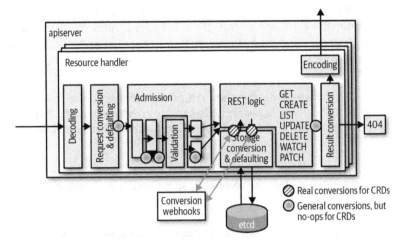

Figure 9-3. Conversion webhook calls for CRs

In contrast to aggregated custom API servers (see "Internal Types and Conversion" on page 168), CRs do not use internal types but convert directly between the external API versions. Hence, only those yellow circles are actually doing conversions in Figure 9-4; the solid circles are NOOPs for CRDs. In other words: CRD conversion takes place only from and to `etcd`.

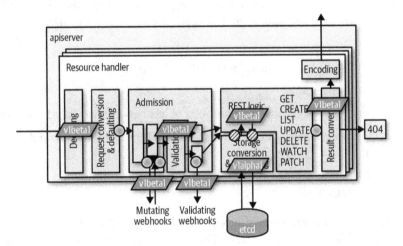

Figure 9-4. Where conversion takes place for CRs

Therefore, we can assume our webhook will be called from those two places in the request pipeline (refer to Figure 9-3).

Also note that patch requests do automatic retries on conflict (updates cannot retry, and they respond with errors directly to the caller). Each retry consists of a read and write to etcd (the yellow circles in Figure 9-3) and therefore leads to two calls to the webhook per iteration.

 All the warnings about the criticality of conversion in "Conversions" on page 172 apply here as well: conversions must be correct. Bugs quickly lead to data loss and inconsistent behavior of the API.

Before we start implementing the webhook, some final words about what the webhook can do and must avoid:

- The order of the objects in request and response must not change.
- ObjectMeta with the exception of labels and annotation must not be mutated.
- Conversion is all or nothing: either all objects are successfully converted or all fail.

Conversion Webhook Implementation

With the theory behind us, we are ready to start the implementation of the webhook project. You can find the source at the repository (*http://bit.ly/2IHXKLn*), which includes:

- A webhook implementation as an HTTPS web server
- A number of endpoints:
  - */convert/v1beta1/pizza* converts a pizza object between v1alpha1 and v1beta1.
  - */admit/v1beta1/pizza* defaults the spec.toppings field to mozzarella, tomato, salami.
  - */validate/v1beta1/pizza* verifies that each specified topping has a corresponding toppings object.

The last two endpoints are admission webhooks, which will be discussed in detail in "Admission Webhooks" on page 226. The same webhook binary will serve both admission and conversion.

The v1beta1 in these paths should not be confused with v1beta1 of our restaurant API group, but it is meant as the apiextensions.k8s.io API group version we support as a webhook. Someday v1 of that webhook API will be supported,[1] at which time we'll add the corresponding v1 as another endpoint, in order to support old (as of today) and new Kubernetes clusters. It is possible to specify inside the CRD manifest which versions a webhook supports.

Let's look into how this conversion webhook actually works. Afterwards we will take a deeper dive into how to deploy the webhook into a real cluster. Note again that webhook conversion is still alpha in 1.14 and must be enabled manually using the Custom ResourceWebhookConversion feature gate, but it is available as beta in 1.15.

Setting Up the HTTPS Server

The first step is to start a web server with support for transport layer security, or TLS (i.e., HTTPS). Webhooks in Kubernetes require HTTPS. The conversion webhook even requires certificates that are successfully checked by the Kubernetes API server against the CA bundle provided in the CRD object.

In the example project, we make use of the secure serving library that is part of the *k8s.io/apiserver*. It provides all TLS flags and behavior you might be used to from deploying a kube-apiserver or an aggregated API server binary.

The *k8s.io/apiserver* secure serving code follows the options-config pattern (see "Options and Config Pattern and Startup Plumbing" on page 160). It is very easy to embed that code into your own binary:

```
func NewDefaultOptions() *Options {
    o := &Options{
        *options.NewSecureServingOptions(),
    }
    o.SecureServing.ServerCert.PairName = "pizza-crd-webhook"
    return o
}

type Options struct {
    SecureServing options.SecureServingOptions
}

type Config struct {
    SecureServing *server.SecureServingInfo
}

func (o *Options) AddFlags(fs *pflag.FlagSet) {
    o.SecureServing.AddFlags(fs)
}

func (o *Options) Config() (*Config, error) {
    err := o.SecureServing.MaybeDefaultWithSelfSignedCerts("0.0.0.0", nil, nil)
```

---

1 apiextensions.k8s.io and admissionregistration.k8s.io are both scheduled to be promoted to v1 in Kubernetes 1.16.

```
    if err != nil {
        return nil, err
    }

    c := &Config{}

    if err := o.SecureServing.ApplyTo(&c.SecureServing); err != nil {
        return nil, err
    }

    return c, nil
}
```

In the main function of the binary, this `Options` struct is instantiated and wired to a flag set:

```
opt := NewDefaultOptions()
fs := pflag.NewFlagSet("pizza-crd-webhook", pflag.ExitOnError)
globalflag.AddGlobalFlags(fs, "pizza-crd-webhook")
opt.AddFlags(fs)
if err := fs.Parse(os.Args); err != nil {
    panic(err)
}

// create runtime config
cfg, err := opt.Config()
if err != nil {
    panic(err)
}

stopCh := server.SetupSignalHandler()

...

// run server
restaurantInformers.Start(stopCh)
if doneCh, err := cfg.SecureServing.Serve(
    handlers.LoggingHandler(os.Stdout, mux),
    time.Second * 30, stopCh,
); err != nil {
    panic(err)
} else {
    <-doneCh
}
```

In place of the three dots, we set up the HTTP multiplexer with our three paths as follows:

```
// register handlers
restaurantInformers := restaurantinformers.NewSharedInformerFactory(
    clientset, time.Minute * 5,
)
mux := http.NewServeMux()
mux.Handle("/convert/v1beta1/pizza", http.HandlerFunc(conversion.Serve))
mux.Handle("/admit/v1beta1/pizza", http.HandlerFunc(admission.ServePizzaAdmit))
mux.Handle("/validate/v1beta1/pizza",
    http.HandlerFunc(admission.ServePizzaValidation(restaurantInformers)))
restaurantInformers.Start(stopCh)
```

As the pizza validation webhook at the path */validate/v1beta1/pizza* has to know the existing topping objects in the cluster, we instantiate a shared informer factory for the `restaurant.programming-kubernetes.info` API group.

Now we'll look at the actual conversion webhook implementation behind `conversion.Serve`. It is a normal Golang HTTP handler function, meaning it gets a request and a response writer as arguments.

The request body contains a `ConversionReview` object from the API group `apiextensions.k8s.io/v1beta1`. Hence, we have to first read the body from the request, and then decode the byte slice. We do this by using a deserializer from API Machinery:

```
func Serve(w http.ResponseWriter, req *http.Request) {
    // read body
    body, err := ioutil.ReadAll(req.Body)
    if err != nil {
        responsewriters.InternalError(w, req,
          fmt.Errorf("failed to read body: %v", err))
        return
    }

    // decode body as conversion review
    gv := apiextensionsv1beta1.SchemeGroupVersion
    reviewGVK := gv.WithKind("ConversionReview")
    obj, gvk, err := codecs.UniversalDeserializer().Decode(body, &reviewGVK,
        &apiextensionsv1beta1.ConversionReview{})
    if err != nil {
        responsewriters.InternalError(w, req,
          fmt.Errorf("failed to decode body: %v", err))
        return
    }
    review, ok := obj.(*apiextensionsv1beta1.ConversionReview)
    if !ok {
        responsewriters.InternalError(w, req,
          fmt.Errorf("unexpected GroupVersionKind: %s", gvk))
        return
    }
    if review.Request == nil {
        responsewriters.InternalError(w, req,
          fmt.Errorf("unexpected nil request"))
        return
    }

    ...
}
```

This code makes use of the codec factory `codecs`, which is derived from a scheme. This scheme has to include the types of *apiextensions.k8s.io/v1beta1*. We also add the types of our restaurant API group. The passed `ConversionReview` object will have our pizza type embedded in a `runtime.RawExtension` type—more about that in a second.

First let's create our scheme and the codec factory:

```
import (
    apiextensionsv1beta1 "k8s.io/apiextensions-apiserver/pkg/apis/apiextensions/v1beta1"
    "github.com/programming-kubernetes/pizza-crd/pkg/apis/restaurant/install"
    ...
)

var (
    scheme = runtime.NewScheme()
    codecs = serializer.NewCodecFactory(scheme)
)

func init() {
    utilruntime.Must(apiextensionsv1beta1.AddToScheme(scheme))
    install.Install(scheme)
}
```

A `runtime.RawExtension` is a wrapper for Kubernetes-like objects embedded in a field of another object. Its structure is actually very simple:

```
type RawExtension struct {
    // Raw is the underlying serialization of this object.
    Raw []byte `protobuf:"bytes,1,opt,name=raw"`
    // Object can hold a representation of this extension - useful for working
    // with versioned structs.
    Object Object `json:"-"`
}
```

In addition, `runtime.RawExtension` has special JSON and protobuf marshaling two methods. Moreover, there is special logic around the conversion to `runtime.Object` on the fly, when converting to internal types—that is, automatic encoding and decoding.

In this case of CRDs, we don't have internal types, and therefore that conversion magic does not play a role. Only `RawExtension.Raw` is filled with a JSON byte slice of the pizza object sent to the webhook for conversion. Thus, we will have to decode this byte slice. Note again that one `ConversionReview` potentially carries a number of objects, such that we have to loop over all of them:

```
    // convert objects
    review.Response = &apiextensionsv1beta1.ConversionResponse{
        UID: review.Request.UID,
        Result: metav1.Status{
            Status: metav1.StatusSuccess,
        },
    }
    var objs []runtime.Object
    for _, in := range review.Request.Objects {
        if in.Object == nil {
            var err error
            in.Object, _, err = codecs.UniversalDeserializer().Decode(
                in.Raw, nil, nil,
            )
            if err != nil {
                review.Response.Result = metav1.Status{
                    Message: err.Error(),
                    Status: metav1.StatusFailure,
```

```
        }
        break
    }
}

obj, err := convert(in.Object, review.Request.DesiredAPIVersion)
if err != nil {
    review.Response.Result = metav1.Status{
        Message: err.Error(),
        Status:  metav1.StatusFailure,
    }
    break
}
objs = append(objs, obj)
}
```

The `convert` call does the actual conversion of `in.Object`, with the desired API version as the target version. Note here that we break the loop immediately when the first error occurs.

Finally, we set the `Response` field in the `ConversionReview` object and write it back as the response body of the request using API Machinery's response writer, which again uses our codec factory to create a serializer:

```
if review.Response.Result.Status == metav1.StatusSuccess {
    for _, obj = range objs {
        review.Response.ConvertedObjects =
            append(review.Response.ConvertedObjects,
                runtime.RawExtension{Object: obj},
            )
    }
}

// write negotiated response
responsewriters.WriteObject(
    http.StatusOK, gvk.GroupVersion(), codecs, review, w, req,
)
```

Now, we have to implement the actual pizza conversion. After all this plumbing above, the conversion algorithm is the easiest part. It just checks that we actually got a pizza object of the known versions and then does the conversion from `v1beta1` to `v1alpha1` and vice versa:

```
func convert(in runtime.Object, apiVersion string) (runtime.Object, error) {
    switch in := in.(type) {
    case *v1alpha1.Pizza:
        if apiVersion != v1beta1.SchemeGroupVersion.String() {
            return nil, fmt.Errorf("cannot convert %s to %s",
                v1alpha1.SchemeGroupVersion, apiVersion)
        }
        klog.V(2).Infof("Converting %s/%s from %s to %s", in.Namespace, in.Name,
            v1alpha1.SchemeGroupVersion, apiVersion)

        out := &v1beta1.Pizza{
            TypeMeta: in.TypeMeta,
            ObjectMeta: in.ObjectMeta,
            Status: v1beta1.PizzaStatus{
```

```
                Cost: in.Status.Cost,
            },
        }
        out.TypeMeta.APIVersion = apiVersion

        idx := map[string]int{}
        for _, top := range in.Spec.Toppings {
            if i, duplicate := idx[top]; duplicate {
                out.Spec.Toppings[i].Quantity++
                continue
            }
            idx[top] = len(out.Spec.Toppings)
            out.Spec.Toppings = append(out.Spec.Toppings, v1beta1.PizzaTopping{
                Name: top,
                Quantity: 1,
            })
        }

        return out, nil

    case *v1beta1.Pizza:
        if apiVersion != v1alpha1.SchemeGroupVersion.String() {
            return nil, fmt.Errorf("cannot convert %s to %s",
                v1beta1.SchemeGroupVersion, apiVersion)
        }
        klog.V(2).Infof("Converting %s/%s from %s to %s",
          in.Namespace, in.Name, v1alpha1.SchemeGroupVersion, apiVersion)

        out := &v1alpha1.Pizza{
            TypeMeta: in.TypeMeta,
            ObjectMeta: in.ObjectMeta,
            Status: v1alpha1.PizzaStatus{
                Cost: in.Status.Cost,
            },
        }
        out.TypeMeta.APIVersion = apiVersion

        for i := range in.Spec.Toppings {
            for j := 0; j < in.Spec.Toppings[i].Quantity; j++ {
                out.Spec.Toppings = append(
                    out.Spec.Toppings, in.Spec.Toppings[i].Name)
            }
        }

        return out, nil

    default:
    }
    klog.V(2).Infof("Unknown type %T", in)
    return nil, fmt.Errorf("unknown type %T", in)
}
```

Note that in both directions of the conversion, we just copy TypeMeta and Object
Meta, change the API version to the desired one, and then convert the toppings slice,
which is actually the only part of the objects which structurally differs.

If there are more versions, another two-way conversion is necessary between all of
them. Alternatively, of course, we could use a hub version as in aggregated API

servers (see "Internal Types and Conversion" on page 168), instead of implementing conversions from and to all supported external versions.

Deploying the Conversion Webhook

We now want to deploy the conversion webhook. You can find all the manifests on GitHub (*http://bit.ly/2KEx4xo*).

Conversion webhooks for CRDs are launched in the cluster and put behind a service object, and that service object is referenced by the conversion webhook specification in the CRD manifest:

```
apiVersion: apiextensions.k8s.io/v1beta1
kind: CustomResourceDefinition
metadata:
  name: pizzas.restaurant.programming-kubernetes.info
spec:
  ...
  conversion:
    strategy: Webhook
    webhookClientConfig:
      caBundle: BASE64-CA-BUNDLE
      service:
        namespace: pizza-crd
        name: webhook
        path: /convert/v1beta1/pizza
```

The CA bundle must match the serving certificate used by the webhook. In our example project, we use a Makefile (*http://bit.ly/2FukVac*) to generate certificates using OpenSSL and plug them into the manifests using text replacement.

Note here that the Kubernetes API server assumes that the webhook supports all specified versions of the CRD. There is also only one such webhook possible per CRD. But as CRDs and conversion webhooks are usually owned by the same team, this should be enough.

Also note that the service port must be 443 in the current *apiextensions.k8s.io/v1beta1* API. The service can map this, however, to any port used by the webhook pods. In our example, we map 443 to 8443, served by the webhook binary.

Seeing Conversion in Action

Now that we understand how the conversion webhook works and how it is wired into the cluster, let's see it in action.

We assume you've checked out the example project. In addition, we assume that you have a cluster with webhook conversion enabled (either via feature gate in a 1.14 cluster or through a 1.15+ cluster, which has webhook conversion enabled by default). One way to get such a cluster is via the kind project (*http://bit.ly/2X75lvS*), which provides support for Kubernetes 1.14.1 and a local *kind-config.yaml* file to enable the alpha feature gate for webhook conversion ("What Does Programming Kubernetes Mean?" on page 1 linked a number of other options for development clusters):

```
kind: Cluster
apiVersion: kind.sigs.k8s.io/v1alpha3
kubeadmConfigPatchesJson6902:
- group: kubeadm.k8s.io
  version: v1beta1
  kind: ClusterConfiguration
  patch: |
    - op: add
      path: /apiServer/extraArgs
      value: {}
    - op: add
      path: /apiServer/extraArgs/feature-gates
      value: CustomResourceWebhookConversion=true
```

Then we can create a cluster:

```
$ kind create cluster --image kindest/node-images:v1.14.1 --config kind-config.yaml
$ export KUBECONFIG="$(kind get kubeconfig-path --name="kind")"
```

Now we can deploy our manifests (*http://bit.ly/2KEx4xo*):

```
$ cd pizza-crd
$ cd manifest/deployment
$ make
$ kubectl create -f ns.yaml
$ kubectl create -f pizza-crd.yaml
$ kubectl create -f topping-crd.yaml
$ kubectl create -f sa.yaml
$ kubectl create -f rbac.yaml
$ kubectl create -f rbac-bind.yaml
$ kubectl create -f service.yaml
$ kubectl create -f serving-cert-secret.yaml
$ kubectl create -f deployment.yaml
```

These manifests contain the following files:

ns.yaml
> Creates the `pizza-crd` namespace.

pizza-crd.yaml
> Specifies the pizza resource in the `restaurant.programming-kubernetes.info` API group, with the `v1alpha1` and `v1beta1` versions, and the webhook conversion configuration as shown previously.

topping-crd.yaml
> Specifies the toppings CR in the same API group, but only in the `v1alpha1` version.

sa.yaml
> Introduces the `webhook` service account.

rbac.yaml

Defines a role to read, list, and watch toppings.

rbac-bind.yaml

Binds the earlier RBAC role to the webhook service account.

service.yaml

Defines the webhook services, mapping port 443 to 8443 of the webhook pods.

serving-cert-secret.yaml

Contains the serving certificate and private key to be used by the webhook pods. The certificate is also used directly as the CA bundle in the preceding pizza CRD manifest.

deployment.yaml

Launches webhook pods, passing `--tls-cert-file` and `--tls-private-key` the serving certificate secret.

After this we can create a margherita pizza finally:

```
$ cat ../examples/margherita-pizza.yaml
apiVersion: restaurant.programming-kubernetes.info/v1alpha1
kind: Pizza
metadata:
  name: margherita
spec:
  toppings:
  - mozzarella
  - tomato
$ kubectl create ../examples/margherita-pizza.yaml
pizza.restaurant.programming-kubernetes.info/margherita created
```

Now, with the conversion webhook in place, we can retrieve the same object in both versions. First explicitly in the `v1alpha1` version:

```
$ kubectl get pizzas.v1alpha1.restaurant.programming-kubernetes.info \
    margherita -o yaml
apiVersion: restaurant.programming-kubernetes.info/v1alpha1
kind: Pizza
metadata:
  creationTimestamp: "2019-04-14T21:41:39Z"
  generation: 1
  name: margherita
  namespace: pizza-crd
  resourceVersion: "18296"
  pizzas/margherita
  uid: 15c1c06a-5efe-11e9-9230-0242f24ba99c
spec:
  toppings:
  - mozzarella
  - tomato
status: {}
```

Then the same object as `v1beta1` shows the different toppings structure:

```
$ kubectl get pizzas.v1beta1.restaurant.programming-kubernetes.info \
    margherita -o yaml
apiVersion: restaurant.programming-kubernetes.info/v1beta1
kind: Pizza
metadata:
  creationTimestamp: "2019-04-14T21:41:39Z"
  generation: 1
  name: margherita
  namespace: pizza-crd
  resourceVersion: "18296"
  pizzas/margherita
  uid: 15c1c06a-5efe-11e9-9230-0242f24ba99c
spec:
  toppings:
  - name: mozzarella
    quantity: 1
  - name: tomato
    quantity: 1
status: {}
```

Meanwhile, in the log of the webhook pod we see this conversion call:

```
I0414 21:46:28.639707        1 convert.go:35] Converting pizza-crd/margherita
    from restaurant.programming-kubernetes.info/v1alpha1
    to restaurant.programming-kubernetes.info/v1beta1
10.32.0.1 - - [14/Apr/2019:21:46:28 +0000]
    "POST /convert/v1beta1/pizza?timeout=30s HTTP/2.0" 200 968
```

Hence, the webhook is doing its job as expected.

Admission Webhooks

In "Use Cases for Custom API Servers" on page 147 we discussed the use cases in which an aggregated API server is a better choice than using CRs. A lot of the reasons given are about having the freedom to implement certain behavior using Golang instead of being restricted to declarative features in CRD manifests.

We have seen in the previous section how Golang is used to build CRD conversion webhooks. A similar mechanism is used to add custom admission to CRDs, again in Golang.

Basically we have the same freedom as with custom admission plug-ins in aggregated API servers (see "Admission" on page 189): there are mutating and validating admission webhooks, and they are called at the same position as for native resources, as shown in Figure 9-5.

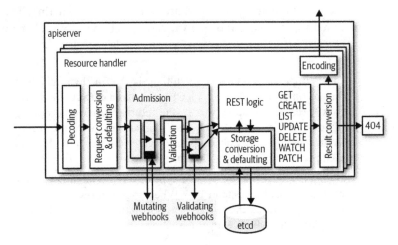

Figure 9-5. Admission in the CR request pipeline

We saw CRD validation based on OpenAPI in "Validating Custom Resources" on page 76. In Figure 9-5, validation is done in the box labeled "Validation." The validating admission webhooks are called after that, the mutating admission webhooks before.

The admission webhooks are put nearly at the end of the admission plug-in order, before quota. Admission webhooks are beta in Kubernetes 1.14 and therefore available in most clusters.

> For v1 of the admission webhooks API, it is planned to allow up to two passes through the admission chain. This means that an earlier admission plug-in or webhook can depend on the output of later plug-ins or webhooks, to a certain degree. So, in the future this mechanism will get even more powerful.

Admission Requirements in the Restaurant Example

The restaurant example uses admission for multiple things:

- `spec.toppings` defaults if it is `nil` or empty to mozzarella, tomato, and salami.
- Unknown fields should be dropped from the CR JSON and not persisted in `etcd`.
- `spec.toppings` must contain only toppings that have a corresponding topping object.

The first two use cases are mutating; the third use case is purely validating. Therefore, we will use one mutating webhook and one validating webhook to implement those steps.

 Work is in progress on native defaulting via OpenAPI v3 validation schemas (*http://bit.ly/2ZFH8JY*). OpenAPI has a `default` field, and the API server will apply that in the future. Moreover, dropping unknown fields will become the standard behavior for every resource, done by the Kubernetes API server through a mechanism called pruning (*http://bit.ly/2Xzt2wm*).

Pruning is available as beta in Kubernetes 1.15. Defaulting is planned to be available as beta in 1.16. When both features are available in the target cluster, the two use cases from the preceding list can be implemented without any webhook at all.

Admission Webhook Architecture

Admission webhooks are structurally very similar to the conversion webhooks we saw earlier in the chapter.

They are deployed in the cluster, put behind a service mapping port 443 to some port of the pods, and called using a review object, `AdmissionReview` in the API group `admission.k8s.io/v1beta1`:

```
---
// AdmissionReview describes an admission review request/response.
type AdmissionReview struct {
    metav1.TypeMeta `json:",inline"`
    // Request describes the attributes for the admission request.
    // +optional
    Request *AdmissionRequest `json:"request,omitempty"`
    // Response describes the attributes for the admission response.
    // +optional
    Response *AdmissionResponse `json:"response,omitempty"`
}
---
```

The `AdmissionRequest` contains all the information we are used to from the admission attributes (see "Implementation" on page 190):

```
// AdmissionRequest describes the admission.Attributes for the admission request.
type AdmissionRequest struct {
    // UID is an identifier for the individual request/response. It allows us to
    // distinguish instances of requests which are otherwise identical (parallel
    // requests, requests when earlier requests did not modify etc). The UID is
    // meant to track the round trip (request/response) between the KAS and the
    // WebHook, not the user request. It is suitable for correlating log entries
    // between the webhook and apiserver, for either auditing or debugging.
    UID types.UID `json:"uid"`
    // Kind is the type of object being manipulated.  For example: Pod
    Kind metav1.GroupVersionKind `json:"kind"`
    // Resource is the name of the resource being requested.  This is not the
```

```
// kind. For example: pods
Resource metav1.GroupVersionResource `json:"resource"`
// SubResource is the name of the subresource being requested. This is a
// different resource, scoped to the parent resource, but it may have a
// different kind. For instance, /pods has the resource "pods" and the kind
// "Pod", while /pods/foo/status has the resource "pods", the sub resource
// "status", and the kind "Pod" (because status operates on pods). The
// binding resource for a pod though may be /pods/foo/binding, which has
// resource "pods", subresource "binding", and kind "Binding".
// +optional
SubResource string `json:"subResource,omitempty"`
// Name is the name of the object as presented in the request. On a CREATE
// operation, the client may omit name and rely on the server to generate
// the name. If that is the case, this method will return the empty string.
// +optional
Name string `json:"name,omitempty"`
// Namespace is the namespace associated with the request (if any).
// +optional
Namespace string `json:"namespace,omitempty"`
// Operation is the operation being performed
Operation Operation `json:"operation"`
// UserInfo is information about the requesting user
UserInfo authenticationv1.UserInfo `json:"userInfo"`
// Object is the object from the incoming request prior to default values
// being applied
// +optional
Object runtime.RawExtension `json:"object,omitempty"`
// OldObject is the existing object. Only populated for UPDATE requests.
// +optional
OldObject runtime.RawExtension `json:"oldObject,omitempty"`
// DryRun indicates that modifications will definitely not be persisted
// for this request.
// Defaults to false.
// +optional
DryRun *bool `json:"dryRun,omitempty"`
}
```

The same `AdmissionReview` object is used for both mutating and validating admission webhooks. The only difference is that in the mutating case, the `AdmissionRes ponse` can have a field `patch` and `patchType`, to be applied inside the Kubernetes API server after the webhook response has been received there. In the validating case, these two fields are kept empty on response.

The most important field for our purposes here is the `Object` field, which—as in the preceding conversion webhook—uses the `runtime.RawExtension` type to store a pizza object.

We also get the old object for update requests and could, say, check for fields that are meant to be read-only but are changed in a request. We don't do this here in our example. But you will encounter many cases in Kubernetes where such logic is implemented—for example, for most fields of a pod, as you can't change the command of a pod after it is created.

The patch returned by the mutating webhook must be of type JSON `Patch` (see RFC 6902) in Kubernetes 1.14. This patch describes how the object should be modified to fulfill the required invariant.

Note that it is best practice to validate every mutating webhook change in a validating webhook at the very end, at least if those enforced properties are significant for the behavior. Imagine some other mutating webhook touches the same fields in an object. Then you cannot be sure that the mutating changes will survive until the end of the mutating admission chain.

There is no order currently in mutating webhooks other than alphabetic order. There are ongoing discussions to change this in one way or another in the future.

For validating webhooks the order does not matter, obviously, and the Kubernetes API server even calls validating webhooks in parallel to reduce latency. In contrast, mutating webhooks add latency to every request that passes through them, as they are called sequentially.

Common latencies—of course heavily depending on the environment—are around 100ms. So running many webhooks in sequence leads to considerable latencies that the user will experience when creating or updating objects.

Registering Admission Webhooks

Admission webhooks are not registered in the CRD manifest. The reason is that they apply not only to CRDs, but to any kind of resource. You can even add custom admission webhooks to standard Kubernetes resources.

Instead there are registration objects: `MutatingWebhookRegistration` and `ValidatingWebhookRegistration`. They differ only in the kind name:

```
apiVersion: admissionregistration.k8s.io/v1beta1
kind: MutatingWebhookConfiguration
metadata:
  name: restaurant.programming-kubernetes.info
webhooks:
- name: restaurant.programming-kubernetes.info
  failurePolicy: Fail
  sideEffects: None
  admissionReviewVersions:
  - v1beta1
  rules:
  - apiGroups:
    - "restaurant.programming-kubernetes.info"
    apiVersions:
    - v1alpha1
    - v1beta1
    operations:
    - CREATE
    - UPDATE
    resources:
    - pizzas
```

```
clientConfig:
  service:
    namespace: pizza-crd
    name: webhook
    path: /admit/v1beta1/pizza
  caBundle: CA-BUNDLE
```

This registers our `pizza-crd` webhook from the beginning of the chapter for mutating admission for our two versions of the resource `pizza`, the API group `restaurant.programming-kubernetes.info`, and the HTTP verbs `CREATE` and `UPDATE` (which includes patches as well).

There are further ways in webhook configurations to restrict the matching resources —for example, a namespace selector (to exclude, e.g., a control plane namespace to avoid bootstrapping issues) and more advanced resource patterns with wildcards and subresources.

Last but not least is a failure mode, which can be either `Fail` or `Ignore`. It specifies what to do if the webhook cannot be reached or fails for other reasons.

Admission webhooks can break clusters if they are deployed in the wrong way. Admission webhook matching core types can make the whole cluster inoperable. Special care must be taken to call admission webhooks for non-CRD resources.

Specifically, it is good practice to exclude the control plane and the webhook resources themselves from the webhook.

Implementing an Admission Webhook

With the work we've done on the conversion webhook in the beginning of the chapter, it is not hard to add admission capabilities. We also saw that the paths */admit/v1beta1/pizza* and */validate/v1beta1/pizza* are registered in the main function of the `pizza-crd-webhook` binary:

```
mux.Handle("/admit/v1beta1/pizza", http.HandlerFunc(admission.ServePizzaAdmit))
mux.Handle("/validate/v1beta1/pizza", http.HandlerFunc(
admission.ServePizzaValidation(restaurantInformers)))
```

The first part of the two HTTP handler implementations looks nearly the same as for the conversion webhook:

```
func ServePizzaAdmit(w http.ResponseWriter, req *http.Request) {
    // read body
    body, err := ioutil.ReadAll(req.Body)
    if err != nil {
        responsewriters.InternalError(w, req,
          fmt.Errorf("failed to read body: %v", err))
        return
    }

    // decode body as admission review
```

```
reviewGVK := admissionv1beta1.SchemeGroupVersion.WithKind("AdmissionReview")
decoder := codecs.UniversalDeserializer()
into := &admissionv1beta1.AdmissionReview{}
obj, gvk, err := decoder.Decode(body, &reviewGVK, into)
if err != nil {
    responsewriters.InternalError(w, req,
      fmt.Errorf("failed to decode body: %v", err))
    return
}
review, ok := obj.(*admissionv1beta1.AdmissionReview)
if !ok {
    responsewriters.InternalError(w, req,
      fmt.Errorf("unexpected GroupVersionKind: %s", gvk))
    return
}
if review.Request == nil {
    responsewriters.InternalError(w, req,
      fmt.Errorf("unexpected nil request"))
    return
}

    ...
}
```

In the case of the validating webhook, we have to wire the informer (used to check that toppings exist in the cluster). We return an internal error as long as the informer is not synced. An informer that is not synced has incomplete data, so the toppings might not be known and the pizza would be rejected although they are valid:

```
func ServePizzaValidation(informers restaurantinformers.SharedInformerFactory)
    func (http.ResponseWriter, *http.Request)
{
    toppingInformer := informers.Restaurant().V1alpha1().Toppings().Informer()
    toppingLister := informers.Restaurant().V1alpha1().Toppings().Lister()

    return func(w http.ResponseWriter, req *http.Request) {
        if !toppingInformer.HasSynced() {
            responsewriters.InternalError(w, req,
              fmt.Errorf("informers not ready"))
            return
        }

        // read body
        body, err := ioutil.ReadAll(req.Body)
        if err != nil {
            responsewriters.InternalError(w, req,
              fmt.Errorf("failed to read body: %v", err))
            return
        }

        // decode body as admission review
        gv := admissionv1beta1.SchemeGroupVersion
        reviewGVK := gv.WithKind("AdmissionReview")
        obj, gvk, err := codecs.UniversalDeserializer().Decode(body, &reviewGVK,
            &admissionv1beta1.AdmissionReview{})
        if err != nil {
            responsewriters.InternalError(w, req,
              fmt.Errorf("failed to decode body: %v", err))
```

```
            return
    }
    review, ok := obj.(*admissionv1beta1.AdmissionReview)
    if !ok {
        responsewriters.InternalError(w, req,
          fmt.Errorf("unexpected GroupVersionKind: %s", gvk))
        return
    }
    if review.Request == nil {
        responsewriters.InternalError(w, req,
          fmt.Errorf("unexpected nil request"))
        return
    }

    ...

    }
}
```

As in the webhook conversion case, we have set up the scheme and the codec factory with the admission API group and our restaurant API group:

```
var (
    scheme = runtime.NewScheme()
    codecs = serializer.NewCodecFactory(scheme)
)

func init() {
    utilruntime.Must(admissionv1beta1.AddToScheme(scheme))
    install.Install(scheme)
}
```

With these two, we decode the embedded pizza object (this time only one, no slice) from the `AdmissionReview`:

```
// decode object
if review.Request.Object.Object == nil {
    var err error
    review.Request.Object.Object, _, err =
      codecs.UniversalDeserializer().Decode(review.Request.Object.Raw, nil, nil)
    if err != nil {
        review.Response.Result = &metav1.Status{
            Message: err.Error(),
            Status:  metav1.StatusFailure,
        }
        responsewriters.WriteObject(http.StatusOK, gvk.GroupVersion(),
          codecs, review, w, req)
        return
    }
}
```

Then we can do the actual mutating admission (the defaulting of `spec.toppings` for both API versions):

```
orig := review.Request.Object.Raw
var bs []byte
switch pizza := review.Request.Object.Object.(type) {
case *v1alpha1.Pizza:
    // default toppings
    if len(pizza.Spec.Toppings) == 0 {
```

```
            pizza.Spec.Toppings = []string{"tomato", "mozzarella", "salami"}
        }
        bs, err = json.Marshal(pizza)
        if err != nil {
            responsewriters.InternalError(w, req,
                fmt.Errorf"unexpected encoding error: %v", err))
            return
        }

    case *v1beta1.Pizza:
        // default toppings
        if len(pizza.Spec.Toppings) == 0 {
            pizza.Spec.Toppings = []v1beta1.PizzaTopping{
                {"tomato", 1},
                {"mozzarella", 1},
                {"salami", 1},
            }
        }
        bs, err = json.Marshal(pizza)
        if err != nil {
            responsewriters.InternalError(w, req,
                fmt.Errorf("unexpected encoding error: %v", err))
            return
        }

    default:
        review.Response.Result = &metav1.Status{
            Message: fmt.Sprintf("unexpected type %T", review.Request.Object.Object),
            Status:  metav1.StatusFailure,
        }
        responsewriters.WriteObject(http.StatusOK, gvk.GroupVersion(),
            codecs, review, w, req)
        return
    }
```

Alternatively, we could use the conversion algorithms from the conversion webhook and then implement defaulting only for one of the versions. Both approaches are possible, and which one makes more sense depends on the context. Here, the defaulting is simple enough to implement it twice.

The final step is to compute the patch—the difference between the original object (stored in `orig` as JSON) and the new defaulted one:

```
// compare original and defaulted version
ops, err := jsonpatch.CreatePatch(orig, bs)
if err != nil {
    responsewriters.InternalError(w, req,
        fmt.Errorf("unexpected diff error: %v", err))
    return
}
review.Response.Patch, err = json.Marshal(ops)
if err != nil {
    responsewriters.InternalError(w, req,
        fmt.Errorf("unexpected patch encoding error: %v", err))
    return
}
typ := admissionv1beta1.PatchTypeJSONPatch
```

```
review.Response.PatchType = &typ
review.Response.Allowed = true
```

We use the JSON-Patch library (*http://bit.ly/2IKxwIk*) (a fork of Matt Baird's (*http://bit.ly/2xfBIsN*) with critical fixes (*http://bit.ly/2XxKfWP*)) to derive the patch from the original object `orig` and the modified object `bs`, both passed as JSON byte slices. Alternatively, we could operate directly on untyped JSON data and create the JSON-Patch manually. Again, it depends on the context. Using a diff library is convenient.

Then, as in the webhook conversion, we conclude by writing the response to the response writer, using the codec factory created previously:

```
responsewriters.WriteObject(
    http.StatusOK, gvk.GroupVersion(), codecs, review, w, req,
)
```

The validating webhook is very similar, but it uses the toppings lister from the shared informer to check for the existence of the topping objects:

```
switch pizza := review.Request.Object.Object.(type) {
case *v1alpha1.Pizza:
    for _, topping := range pizza.Spec.Toppings {
        _, err := toppingLister.Get(topping)
        if err != nil && !errors.IsNotFound(err) {
            responsewriters.InternalError(w, req,
              fmt.Errorf("failed to lookup topping %q: %v", topping, err))
            return
        } else if errors.IsNotFound(err) {
            review.Response.Result = &metav1.Status{
                Message: fmt.Sprintf("topping %q not known", topping),
                Status:  metav1.StatusFailure,
            }
            responsewriters.WriteObject(http.StatusOK, gvk.GroupVersion(),
              codecs, review, w, req)
            return
        }
    }
    review.Response.Allowed = true
case *v1beta1.Pizza:
    for _, topping := range pizza.Spec.Toppings {
        _, err := toppingLister.Get(topping.Name)
        if err != nil && !errors.IsNotFound(err) {
            responsewriters.InternalError(w, req,
              fmt.Errorf("failed to lookup topping %q: %v", topping, err))
            return
        } else if errors.IsNotFound(err) {
            review.Response.Result = &metav1.Status{
                Message: fmt.Sprintf("topping %q not known", topping),
                Status:  metav1.StatusFailure,
            }
            responsewriters.WriteObject(http.StatusOK, gvk.GroupVersion(),
              codecs, review, w, req)
            return
        }
    }
    review.Response.Allowed = true
default:
```

```
    review.Response.Result = &metav1.Status{
        Message: fmt.Sprintf("unexpected type %T", review.Request.Object.Object),
        Status:  metav1.StatusFailure,
    }
}
responsewriters.WriteObject(http.StatusOK, gvk.GroupVersion(),
    codecs, review, w, req)
```

Admission Webhook in Action

We deploy the two admission webhooks by creating the two registration objects in the cluster:

```
$ kubectl create -f validatingadmissionregistration.yaml
$ kubectl create -f mutatingadmissionregistration.yaml
```

After this, we can't create pizzas with unknown toppings anymore:

```
$ kubectl create -f ../examples/margherita-pizza.yaml
Error from server: error when creating "../examples/margherita-pizza.yaml":
  admission webhook "restaurant.programming-kubernetes.info" denied the request:
    topping "tomato" not known
```

Meanwhile, in the webhook log we see:

```
I0414 22:45:46.873541       1 pizzamutation.go:115] Defaulting pizza-crd/ in
  version admission.k8s.io/v1beta1, Kind=AdmissionReview
10.32.0.1 - - [14/Apr/2019:22:45:46 +0000]
  "POST /admit/v1beta1/pizza?timeout=30s HTTP/2.0" 200 871
10.32.0.1 - - [14/Apr/2019:22:45:46 +0000]
  "POST /validate/v1beta1/pizza?timeout=30s HTTP/2.0" 200 956
```

After creating the toppings in the example folder, we can create the margherita pizza again:

```
$ kubectl create -f ../examples/topping-tomato.yaml
$ kubectl create -f ../examples/topping-salami.yaml
$ kubectl create -f ../examples/topping-mozzarella.yaml
$ kubectl create -f ../examples/margherita-pizza.yaml
pizza.restaurant.programming-kubernetes.info/margherita created
```

Last but not least, let's check that defaulting works as expected. We want to create an empty pizza:

```
apiVersion: restaurant.programming-kubernetes.info/v1alpha1
kind: Pizza
metadata:
  name: salami
spec:
```

This is supposed to be defaulted to a salami pizza, and it is:

```
$ kubectl create -f ../examples/empty-pizza.yaml
pizza.restaurant.programming-kubernetes.info/salami created
$ kubectl get pizza salami -o yaml
apiVersion: restaurant.programming-kubernetes.info/v1beta1
kind: Pizza
metadata:
  creationTimestamp: "2019-04-14T22:49:40Z"
```

```
   generation: 1
   name: salami
   namespace: pizza-crd
   resourceVersion: "23227"
   uid: 962e2dda-5f07-11e9-9230-0242f24ba99c
spec:
  toppings:
  - name: tomato
    quantity: 1
  - name: mozzarella
    quantity: 1
  - name: salami
    quantity: 1
status: {}
```

Voilà, a salami pizza with all the toppings that we expect. Enjoy!

Before concluding the chapter, we want to look toward an `apiextensions.k8s.io/v1` API group version (i.e., nonbeta, general availability) of CRDs—namely, the introduction of structural schemas.

Structural Schemas and the Future of CustomResourceDefinitions

From Kubernetes 1.15 on, the OpenAPI v3 validation schema (see "Validating Custom Resources" on page 76) is getting a more central role for CRDs in the sense that it will be mandatory to specify a schema if any of these new features is used:

- CRD conversion (see Figure 9-2)
- Pruning (see "Pruning Versus Preserving Unknown Fields" on page 239)
- Defaulting (see "Default Values" on page 242)
- OpenAPI Schema Publishing (*http://bit.ly/2RzeA1O*)

Strictly speaking, the definition of a schema is still optional and every existing CRD will keep working, but without a schema your CRD is excluded from any new feature.

In addition, the specified schema must follow certain rules to enforce that the specified types are actually sane in the sense of adhering to the Kubernetes API conventions (*http://bit.ly/2Nfd9Hn*). We call these *structural schema*.

Structural Schemas

A structural schema is an OpenAPI v3 validation schema (see "Validating Custom Resources" on page 76) that obeys the following rules:

1. The schema specifies a nonempty type (via `type` in OpenAPI) for the root, for each specified field of an object node (via `properties` or `additionalProperties` in OpenAPI), and for each item in an array node (via `items` in OpenAPI), with the exception of:

   - A node with `x-kubernetes-int-or-string: true`
   - A node with `x-kubernetes-preserve-unknown-fields: true`

2. For each field in an object and each item in an array, which is set within an `allOf`, `anyOf`, `oneOf`, or `not`, the schema also specifies the field/item outside of those logical junctors.

3. The schema does not set `description`, `type`, `default`, `additionProperties`, or `nullable` within an `allOf`, `anyOf`, `oneOf`, or `not`, with the exception of the two patterns for `x-kubernetes-int-or-string: true` (see "IntOrString and RawExtensions" on page 241).

4. If `metadata` is specified, then only restrictions on `metadata.name` and `metadata.generateName` are allowed.

Here is an example that is not structural:

```
properties:
  foo:
    pattern: "abc"
  metadata:
    type: object
    properties:
      name:
        type: string
        pattern: "^a"
      finalizers:
        type: array
        items:
          type: string
          pattern: "my-finalizer"
anyOf:
- properties:
    bar:
      type: integer
      minimum: 42
  required: ["bar"]
  description: "foo bar object"
```

It is not a structural schema because of the following violations:

- The type at the root is missing (rule 1).
- The type of foo is missing (rule 1).
- bar inside of anyOf is not specified outside (rule 2).
- bar's type is within anyOf (rule 3).
- The description is set within anyOf (rule 3).
- metadata.finalizer might not be restricted (rule 4).

In contrast, the following, corresponding schema is structural:

```
type: object
description: "foo bar object"
properties:
  foo:
    type: string
    pattern: "abc"
  bar:
    type: integer
  metadata:
    type: object
    properties:
      name:
        type: string
        pattern: "^a"
anyOf:
- properties:
    bar:
      minimum: 42
  required: ["bar"]
```

Violations of the structural schema rules are reported in the NonStructural condition in the CRD.

Verify for yourself that the schema of the cnat example in "Validating Custom Resources" on page 76 and the schemas in the pizza CRD example (*http://bit.ly/31MrFcO*) are indeed structural.

Pruning Versus Preserving Unknown Fields

CRDs traditionally store any (possibly validated) JSON as is in etcd. This means that unspecified fields (if there is an OpenAPI v3 validation schema at all) will be persisted. This is in contrast to native Kubernetes resources like a pod. If the user specifies a field spec.randomField, this will be accepted by the API server HTTPS endpoint but dropped (we call this *pruning*) before writing that pod to etcd.

If a structural OpenAPI v3 validation schema is defined (either in the global spec.validation.openAPIV3Schema or for each version), we can enable pruning (which drops unspecified fields on creation and on update) by setting spec.preserveUnknownFields to false.

Let's look at the cnat example.[2] With a Kubernetes 1.15 cluster at hand, we enable pruning:

```
apiVersion: apiextensions.k8s.io/v1beta1
kind: CustomResourceDefinition
metadata:
  name: ats.cnat.programming-kubernetes.info
spec:
  ...
  preserveUnknownFields: false
```

Then we try to create an instance with an unknown field:

```
apiVersion: cnat.programming-kubernetes.info/v1alpha1
kind: At
metadata:
  name: example-at
spec:
  schedule: "2019-07-03T02:00:00Z"
  command: echo "Hello, world!"
  someGarbage: 42
```

If we retrieve this object with `kubectl get at example-at`, we see that the `someGarbage` value is dropped:

```
apiVersion: cnat.programming-kubernetes.info/v1alpha1
kind: At
metadata:
  name: example-at
spec:
  schedule: "2019-07-03T02:00:00Z"
  command: echo "Hello, world!"
```

We say that `someGarbage` has been *pruned*.

As of Kubernetes 1.15, pruning is available in *apiextensions/v1beta1*, but it defaults to off; that is, `spec.preserveUnknownFields` defaults to `true`. In *apiextensions/v1*, no new CRD with `spec.preserveUnknownFields: true` will be allowed to be created.

Controlling Pruning

With `spec.preserveUnknownField: false` in the CRD, pruning is enabled for all CRs of that type and in all versions. It is possible, though, to opt out of pruning for a JSON subtree via `x-kubernetes-preserve-unknown-fields: true` in the OpenAPI v3 validation schema:

```
type: object
properties:
  json:
    x-kubernetes-preserve-unknown-fields: true
```

---

2 We use the cnat example instead of the pizza example due to the simple structure of the former—for example, there's only one version. Of course, all of this scales to multiple versions (i.e., one schema version).

The field `json` can store any JSON value, without anything being pruned.

It is possible to partially specify the permitted JSON:

```
type: object
properties:
  json:
    x-kubernetes-preserve-unknown-fields: true
    type: object
    description: this is arbitrary JSON
```

With this approach, only object type values are allowed.

Pruning is enabled again for each specified property (or `additionalProperties`):

```
type: object
properties:
  json:
    x-kubernetes-preserve-unknown-fields: true
    type: object
    properties:
      spec:
        type: object
        properties:
          foo:
            type: string
          bar:
            type: string
```

With this, the value:

```
json:
  spec:
    foo: abc
    bar: def
    something: x
  status:
    something: x
```

will be pruned to:

```
json:
  spec:
    foo: abc
    bar: def
  status:
    something: x
```

This means that the *something* field in the specified `spec` object is pruned (because "spec" is specified), but everything outside is not. `status` is not specified such that `status.`*something* is not pruned.

IntOrString and RawExtensions

There are situations where structural schemas are not expressive enough. One of those is a *polymorphic* field—one that can be of different types. We know `IntOrString` from native Kubernetes API types.

It is possible to have IntOrString in CRDs using the x-kubernetes-int-or-string: true directive inside the schema. Similarly, runtime.RawExtensions can be declared using the x-kubernetes-embedded-object: true.

For example:

```
type: object
properties:
  intorstr:
    type: object
    x-kubernetes-int-or-string: true
  embedded:
    x-kubernetes-embedded-object: true
    x-kubernetes-preserve-unknown-fields: true
```

This declares:

- A field called intorstr that holds either an integer or a string
- A field called embedded that holds a Kubernetes-like object such as a complete pod specification

Refer to the official CRD documentation (*http://bit.ly/2Lnmw61*) for all the details about these directives.

The last topic we want to talk about that depends on structural schemas is defaulting.

Default Values

In native Kubernetes types, it is common to default certain values. Defaulting used to be possible for CRDs only by way of mutating admission webhooks (see "Admission Webhooks" on page 226). As of Kubernetes 1.15, however, defaulting support is added (see the design document (*http://bit.ly/2ZFH8JY*)) to CRDs directly via the OpenAPI v3 schema described in the previous section.

As of 1.15 this is still an alpha feature, meaning it's disabled by default behind the feature gate CustomResourceDefaulting. But with promotion to beta, probably in 1.16, it will become ubiquitous in CRDs.

In order to default certain fields, just specify the default value via the default keyword in the OpenAPI v3 schema. This is very useful when you are adding new fields to a type.

Starting with the schema of the cnat example from "Validating Custom Resources" on page 76, let's assume we want to make the container image customizable, but default to a busybox image. For that we add the image field of string type to the OpenAPI v3 schema and set the default to busybox:

```
type: object
properties:
  apiVersion:
    type: string
  kind:
    type: string
  metadata:
    type: object
  spec:
    type: object
    properties:
      schedule:
        type: string
        pattern: "^\d{4}-([0]\d|1[0-2])-([0-2]\d|3[01])..."
      command:
        type: string
      image:
        type: string
        default: "busybox"
    required:
    - schedule
    - command
  status:
    type: object
    properties:
      phase:
        type: string
required:
- metadata
- apiVersion
- kind
- spec
```

If the user creates an instance without specifying the image, the value is automatically
set:

```
apiVersion: cnat.programming-kubernetes.info/v1alpha1
kind: At
metadata:
  name: example-at
spec:
  schedule: "2019-07-03T02:00:00Z"
  command: echo "hello world!"
```

On creation, this turns automatically into:

```
apiVersion: cnat.programming-kubernetes.info/v1alpha1
kind: At
metadata:
  name: example-at
spec:
  schedule: "2019-07-03T02:00:00Z"
  command: echo "hello world!"
  image: busybox
```

This looks super convenient and significantly improves the user experience of CRDs. What's more, all old objects persisted in `etcd` will automatically inherit the new field when read from the API server.[3]

Note that persisted objects in `etcd` will not be rewritten (i.e., migrated automatically). In other words, on read the default values are only added on the fly and are only persisted when the object is updated for another reason.

Summary

Admission and conversion webhooks take CRDs to a completely different level. Before these features, CRs were mostly used for small, not-so-serious use cases, often for configuration and for in-house applications where API compatibility was not that important.

With webhooks CRs look much more like native resources, with a long lifecycle and powerful semantics. We have seen how to implement dependencies between different resources and how to set defaulting of fields.

At this point you probably have a lot of ideas about where these features can be used in existing CRDs. We are curious to see the innovations of the community based on these features in the future.

---

3 For example, via kubectl get ats -o yaml.

Resources

General

- The official Kubernetes Documentation (*https://kubernetes.io/docs/home*)
- The Kubernetes community on GitHub (*http://bit.ly/2LX2YF8*)
- The client-go docs channel on the Kubernetes Slack instance
- Kubernetes deep dive: API Server – part 1 (*https://red.ht/2IJBDEk*)
- Kubernetes deep dive: API Server – part 2 (*https://red.ht/2RAEv9s*)
- Kubernetes deep dive: API Server – part 3 (*https://red.ht/2NaXgBD*)
- Kubernetes API Server, Part I (*http://bit.ly/2IKh0be*)
- The Mechanics of Kubernetes (*http://bit.ly/2IV2lcb*)
- GoDoc for *k8s.io/api* (*https://godoc.org/k8s.io/api*)

Books

- *Kubernetes: Up and Running*, 2nd Edition (*https://oreil.ly/2SaANU4*) by Kelsey Hightower et al. (O'Reilly)
- *Cloud Native DevOps with Kubernetes* (*https://oreil.ly/2BaE1iq*) by John Arundel and Justin Domingus (O'Reilly)
- *Managing Kubernetes* (*https://oreil.ly/2wtHcAm*) by Brendan Burns and Craig Tracey (O'Reilly)
- *Kubernetes Cookbook* (*http://bit.ly/2FTgJzk*) by Sébastien Goasguen and Michael Hausenblas (O'Reilly)
- *The Kubebuilder Book* (*https://book.kubebuilder.io*)

Tutorials and Examples

- Kubernetes by Example (*http://kubernetesbyexample.com*)
- The Katacoda Kubernetes Playground (*http://bit.ly/31Sydqp*)
- Banzai Cloud Operator SDK (*http://bit.ly/2ZG3OtA*)
- Operator Developer Guide (*http://bit.ly/2Fx4zh4*)

Articles

- Writing a Kubernetes Operator in Golang (*http://bit.ly/2Ei2hCr*)
- Stay Informed with Kubernetes Informers (*http://bit.ly/2Y5OKYX*)
- Events, the DNA of Kubernetes (*http://bit.ly/31Tvey8*)
- Kubernetes Events Explained (*http://bit.ly/2XzwEOM*)
- Level Triggering and Reconciliation in Kubernetes (*http://bit.ly/2FmLLAW*)
- Comparing Kubernetes Operator Pattern with Alternatives (*http://bit.ly/2XxGEYO*)
- Kubernetes Operators (*https://kubedex.com/operators*)
- Kubernetes Custom Resource, Controller and Operator Development Tools (*http://bit.ly/2FpO4Ug*)
- Demystifying Kubernetes Operators with the Operator SDK: Part 1 (*http://bit.ly/2NbGRwZ*)
- Under the Hood of Kubebuilder Framework (*http://bit.ly/2X2NpgX*)
- Best Practices for Building Kubernetes Operators and Stateful Apps (*http://bit.ly/2NdvQeJ*)
- Kubernetes Operator Development Guidelines (*http://bit.ly/31P7rPC*)
- Mutating Webhooks with slok/kubewebhook (*http://bit.ly/2RyScG1*)

Repositories

- kubernetes-client organization (*http://bit.ly/2xfSrfT*)
- kubernetes/kubernetes (*http://bit.ly/2SltTLP*)
- kubernetes/perf-tests (*http://bit.ly/2X556g8*)
- cncf/apisnoop (*http://bit.ly/32u5SqN*)
- open-policy-agent/gatekeeper (*http://bit.ly/2LXCpiX*)
- stakater/Konfigurator (*http://bit.ly/2JBX8HO*)
- ynqa/kubernetes-rust (*https://github.com/ynqa/kubernetes-rust*)
- hossainemruz/k8s-initializer-finalizer-practice (*http://bit.ly/30GzTSF*)
- munnerz/k8s-api-pager-demo (*http://bit.ly/30Ep2IT*)
- m3db/m3db-operator (*http://bit.ly/2XURVi2*)

Index

existing option structs, 161
first start, 166
internal types and conversion, 168
options and config pattern, 160
registry and strategy, 181
roundtrip testing, 177
validation, 179
writing API types, 171
custom resource definitions (CRDs)
accessing, 85
accessing with client-go dynamic client, 86
accessing with controller-runtime client, 92
accessing with typed clients, 87-92
admission webhooks, 226-237
availability of, 71
best practices, 137
defining, 71
discovery information, 73
limits of, 147
printer columns, 80
role of, 17, 71
short names and categories, 79
structural schemas, 237-244
subresources, 81-85
type definitions, 74
validating custom resources, 76
versioning, 209-226
writing with code generators, 95-104
custom resources (CR) (see custom resource definitions (CRDs))

D

declarative state management, 25
decoding, 156
deep copies, 100-102
deep copy, 47
deep-copy
deep-copy methods, 90
deepcopy-gen, 96
DeepCopyObject tag, 100
defaulting, 170, 176, 186, 242
defaulter-gen, 96
delegated authentication, 156
delegated authorization, 157
dep (vendoring tool), 67
deployment (controllers and operators)
access control, 139
automated builds and testing, 142
custom controller observability, 142

lifecycle management, 137
overview of, 131
packaging best practices, 137
packaging challenges, 131
packaging with Helm, 132
packaging with Kustomize, 134
packaging with other tools, 136
production-ready overview, 138
deployment (custom API servers)
certificates and trust, 205
deployment manifests, 199
RBAC setup, 201
running insecurely, 202
sharing etcd, 207
desired state, 25
discovery, 79, 92
endpoint, 167
RESTMapper, 63
discovery client, 52
discovery mechanism, 73
distributed version control, xii
dynamic clients, 86

E

edge-driven triggers, 9
encoding, 156
errors
advanced error behavior of informers, 57
cache coherency issues, 60
conflict errors, 15
connection errors, 56
coping with trigger errors, 10
event handlers, 58
event producers, 9
event sources, 9
events
overview of, 7
watch events versus event objects, 8
extension patterns
aggregated API servers, 147-208
custom resource definitions (CRDs), 71-94
overview of, 4
external version, 169

F

feature gate, 161, 242
field selector, 53
Flant's Shell operator, 129
fuzzers, 178

priority queues, 61
Prometheus, 144
protocol buffers (protobuf), 41
pruning, 239
Puppet, 136

Q

questions and comments, xiv

R

rate limiting, 55
read access, 141
reflection, 65
registry, 164
relist period, 57
remote procedure calls (RPCs), 7
replica integer value, 83
repositories
    API Machinery, 38
    API versions and compatibility guarantees,
      44
    client library, 35
    creating and using clients, 39
    importing, 35
    Kubernetes API Go types, 37
    third-party applications, 66
    versioning and compatibility, 41
request processing, 29-33, 56
resource version, 15
resource version conflict errors, 15
resources
    example Kubernetes API space, 24
    formatting of, 63
    GroupVersionResource (GVR), 23, 63
    namespaces versus cluster-scoped, 63
    overview of, 22
    resources versus kinds, 23
    subresources, 22
REST client, 52
REST config, 51, 58, 86
REST mapping, 23, 63
REST verbs, 35
resync period, 57
role-based access control (RBAC), 32, 81, 139,
    157, 201
Rook operator kit, 128
roundtrippable conversion, 170, 177
runtime.Object, 46, 65, 100

S

Salt, 136
sample-controller
    bootstrapping, 107
      business logic implementation, 108-113
      implementing operators following, 106
scale subresource, 83
schema, structural, 237
schemes, 65
semantic versioning (semver), 43, 69
server request processing, 29-33, 56
server-side printing, 80
service account, 201
shared informer factory, 58
short names, 79
Site Reliability Engineers (SREs), 17
spec and a status section, 50, 82
specifications (specs), 25
state change
    declarative state management, 25
    detecting, 9
status (observed state), 25
status subresources, 53, 81
storage versions, 46
stores, 57
strategy, 184
structural schemas
    controlling pruning, 240
    default values, 242
    IntOrString and RawExtensions, 241
    overview of, 237
    pruning versus preserving unknown fields,
      239
subject access review, 158, 182
subresources, 22, 81-85

T

testing, 142
third-party applications, 66
throttling, 55
    burst, 56
    queries per second, 56
timeouts, 55
triggers
    coping with errors, 10
    edge- versus level-driven triggers, 9
type definitions, 74
type system, 62
typed clients, 87-92

TypeMeta, 47

U
UNIX tooling, for packaging, 136
user agents, 55

V
validating plug-ins, 189
validation, 179
vendoring
    dep, 67
    glide, 67
    Go modules, 68
    role of, 66
    tools for, 66
version control, xii
versioning
    conversion webhook architecture, 213
    conversion webhook deployment, 223
    conversion webhook implementation, 216
    example, 210
    HTTPs server setup, 217
    overview of, 209
    process of, 223
versions, in Kubernetes API, 22, 41

W
WATCH verb, 36
watches, 8, 54, 56
webhooks
    admission webhooks, 226-237
    conversion webhook architecture, 213
    conversion webhook deployment, 223
    conversion webhook implementation, 216
work queues, 7, 61
write access, 141

X
x-kubernetes-embedded-object: true, 242
x-kubernetes-int-or-string: true, 242
x-kubernetes-preserve-unknown-fields: true,
    240

Y
YAML manifests, 132
ytt, 136

Z
Zalando's Kopf, 129

About the Authors

Michael Hausenblas is a developer advocate at Amazon Web Services, part of the container service team focusing on container security. Michael shares his experience around cloud native infrastructure and apps through demos, blog posts, books, public speaking engagements, and contributions to open source software. Before AWS, Michael worked at Red Hat, Mesosphere, MapR, and in two research institutions in Ireland and Austria.

Stefan Schimanski is a principal software engineer for Go, Kubernetes, and Open-Shift at Red Hat. His focus is the Kubernetes API server, especially the implementation of CustomResourceDefinitions, API Machinery in general, and the publishing of the Kubernetes staging repositories client-go, apimachinery, api, and more. Before Red Hat, Stefan worked at Mesosphere on Marathon, Spark, and their Kubernetes offering, and as a freelancer and consultant in high availability and distributed systems. In a former life Stefan did research in Mathematical Logic about constructive mathematics, type systems, and lambda calculus.

Colophon

The animal on the cover of *Programming Kubernetes* is a green sandpiper (*Tringa ochropus*). Both the genus and species name come from Ancient Greek. A small wading bird called *trungas* once caught Aristotle's attention, and *ochropus* breaks down into the Ancient Greek words for "ochre" and "foot," *okhros* and *pous*.

The green sandpiper has only one close living relative: the solitary sandpiper. Green sandpipers enjoy an extremely large range, spanning almost every continent. They are native to Asia and migrate to warmer climates during winter. They wade and feed in a variety of marshy environments. In the ponds, rivers, and wet woodland, green sandpipers find insects, spiders, small crustaceans, fish, and plants to eat.

Green sandpipers have a wide breast and short neck. Their beaks are long and slim. Up close, their greenish-brown wings reveal small, light dots. This feather coloring is the opposite of their eggs, which are buff with brown speckles. A typical clutch averages two to four eggs, which hatch in three weeks. Green sandpipers incubate in the abandoned nests of other birds or even squirrels.

Many of the animals on O'Reilly covers are endangered; all of them are important to the world.

The cover illustration is by Karen Montgomery, based on a black and white engraving from *Shaw's Zoology*. The cover fonts are Gilroy Semibold and Guardian Sans. The text font is Adobe Minion Pro; the heading font is Adobe Myriad Condensed; and the code font is Dalton Maag's Ubuntu Mono.

O'REILLY®

There's much more where this came from.

Experience books, videos, live online training courses, and more from O'Reilly and our 200+ partners—all in one place.

Learn more at oreilly.com/online-learning

CPSIA information can be obtained
at www.ICGtesting.com
Printed in the USA
JSHW010500301020
9184JS00002B/47